THE SAUCIER'S APPRENTICE

THE SAUCIER'S APPRENTICE

One Long Strange Trip through
the Great Cooking Schools of Europe

BOB SPITZ

W.W. NORTON & COMPANY

New York · London

For information about permission to reproduce selections from this book,
write to Permissions, W. W. Norton & Company, Inc.,
500 Fifth Avenue, New York, NY 10110

For information about special discounts for bulk purchases, please contact
W. W. Norton Special Sales at specialsales@wwnorton.com or 800-233-4830

Manufacturing by RR Donnelley, Bloomsburg
Book design by Chris Welch
Production manager: Anna Oler

Library of Congress Cataloging-in-Publication Data

Spitz, Bob.
The saucier's apprentice : one long strange trip through the great
cooking schools of Europe / Bob Spitz. — 1st ed.
p. cm.
ISBN 978-0-393-06059-1 (hardcover)
1. Gastronomy. 2. Cookery, European. 3. Cooking schools—Europe. I. Title.
TX641.S72 2008
641'.013—dc22

2008001331

ISBN 978-0-393-33538-5 pbk.

W. W. Norton & Company, Inc.
500 Fifth Avenue, New York, N.Y. 10110
www.wwnorton.com

W. W. Norton & Company Ltd.
Castle House, 75/76 Wells Street, London W1T 3QT

1 2 3 4 5 6 7 8 9 0

FOR

BECKY AIKMAN,

WHO BRINGS ALL THE RIGHT INGREDIENTS

CONTENTS

LIST OF RECIPES

THE SAUCIER'S APPRENTICE

PROLOGUE

I t's a wonder any of us survived those Friday-night dinners.

They were heated, impromptu little affairs, or at least they had begun that way in the days before the Great Odyssey. Each week I'd invite a revolving gang of friends over, scrape together a couple of dishes using whatever looked harmless in the fridge, and by ten o'clock, with enough wine to pickle a Welsh pony, the atmosphere in my cluttered, steam-filled kitchen seemed perfectly combustible. It was a weatherbeaten little room, dark and stuffy, with a wall of tatty window screens that looked out over a stream. But it was cheerful while we were in it. Warmed by trembling candlelight, we squeezed around a badly stained pine farmhouse table that made no concession for elbows. There was a lot to be said for the informality of it. Everyone pitched in, keeping the traffic flow moving between the stove and the seats. No one minded the rattle and clash. Plates were passed with reckless abandon; I worried about mid-air collisions, and there were always a few near misses. Otherwise, we ate with a desperate greedy desire, jabbering like magpies late into the night.

The world's woes were solved over those meals—capital punishment, the Israeli-Palestinian issue, Clarence Thomas, you name it; we put the entire Cabinet to shame. The next item on our agenda was the Democratic malaise when one night someone, I think it was Craig, made the mistake of saying, "Boy, the food was good." Which, somehow, got scrambled in my brain and translated as: "You're a great cook." And nothing was ever the same.

Thereafter, by Tuesday or Wednesday at the latest, I'd have planned a menu with all the trappings of a state dinner: three courses minimum, plus a cheese platter followed by dessert. A selection of wines was handpicked like pearls to match each dish. Everything else—assisted suicide, the Kurds, even that year's Oscar race—paled in importance. Those dinners took over my life. Thursdays were spent behind the wheel of my car, scouring the county for groceries and fresh herbs; Fridays, I remained imprisoned in the kitchen, where, by noon, the countertops resembled a grisly forensic lab. Tension would always mount as I raced to finish preparations so that by the time my guests arrived, I'd have grown manic. "Who cares about stem-cell research?" I'd screech, scooping up a trail of loose saffron threads as if they were cocaine. *"Taste the fucking flageolets!"*

Things had spun out of control.

Of course, my hysteria shouldn't have surprised anyone who'd come within a mile of me. For several months, I'd been storming around in a cloud of rage, like a bee-stung character in one of those Warner Bros. cartoons. You could almost see the funnel of agitation swirling around me. My closest friends feared I was coming apart at the seams. The causes for my behavior were clear enough. In a relatively short span of time, I'd finished a difficult eight-year book project, a biography of the Beatles, that had left me nearly destitute. To make matters worse, I had fled New York City, which had captivated me like a lover for thirty years. I turned fifty (if only on paper). A fourteen-year marriage ground to an end and lapsed into a bitter divorce, after which I became embroiled in a relationship with a woman . . . but I am getting ahead of my story.

To escape the constant upheaval, I took refuge in the kitchen. Somehow, amid the knives and icepicks, I felt safe there. Comforted by the awful hush of groceries, I attempted to work out my frustrations, chopping, dicing, slicing, and grinding with the kind of vigor one devotes to, say, global *jihad*. And I muttered as I worked, providing a demonic counterpoint to the physical assault. The blade of a chef's knife on wood sounded the backbeat, accompanied by fragments of lyric—*she coulda smiled now and then . . . gave me a hug . . . it wouldn'ta killed her*—that facilitated those purple moods. If art indeed imitated life, then I was doing to pork loins and veal scallops what fate was doing to me.

The dinners themselves, however, gave me something to grab hold of. Nothing else mattered in those precious hours as I labored over a symphony of splattering pots. There was always some clumsy but extravagant concoction in the works: lamb shanks lacquered with a luxuriant pinot-noir sauce bursting with black currants; or sea bass wrapped in prosciutto atop a puddle of *salsa verde*. I'd clipped the recipes from high-gloss magazines whose pictures had seduced me into believing that any healthy biped could follow the instructions and reproduce to perfection a dish that had probably taken a squadron of cooks and food stylists weeks, if not months, to develop. Yet, on the page, at least to me, the creation looked about as demanding as a paint-by-numbers panel. After all, what was so difficult about melting a few spoonfuls of butter, sautéing shallots, adding a bouquet of fresh herbs, and deglazing a pan with chicken stock or Cognac? It didn't take a rodeo star to roll and tie a roast. Or a surgeon to bone a sea bass. There was nothing a bedraggled and broke, ex-metropolitan, middle-aged, divorced, pussy-whipped writer couldn't pull off in the kitchen if he followed directions.

Long before it served to mask my rage, cooking had sustained me. From the age of ten, I was hooked. I took over the family kitchen and tested recipes, mixing ingredients like a mad chemist, and blew up many a chicken potpie. No doubt some of the things I cooked might have qualified as weapons of mass destruction. But I learned how to make veal scallopine, and there was a recipe for steak *au poivre* I'd personalized by adding Cognac and Worcestershire sauce to the pan drippings. For the longest time I served my family something called "Chicken Divine," which I got off a Campbell's soup label. As preparations go, it was child's play: two tablespoons of Dijon mustard and a can of Cream of Mushroom soup slathered over chicken breasts, the top dusted with a mixture of grated Cheddar and bread crumbs. There was nothing to it, no skillful chopping or herbal infusions, but in those days we served it to company as if presenting a *foie gras*.

In the years that followed, my cooking skills improved marginally, a triumph of enthusiasm over finesse. As a writer, I spent too much solitary time hunched over a computer, grinding out copy overseasoned with adverbs. Almost incidentally, after working inside my head all day long, cooking became a sort of daily cooldown. It was a different, more physical means of expression. After work, instead of heading to the gym (where I was long overdue), I did my workout on machinery around the stove. You have to give me credit for effort. I worked on my mussels, lifted pie weights; nothing got my heart rate up like a perfect *crème anglaise*. Meanwhile, I learned hundreds of recipes, all by shorthand, and continued serving them with relentless panache. When things were really cookin', I was filled with joy. I'd crank up some music, dance at the counter, whisk in hand, and occasionally grab my daughter, Lily, and jitterbug from stove to table.

Everything I made turned out just-so—pleasant enough if a bit soulless. It didn't matter that my food lacked excitement or style. My friends loved to eat, and whether I realized it or not, they loved to be fed and feted, even if it meant enduring a series of stovetop experiments that often looked better on the plate than they tasted. We made a ceremony out of it. Every Friday night the gang wandered in at the usual hour, delighted that I'd invited them; delighted to see each other; delighted that I'd kicked out the jams; delighted that I'd put some thought into the menu despite the unreliability of my record. There was a lot of approval in it for me, which accounted for my gung-ho approach.

One day, dreaming of food orgies, I came across a recipe for pan-roasted cod in the *New York Times* Dining section and immediately grew flushed. There was something sensuous about the way it appeared on the page. What I couldn't get over was its aching simplicity, nothing more than a tiny saddle-shaped fillet dressed with a thorny sprig of thyme, looking lost and forlorn in a copper sauté pan. No sauce, no vegetables, just as buck-naked innocent and provocative as the girl next door. Is it normal to gaze at a hunk of fish as if it were the *Penthouse* Pet? I doubt it. Anyway, I decided to serve this little wallflower as the centerpiece the following Friday.

Even so, it had never occurred to me that the meal should be an exercise in minimalism. My friends liked to eat sensibly, so they said, and I was determined not to disappoint them. But I wasn't about to cater to timid stomachs; nothing bored me more than underseasoned food. The cod, on the other hand, gave me a chance to show off with subtle, everyday ingredients and still redeem myself. The week before, feeling extravagant, I'd whipped up a whole roasted beef tenderloin so overcooked it was better adapted to structural than culinary purposes. My guests acted with well-intentioned grace, but they pushed the meat around on their plates until they developed arm cramps. The chickpea *ragoût* went a long way toward solving the country's gas crunch. No one even touched the dessert, a swollen little soufflé that later tore through the trash bag like a Scud missile.

I was encouraged by the simplicity of the pan-roasted cod. Instead of the usual rigmarole involved with saucing fish in an aromatic broth or cream, this fillet triumphed on its own essence. Looking at the recipe, I figured it would be a cinch to pull off. All I had to do was to wash and dry a few center-cut fillets before seasoning them on both sides with salt and pepper. Then I needed to cook them, skin side down, for three minutes in a large skillet filmed with a scant tablespoon of peanut oil, just long enough to crisp the skin. After a short interlude in the oven, the pan got two nuggets of butter to baste the fish until it was cooked through. That was it in a nutshell. My friends would no doubt approve of the accompaniments of sautéed escarole and fingerling potatoes.

Phyllis, for one, rarely left anything on her plate. A healthy-looking woman with kind eyes and a foxy grin, she ate with an endearing nervous

gusto, the result of a housing-project upbringing in the Bronx, where survival of the fittest meant beating siblings to the table. Though she'd since
flourished as a bond trader, a full plate represented something extra, lavish, undue. "No, no, that's too much!" she'd protest as I carried dishes to
the table, pleading with me to give her "half that"—a child's portion. It
never failed that her food disappeared in an instant and she eyed seconds
with longing.

"Phyllis, really," Craig objected, flashing one of those faces that swung
between shock and disgust. "I don't want to hear it tomorrow, when you're
yapping about your stomach."

Every week it was the same. Their routine, I suppose, was cathartic.
Like "Who's On First?" they played these parts so well and so often that
the rest of us knew even the pauses and hand gestures.

The role of straight man especially suited Craig. He was pale and com-
pact, no taller than Phyllis, with the kind of flat Midwestern features that
made him seem like a church deacon, which was misleading. Underneath
the candy-coated shell lurked an ex-marine with a strong sixties portfolio—
Vietnam, drugs, Harleys, the works—contributing to an epic batch of stories. Craig could go on for longer than an opera, with strange rabbitty
anecdotes about diesel-fuel efficiency or the mathematical patterns of
bird flight or . . . weird shit like that, but fascinating. He was a stickler for
precision and punctuality. If dinner was called for seven o'clock, Phyllis
and Craig's car pulled up to the curb at six fifty-nine and a half and as the
clock struck the hour they barged through the door.

Carolyn, on the other hand, always arrived late.

It seemed as if I'd waited hours for her to arrive, although it was probably no more than a few minutes later than the other guests. I stood in the
kitchen instead of going to greet her.

Eventually, I poked my head into the living room and caught her eye.
"Glad you could make it," I said, grinning foolishly to show it was meant
in good fun. She looked at me coolly. Craig took her coat, and she handed
me a bouquet of pale pink peonies wrapped in a paper cone before spiral-
ing back into the gathering, out of my reach.

I laid the flowers on the messy counter. I had hoped Carolyn would help me with dinner, even phoning her earlier to make sure she would be available. "I'll get there as soon as I can," she had said, but her reply had been vague.

"We're drinking pinot grigio," I said now, holding up an open bottle of Carolyn's favorite drink.

"I'll have vodka," she said. She threw me a quick little smile, perhaps as an afterthought, and the impulsiveness of it made my heart surge.

Carolyn was a slim, attractive woman about my age, although she looked years younger. She had a lovely smile that revealed a single bashful tooth turned slightly away from the others, a protest against perfection. There were times I'd seen her in a tailored suit and admired how she carried it off, but for the most part, like tonight, she wore blue jeans and a crisp white linen shirt, with a gauzy scarf of soft pastel colors tied just so at her neck.

For a year and a half, I had been in love with Carolyn. We met by chance, soon after my marriage broke up, and I was completely in her thrall. Smart and intuitive, well-read and well-informed, she could captivate me for hours with her conversation—adult conversation that I craved as I adjusted to life as a single parent. But she was also difficult, difficult as calculus—and I was never that good at math.

She soon wandered back into the kitchen with a short-handled pitcher—the kind that holds just enough water to splash in a cocktail—and began stuffing it with the flowers. The arrangement was wild but beautiful. Carolyn was nothing if not dramatic.

She stood at the other end of the counter and spoke without looking at me. The flowers were worth her attention. I pretended to busy myself stripping a sprig of thyme.

"I hope you're not making anything fancy again," she said. "My stomach can't take those rich sauces."

"Don't worry. We're having a fillet of cod."

Her mouth pursed as she fussed with the flowers, but I could see from a softening of her lips that she was pleased. "Oh. Well . . . that sounds

wonderful," she said, her voice full of relief, even . . . warmth? "As long as
you don't drown it in butter. Fish doesn't need to be so *greasy*."

I wanted to explain that butter would bring a subtle sweetness to the
dish and keep the cod moist and meltingly tender. But Carolyn was the
ultimate challenge for an ambitious cook. For her, meals were a necessity,
not a source of pleasure. She could be satisfied, as she liked to tell friends,
with "a chunk of cheese." There were plenty of holes to punch in this
logic, but if I could win over Carolyn, I'd know I'd arrived as a cook.

I waited until she left the kitchen before turning to the fish. Dinner
would take only a few more minutes to prepare, but I didn't want to feel
hurried by anyone looking over my shoulder. Cooking, for me, was not a
spectator sport. I needed to concentrate on each recipe in order to produce a finished dish. Besides, I was hardly an artist in the kitchen. No one
needed to see me snatch a lamb chop from the floor, finger some eggshell
out of a sauce . . . or stop some bleeding.

Alone again, as the cooking reached a climax, I experienced my usual
crisis of culinary confidence. I'm a fool, I thought, to have slaved all day like
this. I'm a fool, spending all this time and money on groceries and without
a clue as to how everything would turn out. Then I let out a long breath
and swayed slightly where I stood, glancing approvingly at the beautifully
set table, the mauve sunset in the window, and the candles that flickered
like a shrine. A choir of crickets communed outside the screen door.

To put myself at ease I had had more to drink than I should have.
Throughout the late-afternoon prep work, I'd polished off two glasses of
wine and then, with Carolyn's unapologetic lateness, a third. In this condition, I felt lifted above a collective intimacy, like an angel in a Chagall
tableau, and the kitchen seemed to swim up around me.

Since the divorce, I reflected, the world had become a high-wire act
for me. I had felt secure in my family for a very long time. My wife, our
daughter, and I used to gather around the dinner table, eating, laughing,
and sharing our days, and now when I grew nostalgic about the familiar
everyday comforts, I never failed to replay that scene. Occasionally, in a
sentimental mood, I paged through my cookbooks, associating different

recipes with corresponding dinners I had made for my family, or intended to make for them: *coq au vin, boeuf Bourguignon,* fajitas, swordfish with mango and black-bean chutney. Now, I stood on the outside of things, testing each new footstep, like a man who might slip and fall. I felt adrift, lost, clumsy. To regain my emotional footing required courage, and I was a quart low at the moment. Carolyn sensed this, and I'm afraid she saw it as weakness.

At least my daughter gave me strength. Most nights, I still cooked for Lily, and most mornings I sent her off to school with a lunch bag full of leftovers, the most gratifying moments of my day. Only eleven years old, Lily was a chef's ideal at the table, game for trying all my crackpot creations. She was the only kid I knew who'd attack garlicky escargots, a seared *foie gras,* or a dozen raw oysters with fearless relish, yet. I often felt lonely with just the two of us. With Carolyn, I had hoped to re-create that dream of an intact family around the dinner table— or, at least, to make the perfect dinner—but I worried I couldn't pull it all together. It seemed that I was too anxious, not thinking clearly enough, to achieve either goal.

Several minutes passed before I felt like resuming the preparations and began to work in a more decisive manner. Everything had to come together, to flow, in a fine orchestration. Recipes were laid on the counter, like the score of a symphony, each dish a separate movement. The steamed potatoes were nearing doneness; the escarole, slick with olive oil, was approaching the wilted stage; a salad of baby arugula, with roasted beets and pear slices, needed dressing; the wine—a late-model Chablis sweating on a trivet—remained corked; a sourdough baguette awaited slicing. On top of everything else, the fish had to hit the oven at precisely the right moment so that it could cook and be served *à la minute,* still sizzling in its own fragrance.

Everything hovered at the tipping point. Some dishes looked perfect, others needed but a finishing touch. The stove, hot and crowded, with all four burners going full blast, grew more manageable as my confidence rose.

Our friend Lynn hurried in, with another bottle of pinot grigio under an arm and a neatly wrapped gift clutched in the other. She slid the package onto the table and took in the scene as she worked the cork from the bottle.

"Sorry I'm late," she said in a breathy rush. I looked over at the gleam of the straw-colored wine sluicing up her glass. "But fortunately Carolyn was here to help you. Oh, it all looks marvelous. It must have been so much work. You two must have had your hands full."

I didn't have the heart to contradict her. "Could you ask her to come in here for a moment?" I said. "There's a procedure that requires her expert advice."

There was an inquisitive silence from the living room. Finally, Craig called out: "Need a hand in there?"

After a long moment, Carolyn appeared at my elbow. "I've already had as much talk as I can stand about real estate," she said.

I handed her the plates. "Would you mind warming these for me? If you just place them between your thighs . . ."

"Very funny," Carolyn said, fighting down a smile.

While she dealt them onto an oven rack like a hand of cards, I dressed the fillets with thyme sprigs and placed them evenly around a pan. "You know, it'd be nice if you stuck around here until the food is served," I said. "I could use some moral support."

"You seem to be doing fine by yourself." She sounded determined to believe it. "And, anyway, it's *your* dinner party. Big or intimate, simple or splashy, you're in your element. It would be cruel to deprive you of the glory."

"That's kind of a harsh motive to lay on me, don't you think?"

"Don't take it the wrong way. It takes effort to absorb all your energy. You don't even realize it. Really, you should try walking in here one Friday night when you're in the middle of this extravaganza and experience what it feels like from the other side. It'd be a revelation."

"Nobody else seems to mind."

"That's because they'd lose their meal ticket," she said. Carolyn realized the sting of her words and backpedaled. "You know how much they love your food. Everyone looks forward to coming here."

"Everyone except you, it seems."

"Now you *are* taking it the wrong way." With a studied pout, she took a sip from my wine glass, hoping it would distract me enough to reroute the conversation.

I decided to help her out. "You have a nerve looking so lovely tonight." An errant ray from the overhead fixture danced across the bridge of her nose, revealing the palest polleny triangle of freckles.

"It must be the light in here."

"Either that, or someone has a portrait of you stashed in their attic."

"You've obviously had too much to drink." She took the wine glass and smoothly placed it on a high shelf, out of reach. "Maybe it's a cushion for all this work you put in."

"What is that supposed to mean?"

"You know, all of *this*. This melodrama."

She began glancing, aimlessly, lightly, about the room, as though taking a silent inventory, lingering over ingredients that would soon be cooked, looking at the elaborate table setting, the swan's-neck decanter and hand-painted napkin rings. She flinched at some dried stems of lavender left over from last week's dinner party that I'd strewn among some pine branches to make a centerpiece. Depending on the lighting, it looked lifted from either *Family Circle* or *Return of the Swamp Thing*. She shook her head almost imperceptibly. "Why must you always go to so much trouble? You insist on going overboard."

"Because I enjoy cooking—cooking for you. And I love having friends here."

"It's only food. No one really cares whether it's elaborate or not. You could serve. . . ."

"A chunk of cheese. I know, I've heard it before."

"I wasn't going to say that," she said, her mouth registering the appropriate wound. "You could serve hamburgers and we'd be just as delighted."

"We're going to have to order in hamburgers if I don't get this fish going," I said, turning my back. "Would you mind dressing the salad while I get to work?"

Carolyn splashed spoonfuls of a simple vinaigrette over the lettuce, while I seared the cod in a preheated skillet and then slid it into the oven. Invariably, the kitchen filled with smoke from some burned bits and grease that stuck to the pan, but tonight only a sweet, steamy perfume bloomed in the surroundings. There was a lot to be said for restraint, and the aroma in the room was fairly singing its praises.

"There's too much salt in the dressing," Carolyn said, making quick little gerbil noises with her lips and tongue.

"Here," I said, removing a portion from the salad bowl and depositing it on a plate. "Just add more oil and vinegar and put it next to your place setting." I popped the caps on two bottles of fizzy water. "Would you call the gang to the table? It's showtime!"

The kitchen in the house I'd rented since the divorce was comfortable enough for me and my daughter, but with five adults parading through the narrow aisle to the table in back, it felt like the Lexington Avenue subway at rush hour. There was a small electric range with burners that tilted at strange angles, and a wall of plywood cupboards with doors that swung open at the most inopportune times. In any case, it was difficult to maneuver in what little space there was. Lynn and Phyllis squeezed past me at the stove, holding two wine glasses each above their heads, nearly tripping over Craig, who was crouched at the freezer filling a tumbler with ice cubes. My dog, Wink, was underfoot, as usual. Carolyn hesitated in the doorway, as though deciding whether to join us. Silhouetted in the frame, she seemed to me ever more beautiful, serene. I reached out and pulled her toward me. "Let's have a good time," I whispered, lightly kissing her cheek.

"Your fish is going to burn," she said.

This didn't seem to be going well. Yet the room was intimate and full of promise; my friends were already absorbed in conversation, in an obvious good mood, and excited about the food I had prepared.

I was pleased that so much thought had gone into the dinner. It was ambitious, though stubbornly unpretentious food, the baby potatoes encrusted in Provençal spices and the escarole as intensely fragrant and green as the lawn just across the way. When the cod fillets came out of the oven, sizzling in their own juices, filling the entire kitchen with the scent of thyme and the sea, it was impossible, under the circumstances, to let any bad vibes intrude.

I didn't even flinch when Carolyn said, "No potatoes for me."

The plates were passed clockwise around the table, first to Lynn, who added salad and a generous grind of pepper. Forks were poised over the plates: a beautiful still life, I thought.

As he dug in with gusto, Craig broke into a monologue on the return to glory of modern-day Berlin, while the Chablis relayed quickly from hand to hand.

At times like these, I often disengaged from the conversation to let the tide of the experience wash over me. On one hand, there was relief. There had been so many details, planned and fulfilled, and I glowed with the pleasure that comes with such accomplishment. But sometimes the outcome left me feeling rather melancholy, deflated. I drank some sparkling water, hoping to locate my hunger, while heads bobbed around me, keeping rhythm to Craig's sermon: yes, yes, mm-hmm, I see. I nodded once or twice as a sign of fellowship, otherwise my mind skimmed across more personal terrain.

Since the new year, when I'd finished my Beatles book, I'd been bumping around like a stray dog, just reading, cooking for friends, and taking long walks on the beach—that is, doing nothing, *dolce far niente*, as the Italians say. It had been bittersweet, to say the least. In one respect, I'd been celebrating like a madman—the book was finally done. But I was only beginning to understand what a transition I'd undergone, coming to grips with the price I'd paid for the awful descent of my marriage and the fears and excitement of starting anew. My friends had only caught glimpses of this dark domestic drama from which I still hadn't recovered. I had been forced to take a good hard look at myself, to reevaluate my ability as a writer and my place on the planet.

Turn and face the strange . . . But all those *ch-ch*-changes at once seemed extreme for one man to absorb.

And where did Carolyn fit into all this? Her brains and beauty seemed a gift, the perfect antidote. But a relationship needed to grow, to reach the next level gracefully, and there wasn't anything graceful about this one.

I did expect her to say something about the food. Phyllis's plate was nearly empty. Rather than ask for more, she seemed content to nibble from Craig's while he rambled on about café life along Nollendorfplatz. It was Lynn who weighed in first.

"Hats off to the chef," she said, raising her glass in my direction. "Everything is delicious."

"As usual," Phyllis agreed.

"As usual I've been jabbering too much," Craig apologized. Ceremoniously, he picked up a fork and reeled at the evidence of Phyllis's hunger—the mangled fish, some shredded escarole, the nubby remnants of a potato. "Jesus! It looks like a cyclone blew through here."

Carolyn followed the action like a spectator at a play, her expression guarded. "How you doing over there?" I asked her, as one might a new acquaintance.

"I'm fine."

"Because it looks like you haven't touched anything. I just wondered if it was okay."

"I could ask you the same question," she said, nodding at my place setting.

I continued to stare into her silver-blue eyes, shaken by the lingering mystery that continued to attract me. Absentmindedly, I placed a bite of the fillet in my mouth.

My heart sank for the second time that night. From the first forkful I knew that my dinner was anything but a triumph. For one thing, it was obvious that the cod had cooked too long. Somewhere in the last few minutes, the fat had leached out, and with it the supple, briny, moist consistency that turns fish into an ethereal confection. This cod tasted, astonishingly, like any other piece of fish. There was nothing exciting about it, nothing sensuous. That isn't to say it was not satisfying, but I *hated* satisfying, unless there was something more, something that made me cry, *"Holy shit!"* when I bit into it. It needed a boost—perhaps leeks sweated until they were jelly, some enriched stock, and a splash or two of dry vermouth. Perhaps a trip out the window courtesy of my Rubbermaid spatula.

"Oh, this is just luscious," Craig said, momentarily coming up for air. "The flavors are extraordinary. You've outdone yourself, my friend. I applaud you."

Struggling to maintain my game face, I speared a few leaves of sautéed escarole and lapsed into darker desolation. The once-beautiful greens had taken on a slightly metallic aftertaste, and their texture was all wrong. Ideally, they should have held their shape, which would have brought out a concentrated sweetness; instead they were limp and soggy.

"I especially like the cooked lettuce," Craig continued helpfully.

"Escarole," I muttered. "Sorry, but it should have come off the stove much sooner."

"Oh, it's perfectly fine," Carolyn said, sighing. "Why do you always have to find fault with everything you make?"

"It's supposed to be crisp, that's all. It would taste different if it were cooked properly."

"Nobody knows the difference."

"*I* know. And I know that the fish is overcooked and the potatoes are tasteless. How's that for fault-finding, babe?" I didn't give her a chance to answer. "The problem is, I *love* good food. I love the ingredients, the process, the smells, the way everything tastes. But like music, it has to hit all the right notes. You can't cut corners." Suddenly my voice was two octaves higher. "There are no compromises. You can't settle for 'fine' or 'good enough.' I want the fish to melt in my mouth, the escarole to be tender, and potatoes to be full of flavor. Anything less, I feel cheated."

The dog began to slink away.

"Well, I certainly admire your passion," Carolyn said. Everyone else looked down uncomfortably.

My passion had gone the way of my appetite, which was to say south. Carolyn, on the other hand, proceeded to eat. I watched her devour the cod with real determination and realized there was nothing more I could do to express how I felt. Our relationship and my cooking turned on the same sorry axis: How could either find balance if I didn't understand the first thing about them? My passion for Carolyn was deep and irrational. Cooking, I had hoped, was easier to embrace. Perhaps it was not too late for me to conquer that passion, or at least ground it in some kind of tangible skill. Maybe I should think small—start with learning how to cook and leave the rest alone for now.

Thinking about the dinner I had intended to make, I agonized over the dinner I had just served. I felt its clumsy mechanics in every dish. There was nothing imaginative about it, no flair. It was obvious I didn't know much about cooking. I had the urge to express myself in the kitchen, but I was only executing recipes, hoping they would turn out all right. No matter how good a recipe, how accurate the descriptions and instructions for preparing a dish, I realized that it required that I add something of my own, something basic and probably indescribable, and that meant developing enough versatility to trust my instincts.

I confessed as much to my friends while they helped themselves to more salad. The sad fact, I admitted, was that I needed to learn how to cook, really cook—to grasp the mysteries and magic associated with the process. "Not like this coffee-shop fish on your plates. It takes more than a fancy knife and expensive pans to make delicious food. I need to learn what a chef needs to know and what the secrets are of truly great cooking." Avoiding Carolyn's eyes, I said, "Besides, I need to get away for awhile. I need to get my life back on track."

The table fell silent, waiting. I had veered onto a road inhabited by snipers and land mines. Across the table, the creamy contours of Carolyn's face changed shape, then stiffened, as she concentrated on pouring more wine. "It sounds like you're headed for a midlife crisis," she said, without looking up.

"Maybe you should buy a new Cuisinart," Lynn offered. "I saw them on sale at Bed, Bath & Beyond."

Craig was more generous: "Or a few weeks in a cabin, with no phone and a stack of books. Isn't that what it takes to recharge the ol' batteries?"

"Something like that," I said.

Actually, I knew what had to be done, had been dreaming about it for a long time. I'd been distracted, preoccupied for the last eight years, but now seemed like the perfect time to pursue my odyssey, to follow my heart. With any luck, it'd help put my relationship with Carolyn back on track.

"I am getting out of here," I announced. "I'm going to Europe, to learn how to cook."

The announcement struck them as absurd, and not even the dog believed it.

Chapter One

RUE DU LAC

If I believe in anything, I believe this: Life is no chunk of cheese. Ask any guy over forty and he'll tell you the same thing. Life is a goddamn feast. Everything that comes before is just a burger, the basics—a place to live, a job, a ball game on TV, getting laid. But crawl over that forty-yard line and, brother, that burger is just so much ground chuck. At a certain point, you want the finer things. If I didn't, I'd still be stumbling around the kitchen in that cottage back in Connecticut, cutting out coupons. At least, that's the conclusion I'd reached during an interminable flight to Milan. Alitalia had booked me in a seat next to the

window, and as the plane banked over Mont Blanc, I attempted to zero in
on the things that mattered to me now.

How, you might ask, did I wind up in this spot? Last seen, I was cooking for some friends in my kitchen back home; next thing I know I'm on
a plane bound for Italy. It hadn't taken much to set things in motion. The
more I thought about it, a getaway sounded like the perfect tonic for the
frustrations of midlife—my midlife, that is, a scene out of *The Heartbreak
Kid*. Three or four months of barnstorming through Europe, working in fabulous kitchens, cooking alongside master chefs—at first, it seemed crazy,
a fantasy run wild. I'd been dreaming about just such an adventure for a
long time. Suddenly, it made perfect sense. The time was right; something
told me it was now or never. Yes, I wanted to learn how to cook, but that
well-made goal came wrapped in the more fundamental pursuit of a spiritual, soul-nourishing antidote to modern living. The previous few years had
been a nightmare. Yet, I'd survived and managed to reinvent my life. So a
trip through European cooking schools would be less an avenue of escape
than an exploration—of life, of new opportunities, of misplaced passions
and desires.

The pursuit of passion. It sounded like an *Esquire* article: what it is,
how to get it, what to do with it once you have it. Most men my age are
still obsessed with these questions. They're still searching for the things
that make life special—something extra, something more. Guys I know
pursue countless flaky obsessions—a single-engine Cessna, a kitschy tat-
too, that twenty-four-year-old trophy wife. Many of us today have the luxury and disposable income to pursue fantasies in ways our fathers never
could. Somehow, with everything else falling apart around me, the one
passion I was still sure of was cooking.

I love making food. It makes me happy, gives me pleasure, provides a
source of creativity. The pull of the stove is very hard to resist. The urge
to express myself, to prepare a great-tasting dish, is as good as it gets, and
when all goes according to plan, I get as turned on as a teenager. Twenty
years ago, a guy admitting that might have been treated as a crackpot.
But somewhere along the way, cooking became a cool pursuit. Perhaps a
culinary adventure would help me sort out my situation.

My Alitalia seatmate, however, didn't see it that way. Discreetly, I had tried it out on Dan, a Fiat distributor on his way to Turin, who was convinced that European cooking schools were Interpol's version of the Witness Protection Program.

"Where do you think they've stashed Ratko Mladic?" he asked, glancing up from a paperback page-turner. "Put a guy like that in a restaurant kitchen and no one'd ever find him."

Omens are powerful mojo. Any person in his right mind would have regarded this nutjob as a sign from the gods and hopped the next flight back to the States. In the event that wasn't incentive enough, the throbbing in my hand should have convinced me. Two days before leaving home, I had broken a fall, along with two small bones in my right—chopping, dicing, and slicing—hand, which had swollen to the size of a papaya, making cooking lessons all but absurd. A cast was out of the question. Between a truckload of luggage and essential kitchen paraphernalia, my limbs were already mortgaged to the hilt. Determined to flout the Fates, I paid no heed to either omen; instead, I thanked my seatmate for his insight, even shook his hand.

Nothing short of Armageddon was going to derail my adventure. In slightly under a month, working feverishly, I had managed to knit together an impressive itinerary that would take me from northern Italy through France and back to Italy for a nightcap. There were eighteen cooking schools where I could do what is called a *stage,* or internship, to learn basic skills from the masters, eighteen glorious kitchens in which to exercise my fantasies without fear that a fillet of fossilized cod would reach an unsuspecting dinner guest. It would be instructive beyond my dreams. Besides, I was going to have the time of my life, according to my friend Sandy D'Amato, who owned the restaurant Sanford in Milwaukee and happened to be one of America's finest chefs. "Cooking schools are the new Club Meds," he told me, during a break in the advance work. "Imagine the kinds of characters you're going to meet along the way, not to mention a fair amount of horny single women." Visions of Gauguin in Tahiti danced in my brain, quickly marginalized by the cold light of kitchen galleys presided over by stoop-shouldered women with mustaches better than my own. And anyway, I had finally talked Carolyn into joining me.

She seemed reluctant, at first. Her exact words, I believe, were: "You must be out of your mind." The kind of trip I proposed, she said, was for dreamers and dilettantes, but in any case not her sort of fantasy. There were other issues, as well: She hadn't spoken to me in more than two weeks, she hated to cook, and the prospect of spending three months on the road with me—and, god forbid, sharing a room with me—unsettled her. We fenced for days without resolving anything. Finally, in an effort to avoid a real confrontation, she ran off to Nantucket, hiding out there with friends until, ostensibly, I'd left the country.

Hurt by our inability to compromise, I was unprepared for Carolyn's call in the days just before departure.

"I'm coming with you!" she cried, through the eddy of cell-phone static. I gingerly withheld a response, in case I'd mistaken what she had said. *Yawn coming. Itch you? Oncoming witch ewe.* Was my ear playing tricks on me? One thing was clear: The surface of her armor had cracked. I heard elation in place of her usual careful reserve.

A weight fell off my chest.

She'd just needed time to come to her senses. "I've been turning it over for days and realized this was the trip of a lifetime," Carolyn said. "If I didn't go, I'd probably regret it forever." *And?* "Think about it: It'll be just the two of us. Our own private world. Exactly what we've needed."

Taxiing toward the Milan Malpensa terminal, I reflected on her excitement that afternoon, and mine. I could only imagine what it must have taken for Carolyn to arrive at that decision. Nothing, other than loneliness, came easily to her. Somehow I seemed to have breached security, and it must have unnerved her. The exposure made her unstable, as unpredictable as the weather.

In the interim, she had spent many days at the beach poring over maps, tracing our route for the next three months. On paper the trip seemed idyllic: a train ride over the Alps from Milan to Lyon, then farther into Burgundy, rural Provence, Nice, Bordeaux, Paris, and Cannes in succession before pushing back south into Italy. The details made her head spin. "I'll never be able to pack in time," she sighed. "But you go ahead. Do some cooking, get your feet wet, and I'll meet you in Nice."

Something else hung in the air, and it took some effort to pry it out of her. *I can't. . . . Just forget it. . . . Really, never mind. . . .* Carolyn's giggle was a smokescreen. After some exaggerated hedging, she broke like a dam. "I just got off the phone with my mother," she confessed, "who, believe it or not, encouraged me to go with you. She only had one worry. She said, 'Now don't you two run off and get married while you're in Europe.'"

So my hopes were high about Carolyn, but I was already missing the other woman in my life, the one who liked my food. Lily and I had endured separations before, when I'd traveled for work. Now it was happening again—only, this time, it would be for a few months. Through plenty of tears, we agreed to stay in constant touch. Ever loyal, she said she couldn't wait to try my new recipes.

The itinerary had fallen neatly into place. As I sorted through websites devoted to culinary instruction, the loose fabric of a cooking-school circuit materialized in some of the most exotic locales in Western Europe. There were dozens of programs to choose from—one type in which you take classes with a group of like-minded enthusiasts; other classes I could arrange with great teachers in their homes. Using contacts I'd made as a magazine writer, I also set up some private sessions with master chefs at fabulous restaurants such as Arpège in Paris and Moulin de Mougins near Nice. I've been drooling over websites promoting a riot of cuisines, fabulously seductive menus. "Join us for five fun-filled days of cooking deep inside Provence. . . ." "Our 18th Century farmhouse nestled in an olive grove provides a superbly-equipped kitchen. . . ." "Authentic regional cooking developed and handed down over generations set in a restored Tuscan villa. . . ." "Top chefs." "Hands-on, one-on-one instruction with a Michelin-starred virtuoso. . . ." "Cook with confidence and passion for your family and friends. . . ." "Once back home, you will be able to reproduce what you've learned here with ease and style. . . ."

The accompanying pictures bordered on the obscene. Plump little flans shuddered on antique saucers, casseroles burbled like Vesuvius, mussels oozed enough butter to clog the Alaska pipeline. One woman, her face surrendered in ecstasy, lowered a fat, juicy spear of asparagus into her mouth with a finesse that would have impressed Marilyn Chambers. This was Internet porn at its finest.

The come-ons and delicacies made it difficult to choose; everything was bathed in a soft-focus splendor. Many programs showcased groups of attractive, well-tanned couples holding wine glasses aloft on some candlelit terrace. Or at a picnic feast spread out in tall grass, awash in summer light that would move a poet to tears. A link whisked me unexpectedly to a cliffside retreat above Mykonos, where the *dolmades* looked like stubby Cuban cigars. With so much variety, how could I expect to limit a culinary odyssey to any one segment of the globe? I wanted it all and decided to hopscotch around Western Europe, hitting one fabulous school after another.

My approach was unorthodox, I knew. There are other ways to learn to cook. I could have stayed in one place and taken one long course, from basic to advanced, but I wanted to experience the best. I wanted to tap into the imaginations of great chefs. I knew my plan could get crazy. I'd risk running into some strange situations; some duds; some flamboyant, tetchy personalities—they were chefs, after all. When it worked, though, it could be amazing, life-changing. Who could use that more than I?

"Stick to France and Italy," Sandy D'Amato had suggested. "The twin pillars of Western cuisine."

That sounded a bit parochial coming from a world-class chef. I argued for stops in Spain, Greece, and Portugal, to say nothing of Japan, China, and India, where exotic spices challenged even the most experienced cooks. "You can't jump-start a lamb kabob without curry," I said.

"That may be so," retorted Sandy, "but there has to be some focus to the cooking. Start with the basics. The French and Italians both have a grand cuisine and a peasant cuisine, unlike the rest of Europe, where there is only generic cooking. Their fundamentals of building flavors are similar, their lifestyles are complementary and intertwined. Moreover, their chefs share intimate relationships—and rivalries—that date back generations."

The Italians, I learned, claimed credit for the prominence of French cuisine. Legend has it that Catherine de Medici, a figure of wide influence, brought her cooks and pastry chef from Florence to the court of Henri II on the presumption that the food in France was undistinguished, if not entirely inedible. As French kitchens began filling with such Florentine delicacies as butter and truffles, Catherine's subjects had no choice but to embrace her haute cuisine. Which is why many Italians, to this day, believe that the French are basically eating Italian food.

No way was I wading into those bloody waters, but the aspects that were interchangeable in their cooking were intriguing as hell. Even after all the years at the cutting board, I could not tell the difference between a *mirepoix* and its ancestral *soffritto*, necessitating guidance to keep me from fouling up yet another *ragoût* (or, as the case may be, a *ragú*. I had never been sure).

France and Italy: I had been infatuated with both countries since childhood, cherished them as an adult. There wasn't a custom, aside from maybe hairy female armpits, that didn't enchant me. In the last two decades, I had never let a year pass without making a pilgrimage of some sort, whether it was holiday travel or a mad weekend of restaurant bingeing. My French was decent enough, I suppose. In preparation for the trip, I'd picked up an audio course that promised to make me fluent in Italian after just thirty days—and it might work at that, as long as the chefs limited their conversation to sentences like "*Buon giorno*, Carlo. It is a beautiful afternoon. What time does the bus depart for Livorno?" No matter, we'd find some way to communicate. In the meantime, I was memorizing such key words and phrases as: salt, extra-virgin olive oil, tourniquet, and resuscitator.

It has been my long-held belief that everything to be found in France and Italy is more intense and romantic than in any place else I know or care about. Of course, I am not entirely alone in this opinion. A great many people have said the same thing, perhaps in more expressive ways. People-watching from a seat in any French or Italian outdoor café is like theater; everyone has a surround of chic or clangor that is impossible to ignore. The food there is richer, more delicious, more alive on your tongue. Wildflowers seem more vivid, their musky essence as intoxicating as a highball. If you happen to stumble there, you feel more foolish than you would in, say, London, and if you soar, you fly higher than anywhere else. In the same respect, there is no place on earth where passions are more in play, which means that heartbreak, when it happens, is crueler and more tragic than one had imagined possible.

I was betting that France and Italy would work their magic on Carolyn and cast a golden spell over our relationship. So it seemed pointless or masochistic to take the train over the Alps alone. That little detour had been designed specifically as an aphrodisiac to put Carolyn in the mood. Without her, those breathtaking views would be nothing more than mountains and trees. So I cashed in my ticket for a seat on the next puddle-jumper out of Milan and arrived in Lyon before nightfall.

There was nothing coincidental about the gateway to my adventure. Most towns where cooking schools are located have some pivotal tie to cuisine: a three-star restaurant, a market, an indigenous crop, an Eiffel Tower. But only Lyon claims to be the capital of French gastronomy. The surrounding hillsides are simply infested with places to eat—a handful of groundbreaking restaurants and first-rate bistros, as well as the local version of down-home country-cookin' joints, the *bouchons* that serve platters of transcendent Lyonnais specialties so buttery rich they could stop a man's heart before dessert arrives.

Then, of course, there is Paul Bocuse. Word had it that the so-called Chef of the Century was rarely at his place down the road anymore, although it still dished up the most inspired food this side of the equator. I'd once had dinner with him in New York, and he was such a gnarly old bastard that I swore I'd never put another forkful of his food in my mouth. Then, again, I took a similar kind of oath when George W. was elected president and I hadn't yet moved to that cliffside shack in Tierra del Fuego. I wondered if a table *chez* Bocuse was to be had. If a *quenelles mousseline* or *tête de veau bourgeoise* can only be savored as they were meant to be in his restaurant, then I was going to have to swallow my pride and book a seat right away.

Bocuse gave Lyon a guru. And two of France's best-known wine-growing regions—Beaujolais to the north and the Côtes du Rhône to the south, both only a stone's throw away—gave the city their blessing. There wasn't a reason for anyone interested in food—serious food, that is—to set a big toe even a silly millimeter beyond the town line. The outdoor market stretched on for what seemed like miles, jammed with people picking through stalls of picture-perfect vegetables; fat *saucissons*; chickens the size of newborn babies roasting to perfection on the spit; mounds of wrinkly, sun-cured olives; cheeses I'd never heard of; to say nothing of the huge variety of local specialties that will never make it to the next region, much less to a Stop & Shop.

Lyon's legacy of cooking was as old as its Roman heritage, which was still alive on the banks of the two great navigable rivers that run through the city. In 43 BC, Caesar ordered the city built where the Rhône and the Saône converged like an hourglass full of energy and bountiful light. Calling it Lugdunum, he invested it with the kind of practical Roman foresight that inspired rapid development: functional roads, a series of aqueducts and bridges, and an amphitheater where lions presumably dined as well as the emperors.

The sense of antiquity in Lyon is evident in and around the rivers, especially at night, when the castles, palaces, and cathedrals cast glowing reflections on the water's slatelike surface. The romance and beauty of the nightscape are a magnet for crowds who promenade along the riverbanks with a formality that evokes the city's glorious past. Saturday night, when I arrived and set out for a walk, the footpaths seethed with well-dressed couples making a slow, ceremonial procession. It resembled the set of a Merchant-Ivory film, and I supposed, with a little imagination, this was how Paris might have looked in the thirties, before the commotion of lights and technology arrived.

The next morning, I made a beeline for Old Lyon, the medieval *quartier* on the western bank of the Saône, preserved as it was when Agrippa designated it the starting point of the principal Roman roads throughout Gaul. I had been here twice before, dreaming of it often in the intervening years. Everything was exactly as I'd remembered: quaint and enchanted. I felt my spirits rise. The natural contours of the *quartier* made it seem almost miniature in scale, restricted by the backdrop of Fouvière hill, a steep cliff looming like unfinished sculpture above the terraced, rose-col-

ored buildings. Beneath its expanse was a patchwork of narrow, brick-
lined streets stacked one just above the other, running headlong into wide
squares before snaking off again like those blasted concourses in modern
airline terminals. Because of the tight, boxed-in façades, the streets surrendered to a current of ever-changing shadows reminding me of those
early monster films when Rodan or Mothra flew overhead. But when the
sun began to rise over the towers of modern Lyon, a brilliant glare blew
away the cobwebs with blinding indifference.

On Sundays, the *quartier* slept late under a blanket of shade. It was
a sultry August morning, already uncomfortable. Restaurants were shuttered until well past ten, the streets all but deserted. A brigade of scruffy
cats patrolled the gutters in pursuit of scraps, while overhead a column of
pigeons stood sentry on the lips of awnings, waiting their turn.

I had arranged to meet an acquaintance for brunch in the Rue St.-
Jean, just around the corner from the Gothic cathedral. There were still a
few hours before I was due to leave for Burgundy, where my first cooking
instruction was situated, and a Lyonnais meal seemed the best way to fill
the time.

David was like most expatriates who'd hitchhiked through Europe
after college and had never gotten around to returning home. There was
some long, sad story about a tyrannical father that I wasn't prepared to
hear. In the interim, he had carved out a new identity that owed nothing
to his family—or to his country, for that matter. Tall and shaggy-haired, he
had even lost the well-upholstered gloss that characterized other young
American tourists, who now regarded him dismissively as if he were
another baffling Frenchman.

Living practically hand-to-mouth in Lyon, David got by teaching
English in a local university, and, as befits most instructors of a certain age
and self-esteem, he had fallen for one of his students.

Lucy was the kind of French girl I'd idealized from boyhood: slim,
high-breasted, sensual, and supremely confident, showing enough bare
midriff to warrant the warning: This belly was specially reformatted to fit
your television screen. The daughter of a local line cook, she was bursting
with schoolgirl ripeness, a quality made evident by David's lickerish stare;

I could tell that she was amused by him but that it would soon grow old. At least her English was good; David had done his job well.

"Bocuse is shit, a turd," Lucy said when I suggested a place to eat. "He couldn't cook his way out of *une papillote.*"

"A paper bag," David corrected her.

"Yes, exactly. That's what I said."

Lucy had her heart set on a bistro in Old Lyon where she predicted the breakfast would deliver an unforgettable experience. "We'll have *huitres* and white wine and then something larger from the sea."

David looked ashen. "I couldn't put that in my mouth right now, Luce," he said, checking his watch, which read slightly past ten. "How about later?"

"But it's the *perfect* breakfast," she insisted, her mouth drawn into a spoiled pout. "I bet Bob is more adventurous."

Actually, oysters sounded heavenly no matter what the hour. There were few things able to make my saliva run at the very mention of a name. "But it's August," I sighed, "and about eighty-five degrees already. How about if we just swallow Drano instead?"

"What can be the matter? Ah, you Americans are such—how do you say?—*chats.* "

That could have gone either way. My money was on pussies, but David let it slide. He's picking his battles, I thought admiringly, as Lucy led us around the corner like a streetwalker with two excited johns.

The restaurant was a typical Lyonnais *boîte,* the kind that revels in funky organ meat but serves a selection of tamer dishes for the tourists, with a small bar and five or six banquettes grouped below a mural of the Champs Elysées. The painting was yellow from smoke and hideously old-fashioned, but it didn't matter, because no one other than the owner's family ever sat indoors. We parked ourselves at one of the sidewalk tables just off the curb and waited while a blank-faced waiter took his sweet time rearranging the rows of chairs. We might as well have been invisible. There was no one else at the place, but his routine had been disturbed by our early arrival, for which the penalty was to be ignored.

I was starving. I had last eaten during the flight from New York, not counting a midnight raid on the hotel mini-bar, which I'd plundered in an effort to stanch my hunger. Over and above that (and being fairly exhausted), I felt an awful need for something satisfying, something simple and honest and unforgettable, to inaugurate my cooking odyssey. That is, if the waiter ever made an effort to acknowledge us.

"*Bouge ton boule,*" Lucy muttered under her breath, her eyes downcast and expressionless, as though she were talking to herself.

I looked at David, who grinned before translating. Literally, *bouge ton boule* means "move your ass." But the proper phrase, according to him, should have been *bouge tes fesses.* "You see, in America," David explained, "you have one ass. But the French—superior beings that they are—have two asses: a left ass and a right ass. So the only way you can properly express this is by using the plural, *tes.*" Even so, Lucy assured us, *bouge ton boule* was a much hipper way of putting it.

In due time, the waiter dragged his *fesses,* both of them, over to our table, propping a blackboard on one of the empty chairs. The daily special was *cabillaud en papillote,* cod wrapped in parchment, which sounded promising if reasonably safe. David ordered for the three of us, careful to include an appetizer that would keep his girlfriend happy.

As Lucy slurped down a dozen Belon oysters, we could only shrug with admiration. She had her own enviable technique, grabbing each slippery mollusk between the tips of her tiny Chiclet teeth, pulling gently, and then wrapping her tongue around it in a circular extracting motion. That girl was part gull, I decided. Or something else altogether.

As if reading my mind, David said, "I'm telling you, man, you ought to spend some serious time in Lyon. Aside from the tourists who swarm the streets on the weekends, there is plenty here to keep you entertained. Lucy's got a killer group of friends. Take it from me, it could change your life."

Watching Lucy's kitten face dip childishly into the plate, an incentive of that sort couldn't have been farther from my mind. She was an appealing girl, no doubt about that, but she had nothing on Carolyn, who had a gilded cameo quality about her that cheapened Lucy's youth. And her friends had the appeal of a rice cake. I was careful not to let this show; the last thing I wanted was to hurt anyone's feelings. Instead, I thanked David for the invitation and tried to explain why lingering in one place would be impossible for a while.

That first morning in France I was filled with expectation, but there had been times, I had to admit, when such an offer would have made me sweat. The temptation to disappear into another country, to reinvent myself, was powerful, especially at night when insecurity lurked in the shadows. Heart racing, I'd convince myself that the situations in my life, every last one of them, were completely and utterly hopeless. When that happened, all I could think about was the sudden freefall of my bank account, the screws turning in my never-ending divorce action, editors pounding on my door demanding that long-overdue manuscript, the failure of Carolyn to commit herself to my heart—every horrific responsibility and obligation pulsed through my body until only the prospect of flight from it all invited the refuge of sleep. I'd lock the door behind me and get on a plane, with only a change of clothes and that battered copy of Trollope's *The Way We Live Now* to keep me entertained. There were always sirens like Lucy in those scenarios. And endless dinner parties in fabulous villas.

It occurred to me that perhaps the dream had gained some kind of purchase on my life, with cooking schools pinch-hitting for that elusive gold ring.

"I don't know, man," David said, as our plates of food arrived. "It sounds to me like you could stand a little fun. All those lessons are just gonna wire you in a different way. Really, how long is it going to be before you want to escape from those as well? Two weeks? *Four?* Listen, any time you get fed up with it, you can always come back here and crash on my couch."

I felt sorry but said nothing to David, who seemed to sense what I'd gone through and was eager to help. But he had his own sorrows to contend with, and they clouded his judgment. He assumed we were brothers-in-arms, refugees from some train wreck of a life that needed a fresh start in a fresh place with a fresh set of dreams. He assumed that a young, saucy woman would cure all my ills. But he'd gotten me wrong. I wasn't running away from my past, or even my heart, for that matter. I wanted to cook, but I wanted Carolyn with me, too.

"You know," he said, with a sudden change of voice, "this might turn out to be an instructive meal for you. Hopefully, it'll give you something to measure other meals against. Lyonnais cooking is a cut above the stuff you're going to eat in other parts of France, like the *cassoulets* in Bordeaux that are so typical."

He couldn't have meant the lunch set in front of us. It was beautifully prepared, but unlike anything that usually came out of a Lyonnais kitchen. The *papillote*, for one thing, was aluminum foil rather than parchment, and the vegetables were straight from a Middle Eastern garden—a delicious sort of chickpea relish with roasted peppers and whole garlic cloves swimming in a cumin-infused olive oil. I began to peel away the fine layer of skin attached to the fish, but David and Lucy wolfed it down, skin and all. The French consume everything: eyes, knuckles, toes, the works. I half-expected them to eat the foil as well, but they either missed it or left it behind.

"This makes up for that awful airplane food you had," Lucy said, looking approvingly at my empty plate.

The fish, as I had thought, was sufficiently satisfying, and the *pastis* we drank with it proved a cure-all for my blahs. A slice of very young Comté, the ubiquitous French hard cheese, acted like a stimulant on my tongue. I could feel my body coming to life again.

We talked until almost three, discussing my cooking-school odyssey in a vein that was as lively and refreshing as the rosé we were mainlining. Time was marked off by the waiter's dagger stare. I could tell that beneath their veil of interest, David and Lucy surely thought I was tilting at windmills.

"You're the embodiment of the galloping gourmet," David said, struggling to swallow a smile. "With apologies to Graham Kerr, of course."

"Maybe afterward," said Lucy, "you can do something about the food *chez* Bocuse."

We laughed easily, as the waiter delivered the check with an emphatic flourish. Several itchy looks passed between my friends. They were relieved when I covered it with my credit card.

"You must come back here and cook for us after you have had your instruction," Lucy went on. "We will be very interested to see what you have learned. It is not often a *ville* like Lyon receives a chef who has trained in so many important kitchens. It will be a great treat for us."

It took me a moment to realize she was poking fun at me. But, all things considered, I probably deserved it. In a place such as Lyon, a cooking apprenticeship was like entering the priesthood. I had to be careful not to take this thing too seriously.

"You can count on it," I assured her. "Six months from now, I'm going to make you the best chili cheese dog you've ever tasted."

⁕

On a warm Sunday evening at dusk, there are two types of people lurking in Lyon's Place Bellecour: the honors class from the local mugger's college—and their intended victims. I had the distinction of resembling the poster boy for the latter as I crept into the shadowy square dragging an overstuffed suitcase and a shoulder bag with a shiny new laptop peeking through the top. The instructions I'd been given were explicit; my liaison from the Robert Ash Cookery School would meet me by the statue of Louis XIV, a massive equestrian bronze depicting the Sun King in splendid battle attire.

When I arrived, the square was eerily deserted. From the comfort of my couch at home, it had seemed that the guidebooks must be exaggerating its grandeur as one of the best people-watching spots in France; now, the magnificent emptiness of Bellecour had a stomach-lurching power that caught me by surprise. It was indeed a beautiful site, surrounded on three sides by fortresslike buildings with classical façades. Underfoot, a coral-colored gravel carpet gave the square a ruddy warmth. The statue was located on a tiered platform, near the entrance to the subway. From its steps, I could keep a nervous eye out for the predators.

The first hour passed without incident. It was actually dark and peaceful. From where I stood, facing the city, the view across the river shattered any sense of antiquity. Modern Lyon was posed against the dying sky like

Oz, its thousands of lights flickering in distant windows. But it was a calming radiance, unlike the restless neon skyline over cities—the City—back home. There was no loud soundtrack, no throbbing pulse, aside from the faint shuffling of gravel in the immediate vicinity. Nothing to worry about, though, as couples were merely cutting across the square like ghosts in the dark, on their way to and from neighborhood bistros.

The only dicey moment arose later, when a scrofulous-looking man in jeans and sneakers stepped out of the shadows and stumbled toward me. He had hair like a worn-out Brillo pad and the kind of bushy eyebrows that could have been mistaken for large furry insects. I stood perfectly still, my hand tightening around the shoulder-bag handle, mind racing in several directions at once, like any respectable victim. In the ensuing panic, I nearly missed his saying my name. "Hope you haven't been waiting long," he apologized, reaching for my suitcase.

I shot out an arm to stop him but recovered in time to make it seem like a handshake.

He was Roger Pring, a Brit who pronounced his last name with the same snappish accent his countrymen might have used to say *prawn*. I liked him at once. He was friendly and awkward, a big teddy bear of a man, like Jerry Garcia, I thought, without the buggy stare. Walking toward a parked van, I asked, "Student or cooking teacher?"

"I'm the general assistant, fake sommelier, jack-of-all-trades, and shit-shoveler," he said quickly, making it sound rehearsed.

As Roger loaded my gear in the boot, a woman in the van made room in the back for me. Her name was Helen, another Brit, perhaps a few years older than I, with a dark-complected elegance that originated from somewhere between Greece and Egypt. She introduced herself as a long-time admirer of the chef's food. I couldn't help feeling surprised to learn that she was enrolled in the program.

She seemed almost wary of learning how to cook. "I'm afraid I won't be much help with the nitty-gritty," Helen confessed.

"That's nothing to worry about," I said. "We're all pretty much in the same boat." I glanced briefly at her face and noticed a flutter of uncertainty. "You are eager to learn, though?"

A smile played nervously at the corners of her mouth. "I'll probably do better as an observer," she said. "Besides, I'm not actually a full-fledged member of this team. My status is more guest than student."

I wasn't sure what she meant, but as we drove south along the *autoroute*, rattling from Lyon into Burgundy, a heavy foreboding hit me as Roger and Helen made little jokes about some minor dramas at the cooking school. The car became full of crossed parenthetical remarks. From what I could piece together, there were still many last-minute arrangements being ironed out, among them the food for tomorrow's menu and room assignments and a shortage of burners on what the Brits called the cooker, which I took to mean the stove. It sounded as though they were feeling their way through the process.

"Is this the first session of the season?" I asked innocently, trying not to betray my concern.

"The first?" Roger echoed. "Oh . . . yes . . . definitely . . . you could say that." He threw Helen a funny little glance.

"It's the first one," she said, smiling weakly, ". . . ever."

It took me some time to realize this wasn't a joke. This was their maiden effort, a test run to see if they could get the Robert Ash Cookery School off the ground. Somewhere in the back of my mind, I heard Donald O'Connor saying, "Hey gang, wouldn't it be great if we could put on a show?" My heart sank. How could I have made such a colossal mistake? The website for the school had made it sound like a well-established affair. It described an eminent chef and his wonderful kitchen—no, a *"main teaching kitchen,"* which had impressed me no end—"equipped to a high standard, with every conceivable tool of haute cuisine." There were gorgeous pictures of food and of previous classes, which, I was to learn much later, belonged to another cooking school in another country. In the calmest voice possible, I asked, "How many other students will be there besides me?"

After a long pause, Roger said, "I'm afraid you're it for now, mate. But that shouldn't be a problem. We've invited a few friends down from London to fill in the ranks. It's going to be a lot of fun."

Fun was nowhere on my list of perks. Fun was skiing the back bowl at

Vail. Or combing the stalls of rural flea markets. Cooking school was supposed to teach the mastery of skills and discipline, perhaps be artistic, even
a bit philosophical. Only fun in the sense that we could eat our mistakes.

I sat in the enveloping silence and tried to organize my feelings.
There were reasons I'd chosen this particular school to begin my odyssey. The hills of Burgundy held a very special place in my heart. Years
ago, I'd crossed them on a bicycle, drinking in the ancient beauty as
well as the best of its wine. Nothing had prepared me for the experience. The landscape surrounding that weave of roads unlike any I
had ever seen, the colors more dazzling and intense: the greens were
greener, yellows yellower, with ripe fields of purple, brown, and red
sewn like a big patchwork bedspread. The hills that plunged down to
the flatlands were covered with gnarled vines. And its cuisine was in a
category all by itself. A wanderer coming upon unexpected treasure, I
had gorged myself on the rustic, hearty comfort food found in typical
Burgundian kitchens—the beef stews and *coqs au vin;* the encyclopedic
cuts of *charollais* slathered in rich wine sauces thick with onions, mushrooms, and *lardons;* the slices of *jambon persillé;* and the knuckle-size
escargots roasted with garlic and oil.

It seemed fitting to start here. The food would be straightforward, honest, free of the long, elaborate preparations that complicate so much of
French cuisine. I'd feel more confident learning to make reductions and
pâtés and soufflés after a week or two with the basics. Besides, Robert
Ash was English, which meant that I could ease into the instruction without having to hurdle the language barrier. My French was decent, not
great; translating each drill would slow things down and exhaust me. And
Ash himself sounded like a wonderful character. The website described
him as "chef-patron of London's legendary and award-winning Blythe
Road Restaurant." The place meant nothing to me, but I loved the sound
of *chef-patron,* the whole idea of paying homage to a master.

I just wished to hell that he'd taught cooking before now.

Roger assured me that Ash was the real deal, but I wasn't so sure. I was
picturing myself as a guinea pig for these aspiring foodies, Chef Ash and
his Merry Men.

I felt better when we turned off the highway onto a wobbly country road flanked by farms and vineyards. The land on both sides looked deep-set and hidden. I squinted through the dark into the shapeless night. It was only through some effort that I could glimpse a village. Beyond the rise of the hills, the treetops were tipped in silver moonlight; otherwise, it was difficult to make out much in the head-lamp's pencil glare. My memory, such as it was, had to fill in the blanks. The last time I was here, they had just finished the grape harvest, the *vendange*. It was in the fall, right after the trees had turned color, and there was a soft rushing as dozens of farmers hurried from vineyard to vineyard with the stubborn preoccupation of accountants at tax time. Sunlight shot through the vines with tendrils of honeyed hues, and the scent of wine, faintly tart and tangy, hung over everything. There was so much to absorb. I had just gotten married, and it was difficult to reconcile my thoughts and feelings about this surfeit of beauty. From that point on, one thing was clear: My heart no longer belonged solely to the woman on my arm but to this glorious countryside as well.

I recalled all of this as the car trundled on, past the turnoff to Villefranche-sur-Saône and a skein of tiny villages nestled below the Beaujolais slopes. Through the open window, the night air felt cool and thick, with a peaty musk that suggested eternity. My spirits continued to rise with every mile.

"You're going to love this place," Roger said, and I couldn't help but agree as we cruised through the intersection at Les Massonnays and turned onto a gravel road, beyond a gatepost that said RUE DU LAC.

Of course, I couldn't see the lake through the copse of trees, but I could feel its presence. The house, however, was bathed in light. Far from the noble twelfth-century farmhouse promised by the cooking-school agent, it was a modest stucco affair framed with blue shutters and surrounded by a moat of gardens that appeared to be in full bloom. Its appearance, from what I could see, radiated bourgeois caution. A middle-aged man with a kind face opened the door, and suddenly I was in a bright, airy kitchen on whose counters stood perhaps two dozen bulging grocery-store bags tilting under the strain. "Forgive the mess," said the man, Paul, herding us into a pleasant parlor. "Bob just got back from the local Carrefour, and we haven't had time to unpack."

"But you left four hours ago," Roger said, fingering through one of the cartons.

"Five, actually—not that it mattered. You should have seen him. Bob was like a kid in a candy store, marveling at melons and aubergine. 'Look at this fennel! Smell this *Époisse!*' I couldn't get him out of there. If the store hadn't closed, we'd still be shopping."

I settled into a club chair and took off my jacket. "Is he here? I'd love to meet him," I said, glancing about for a suitable suspect.

Not a chance, I was told, not tonight anyway. Chef Ash was secluded following his ordeal, resting up for tomorrow's lesson. It crossed my mind that he might be off somewhere rereading the *How to Teach Cooking* manual.

I had a restless night's sleep. The ancient pipes under the floorboards wheezed at a frequency so low and husky it sounded like snoring in the next room. Toilets flushed in SurroundSound. From somewhere in the snug house came a lullaby of ticking, perhaps a clock or someone's ham radio making contact. Of course, none of these compared with the jangle in my head. I heard from the full cast of characters barnstorming through my life, their words of advice and warnings, their complaints, demands, opinions, ultimatums, even their *recipes*—for success and failure, Dr. Freud might have suggested—and for several hours insomnia coursed through my body nerve to nerve.

No one else was up when I crawled out of bed sometime after daybreak. The house was cold, clammy with rural damp. I took a short walk through the small, medieval village—a cluster of decrepit houses—and around the lake, where a few greedy fishermen had already thrown their lines in the water, hoping to surprise their catch. As I walked, the morning revived me. The cool air was refreshing and filled with a grassy extract that tickled my nose. When I got back a half-hour later, the kitchen was in full swing.

"We thought you might have hitchhiked back to Lyon," said a pale, dainty brunette with a sort of Gainsborough brittleness who introduced herself as Susie Hands-Wicks. A neighbor of the chef from a London suburb, she and her husband, Paul, had offered up their vacation time to assist in the cooking school's launch. "Roger suspects you are disappointed with the setup."

"Not at all," I lied.

"In which case I can promise that you won't be disappointed with the food. Bob makes the single best guinea fowl I have ever tasted. And his duck *confit* . . ." she said it while touching her heart as if blessing a sacred fire . . . "his duck *confit* is a minor miracle. You could close your eyes and think you were eating . . ."

"Duck *confit*."

The voice had come from behind me, and I turned to find a tall, wide-shouldered man battling schoolboy plumpness, his forehead jeweled with sweat. He had an impressive quiff of salt-and-pepper hair that appeared to be lacquered in place, making him look like a doo-wop star on the revival circuit. Above the pocket of the white chef's coat, stitched in script, was *Robert Ash*. He gripped my broken hand with an excessive firmness that served as advance notice of our teacher-student relationship.

"Don't believe anything Susie tells you," he said affectionately, throwing a quick, professional glance at the vegetable she was chopping. "She's paid to say that. Meanwhile, check out her scrawny waistline. Mother of two teenagers. Does it look like she's eaten very much rich food lately?"

Susie rolled her eyes skyward and touched his sleeve.

A look of concern tightened on Ash's face. Leaning over the cutting board, he said, "A little finer, darling."

The attention to detail was reassuring. On first impression, it would be safe to say, his appearance didn't inspire. Ash seemed young to be considered a *chef-patron*, let alone having the distinction of being called master, although I am sure he had tended his fair share of stovetops all over the world. And he had a restless spirit that made him seem distracted in regard to the rigors of French cooking. I stared with a kind of foreboding at his florid, rakish face, wondering if there wasn't some excuse I could make to leave a few days early. The last thing I needed was to waste time studying with a guy who was only as good or as technically inventive as I was.

They were in the midst of some preparation for our lunch, which I was told we'd begin cooking in earnest during the morning class. In the meantime, Roger—who, it turned out, owned the house at Rue du Lac and was letting his friend Ash use it for the school—recruited me for a croissant run to the next town. The prospect of freshly baked French rolls was an indulgence I'd been craving, but the *pâtisseries* in Pontanevaux and Les Maisons Blanches were closed when we got there. Monday, apparently, was the baker's day off. Supermarket baguettes loomed in our future until we stumbled across a hidden *pâtisserie* in Crêche-sur-Saône. In the main square of the town, we picked up the insanely sweet scent of butter and followed it into a side street, where we found the bakery.

The place was filled with desperate characters like us who had come looking for their morning fix. When it came our turn, Roger ordered a half-dozen *bressans*, peculiar breast-shaped loaves named after the town of Bresse, which are heavier than brioches and made from maize. The old woman behind the counter dumped them from her baking paddle into Roger's hands, initiating a clumsy juggling routine. "Shit . . . Jesus!" he sputtered, shoveling them onto the glass. "She must have just taken them out of the oven."

The woman regarded us with amusement. Roger gave her a look that verged on murder. She held out a bag, and for a moment I worried that he might hit her. He swept the loaves into the bag, grabbed a few baguettes, and paid. "Thank you," he said, turning his head away before muttering, "Cheeky little fucker."

To soothe Roger's trauma, we shared a hot *bressan* in the car, eating the halves much too fast and knowing that we had never feasted on such dense, creamy bread. It fairly wept butter. A brief debate ensued, during which we swore an oath not to break into another one, although there came a point when it seemed that only manacles would keep us from tearing open the bag. We rolled down the windows, hoping it would help to discourage temptation. Still, the smell of the bakery followed us all the way back, making my stomach churn with hunger.

As we turned into the driveway of Rue du Lac, I commented on the unusual siting of the house. The property, which stood less than a thousand feet from the Saône, looked over a small lake on the other side. There was an unobstructed view of the Beaujolais hills: Fleurie loomed to the east; its northern edge tilted gently toward the vineyards of St.-Amour; and the westerly treeline was opened a hair, thanks to an obstinate wind, exposing the slopes of Chenas. Without even looking, I knew the back of the house faced the vaunted soil of Pouilly-Fuissé, whose grapes had fueled many a festive glass of mine. None of this, of course, had been visible upon my arrival. But in the daylight I could see the remains of the crumbling rock formation on which the house now stood proudly.

Roger explained that it had been abandoned in 1986 by a pork butcher from Mâcon who went a bit crazy, tried to shoot his wife, and ended up going bankrupt defending himself at trial. "In the time-honored English tradition, we bought the house from his creditors," Roger said.

Built in 1820 and renovated by Roger and his wife, Sarah, the house was cozy, with rectangular low-slung rooms, chair rails and molding fashioned from apricot-colored woods, and worn irregular squares of terra-cotta on the floors. The upstairs hallways were lined with a warren of simple, monastic rooms. It was heartening the way the house invited lemony shafts of sunshine during all intervals of the day. Adjacent to the living room, Dutch doors opened onto a terrace, one of the most relaxing oases I had ever seen, with a reflecting pool and a few chaises longues and wisteria intertwined with orange vines dangling from trellises. If the wind was blowing in and you listened hard, very hard, it was possible to hear the slow lap of the lake, or at least a sound that could be reasonably interpreted as water.

The kitchen was spread out, with a tiled checkerboard floor and two windows over the sink looking out onto the pleasant little garden and a pond beyond that. An eye-popping supply of cookware teetered in the overhead cupboards. There was a light supporting symmetry to it all that seemed custom-made for cooking. As we sat down to coffee, I saw in one easy glance that the room had yet to be put to the test. The counters were still shiny, the sink a stainless white shell. The stove (or should I say the *cooker*?) seemed just to have come out of the box.

Robert Ash fussed through the kitchen noisily while we ate the *bressans*; he had apportioned the room into workstations by the time breakfast was finished. Chopping boards and utensils were laid out by each position, close enough together so that Helen, Susie, and I could observe each other's work yet cook without bumping into each other. (Paul and Roger were content to hover, as opposed to cook.) Bowls stuffed with fragrant herbs rested on a trivet in the center, and in the sink was a metal funnel-shaped gizmo I'd never seen before. Each of us received a crisp white apron and a blue notebook full of sleeves into which we could slip our recipes. Like a symphony conductor delivering the score, Ash handed out an inch-thick sheaf of instructions for the upcoming session.

"Well," he said, wiping his hands on his apron, "we ought to get started right away if we intend to have lunch ready by one."

The menu was ambitious. If I read it correctly, we were making a salad of endive and roasted almonds garnished with bacon, avocado, and feta cheese, followed by that old Lyonnais standby, salmon cooked *en papillote* with braised vegetables, and a dessert of pears poached in port. To my thinking, it seemed like a wonderful way to begin our work. We were excited, the way that children get on the first day of the school year, when everything is new and the freshly scrubbed classroom looks like the backdrop for a Norman Rockwell painting.

If lunch alone had been our goal, we might have breezed through the preparations. But Robert Ash, as it turned out, was almost singlemindedly obsessed when it came to cooking, *teaching* cooking, and from the outset the workload was more than any of us had bargained for.

Our first order of business was to formulate a "house dressing" that Robert said becomes a cook's signature—one used not only on salads but also as a base for almost every kind of dish, hot or cold. When made thoughtfully, dressings morphed into marinades, starters, *jus*, or dipping sauces. Naturally, this required certain basics—a good, fragrant olive oil and red-wine vinegar, a half-teaspoon of coarse-grain mustard, and plenty of salt (even a little too much for my taste). As for pepper, Chef demanded we use the stronger white variety on everything, for mostly aesthetic reasons, along with a little sugar to balance out the acidity. Although still fairly unaccustomed to each other, we decided to exert our independence by including a handful of chopped shallots, blended thoroughly with enough raspberries to give the mixture a decadent blush.

Ash didn't seem pleased. He eyed the dressing suspiciously, as one might a dinner guest who showed up in a monocle and bow tie. The shallots didn't bother him, but the creamy pink, he said, seemed prissy, undignified. And it made the dressing thick. To compensate, he drizzled a scant two tablespoons of it over a truckload of endive, then used his fingers to toss it, coating each leaf with dressing.

Helen wrinkled her nose at the jungle procedure. Instead of following suit, she mixed her portion with two soup spoons, clacking them like castanets against the metal bowl. Wordlessly, Ash took the spoons out of her hands and flung them into the sink, watching as she joylessly but grudgingly dipped her fingers into the brew, which, I suppose, was the same approach Helen might have taken the first time she went skinnydipping.

"From now on," Ash announced, "everything we do is going to be hands-on, in the strictest sense. We're working with food here, and that means we have to touch it, smell it, feel it, taste it. This kitchen is no place for the squeamish. Trust me. If you handle the ingredients timidly, it's going to come through in the final result. Now let's roll up our sleeves and have a go at it."

Ash's tactful rebuke blew right past Helen. After he demonstrated how to juice lemons and separate eggs through our fingers rather than the more conventional ways, she rushed to duplicate it, cooperating but also pointedly washing her hands after each procedure. Helen was a terrific sport, and so was Susie, who had good homemaker's instincts for the practical, the efficient, the necessary. I had pegged them both as earnest British university grads who, forsaking any real ambition, had settled comfortably into the background of life. Had they been less congenial or part of a larger group, I probably wouldn't have developed a rapport with either one of them. Our intimate cooking arrangement, however, was an excuse for me to appreciate their engaging lightness. Both women brought with them a style, an unself-conscious amiability that relieved the burden of formality.

Our long morning session, with Roger providing off-color commentary, gave all of us an appreciation for time management, considering Chef's breakneck schedule. The four of us worked like mad, in constant motion. We made a big salad and began a preparation for duck *confit* that would stretch over three days, necessitating daily tweaks. After tea, Bob presented us with two whole sides of wild salmon, enough, I thought, to feed the French fleet, and explained that we would be using every inch of the fish for several different dishes.

I love salmon, but the kind I got back home was mostly farm-raised—as pale as a redhead on the beach, with only a suspicion of flavor to suggest its seaworthy origins. These babies announced their pedigree before they even hit the table. They smelled like honest-to-god fish, just briny enough to recall that last low tide at noon, leaving the faintest hint of sweetness on the nose. If I hadn't had my glasses on, I would have sworn they were painted, they were that intense, a deep carroty orange streaked with red and rippled silver. They felt satiny after we washed them, with a spring to the touch, not the kind of fish that bent like a rubber hose.

Bob sliced six fillets, each about an inch thick, from the fattest ends of the fish. These we reserved for the next day's lunch. We were instructed to skin another portion by holding the tail end with our fingers, making a small incision in the fish, and simply pushing the knife through, in the hairline crevice between the flesh and the skin, at a thirty-degree angle. Like magic, the two sides separated without leaving so much as a fleck on either piece. (I began keeping a list of things to do once I returned home, and at the very top I wrote: sharpen knives.) We cut these into half-inch slices and layered them in a Pyrex bowl, for an appetizer of salmon ceviche—Bob pronounced it *sah-vitch*—cured with a citrus fruit marinade. Leaving nothing to waste, we packed the tail ends under a thick bed of salt, sugar, and dill for gravlax, to be served a few days down the pike, alongside a honey-mustard dill mayonnaise.

As we prepared each of these recipes, Chef interrupted often with a bonanza of technical tips. For example, much later, when readying the ceviche, Bob showed me a nifty little flourish to enhance the presentation. We found a beautifully shaped cucumber, pulled the zester over it from stem to stern, then cut it in half lengthwise and scooped out the seeds. We then shaved each half into paper-thin moons, which we over-lapped in the center of the plate to create an impressionistic flower shape, before mounding the fish on top. The pale green and orange provided a stunning contrast, in addition to the fashion statement the dish made when it was presented at table.

Those recipes would stay with us always, as convenient go-to options. We'd make them effortlessly, without much forethought, knowing they'd turn out as perfectly as a peanut-butter-and-jelly sandwich, and with about as much originality.

The salmon *en papillote,* however, was a revelation. The exotic locale not-withstanding, it more or less justified the entire cooking-school experience—and this, as hard as it is to believe, on my first day out of the box. This was just what I'd had in mind. I congratulated myself for coming here—my fantasy was beginning to take shape. I had made this dish often at home, but my preparation was a car wreck. Roger, who hovered like an evil insur-ance inspector while we cooked, hit it right on the head when he said, "It seems like you just stuff all this shit in a paper envelope and throw it in the oven—bang, bang, bang!" My salmon at home wasn't even that elegant. I used aluminum foil as my *papillote* and piled on any odd vegetable lurk-ing in the kitchen. If the celery looked about shot, I chopped it up and chucked it in. A can of chickpeas left over from the last century? Sure, why not. I once even threw in a sorry-looking flap of roasted pepper I found floating in a jar of sulphur-yellow liquid. By the time I folded up the sides of the foil, it resembled a stealth bomb.

Robert Ash's version carried with it the elegance that such a dish would embody were it ordered in a fine-dining establishment, and there are those brave souls who wouldn't shrink from his rule of placing the unopened pouch in front of a guest and ceremoniously slicing through it so that everyone at the same time sees how it turned out. A stunt like that takes courage, considering the disasters I've turned out, but from all evi-dence based on our endeavors, it never fails to produce sensual delight.

It required a little more effort than my lethal attempts, but the result was well worth it:

SALMON *en papillote* WITH BRAISED VEGETABLES

4 Tbl. butter

1/2 cup carrots, shredded

1/2 cup leeks, shredded (white
part only)

1/2 cup red onion, julienned

1/2 cup mushrooms, julienned

2 tsp. chopped fresh tarragon

4 sheets of parchment cut into
14-inch rounds

olive oil

1 lb. 4 oz. fresh filleted
salmon, cut into 12 equal
pieces

salt and white pepper

12 tarragon leaves

4 knobs (1–1 1/2 Tbl. each)
butter

4 Tbl. dry white wine

4 Tbl. chicken stock

4 tsp. finely chopped shallots

Melt the butter in a skillet and add vegetables with the chopped tarragon. Sauté gently until soft. Make this beforehand and set aside so it cools, to keep the vegetables from tearing the paper parcels.

Preheat the oven to as hot a temperature as possible—450° or hotter.

Fold each of the paper rounds in half and brush with oil. Lay the rounds flat and place one-fourth of the vegetables on the front half-moon of each disc, then lay three pieces of fish on top at a 45-degree angle to the fold. Season both sides of the salmon with salt and pepper. Press a tarragon leaf on each piece of fish, add a knob of butter, 1 tablespoon of white wine, and 1 tablespoon of chicken stock, then strew 1 teaspoon of the shallots over the top. Seal the paper parcel by folding over and crimping the edges—making a 1/2-inch fold, moving 2 inches up and folding over again, pressing down tightly, then repeating until fully sealed.

Set the parcels, well spaced, on a baking sheet, and bake 4 to 5 minutes, or until they puff up. Serve immediately by cutting them open. (Lots of steam emerges; use extreme caution.)

Serves 4

How in God's name, you might wonder, are you supposed to measure a knob of butter? This is something that can't be answered with any precision. Bob just lopped off hunks of the butter bar and judged them to be suitable specimens. "Smaller than a door knob," observed Roger, "and larger than my wife's." To my eyes, on average, they looked about the size of a man's knuckle. A reasonable knob of butter melts through the entire serving, layer upon layer, and delivers a sweet, richly flavored fillet that stands up to the savory combination of ingredients competing for attention.

The great thing about this recipe is its efficiency: It can be assembled ahead of time and slipped into the oven just as everyone is unfolding napkins. Bob encouraged us to improvise: Susie added fish stock instead of the chicken, and a splash of dry sherry; I replaced one piece of salmon with two shrimp for variety; and Bob said that monkfish or even halibut worked to great effect. Meanwhile, we attended to the other dishes in various stages of development and banged out our dessert.

We worked so furiously that morning, about as fast as my mind could follow, that when Chef announced lunch, it seemed more a reprieve than a reward.

Everyone gathered around a picnic table on the terrace, which had been set by Paul. Framed by the lovely garden, it was a most agreeable spot; we had sun on our faces and the thin scent of orange blossom swollen by heat and Carole King who serenaded us from hidden outdoor speakers. It was my impression that this group of friends sat down to eat often together. Everything revolved around Bob Ash's cooking, but his virtuosity, rather than glorifying him, had a clubby, embracing effect. It was generous of them to include me in their gay familiarity, considering I'd known them for under twenty-four hours.

Paul, especially, seemed like a good sort. He was the type of middle-aged man I recognized from those quirky British TV mysteries, the kind who lives alone in a Midlands cottage, wears cardigans, smokes a pipe, maybe raises pigeons, and happens to overhear a neighbor confess to his wife's murder. A surveyor by trade, Paul introduced himself to me as the *sous-plongeur* (Roger being our chief dishwasher), a noncook, "just an eater," as he pointed out, who was prepared to handle any grisly job so long as he could gorge himself on Bob Ash's food. "I've waited weeks to enjoy this lunch, even if a bunch of rank amateurs are preparing it," he despaired.

Roger proposed a toast. "To our valiant chefs in the kitchen. Lord have mercy on us all."

The meal, to our credit, had come together into a well-constructed affair, and we cleaned our plates with crusty bread from the bakery in Crêche-sur-Saône. I can't remember now how many different wines we tasted with lunch, an endless supply of bottles from the area's best producers, including a gorgeous sweet Muscat de Beaumes-de-Venise that accompanied a platter laden with special cheeses. By the time we got to dessert, I could only poke wearily at the plump-bellied Anjou pear lolling in a puddle of spices and port wine. It seemed indecent to leave it on my plate after all the care that went into making it:

POACHED PEARS IN PORT

6 Anjou pears, peeled	ground allspice, big pinch
3 or 4 whole cloves	sugar, to taste
1 750 ml. bottle cheap port	chervil sprigs, for garnish
4 cinnamon sticks	

Choose good, well-shaped pears with fat bellies so they stand up in the pan; otherwise, take a little slice off the bottom to ensure they stay upright. About 1/2 inch from the top of the pear, make a small horizontal incision with a knife, being careful not to cut all the way through the pear, so that it can be cored without taking off the top. Then trace a circle in the bottom of each pear with the corer, following the circle inside, deeper and deeper, as you core it until you hit the incision and can remove the core.

Choose a pot that will hold all 6 pears yet is small enough so they fit snugly. (If necessary, add an extra pear in the middle of the pot.) Add

*the bottle of port and the spices and top with enough water so that the
upper quarter and stem of each pear remains dry. (If there is any old
red wine around, throw that in, too.) Bring to a boil and reduce to a
trembling simmer until the pears are tender.*

*Remove the pears from the pan and bring the liquid to a rapid boil,
reducing until it is the consistency of maple syrup and coats the pears.
(Add a tablespoon or two of sugar if the reduction isn't sweet enough.)
Spoon the port reduction over the pears, drape a little chervil around
each stem as a garnish, and serve warm.*

Serves 6

After dessert, I made my way upstairs for a well-deserved nap. Everyone
else, except the chef, tromped off to a wine tasting at a nearby chateau,
where, after subhuman moans of indisposition, they reportedly drank
more wine and ate more food. It is anyone's guess what I dreamed about
during that interlude, although it is safe to assume it involved at least
three types of antacid and Carolyn, immodestly clad.

Stupefied though I was by food and drink, I slept fitfully. Lunch was
fermenting in my stomach like an underground nuclear test, and I hadn't
heard from Carolyn since arriving in Europe. I checked in via Roger's
Internet setup and came up cold; she was either too busy packing or shopping for the trip. So I emailed Lily a description of everything I'd learned
so far, even though we'd spoken on the phone a few hours earlier.

Around four o'clock, I heard a rumbling downstairs in the darkened
kitchen and was surprised to find Bob ransacking the cupboards like a
hungry raccoon. When he saw me loitering on the periphery, he thrust a
glass of wine at me and bellowed, "Let's get going. We've got a dinner to
prepare."

This turned out to be a stroke of wonderful luck: just the chef and
I, one-on-one in the kitchen. The syllabus designated tonight's menu as
guinea fowl with pancetta in a *cèpe* sauce, and I offered my services like an
obedient slave. Even squeamishness could not shake me from the anat-
omy lesson at hand. Ash taught me the proper way to remove the breast
from any game bird: making an incision in the skin at the top of the breast

and gradually paring the meat away from the bone, working my way down the breast with short, delicate strokes from a seriously sharp knife to separate the connective tissue. Once that was done, I clipped off part of the wing and then went through the joint at its socket and cut out the wishbone before removing the entire piece. It was much easier than I'd expected—and it paid dividends. For years, I'd watched the butchers at Stop & Shop take apart my birds with several flashes of their knives and admired how they made the trimmings disappear, like David Copperfield. Ash nearly tackled me as I attempted to launch our odds and ends into the trash bin.

"Are you out of your mind?" He cradled the spoils like treasure. "This gives us the start of a beautiful stock." He wrapped the discarded chicken in butcher paper and returned it to the fridge. Then he leaned into the trash, sorting through it with ferocious vigilance, to make sure I hadn't deep-sixed more of his precious waste. "Everything gets recycled. Nothing is thrown away until we've wrung every last use out of it."

Before the serious cooking got under way, Ash clapped his hands sharply like a stern headmaster and waved me toward the door: "Would you go out to the car and get *Pet Sounds,* please?"

There was a longstanding tradition in his kitchen that prep work jumped to the tempo of the Beach Boys. As I cranked the volume, Bob left the stove to hammer out a few chords of "Wouldn't It Be Nice" on the upright piano standing against one wall of the dining room. He played with the same flair with which he cooked: confident, graceful if a bit sloppy, with a nice economical groove that danced all over the incongruities.

"This is the album that did it for me," he said, returning to the *mise-en-place* with almost post-coital pleasure. "Never fails. Those amazing Brian Wilson licks and harmonies give me such a charge."

I protested only to myself, recalling how, for most musicians, this album was the Holy Grail. Paul McCartney once told me that his goal for *Sgt. Pepper's* was to produce something as musically compelling as *Pet Sounds,* but truthfully most of it bored me silly. As "Wouldn't It Be Nice" gave way to "Don't Talk" and "Let's Go Away for Awhile," I was unable to hold my tongue any longer, railing at the whiny filler between a few glittering gems. This fired up Ash even more, and we sparred through the rest of the cooking session, talking about the things that mattered most in life: food and rock 'n roll.

As the afternoon wore on, the two of us developed a companionable rapport. We were exactly the same age and had spent most of the seventies in service to rock 'n roll: Ash playing guitar behind Jimmy Ruffin and Rick Wakeman, and me with Bruce Springsteen. "From the time I was eighteen, I played in a band that backed American artists, groups that had one hit and came to England for personal appearances without their own musicians," he said, ticking off Martha Reeves, Doris Troy, and Desmond Dekker, to name a few. Performing invigorated him and brought in decent money, which provided the freedom to pursue other fancies. When I asked him why he gave it up, he just shrugged in that weary way only another musician understands.

Food—good food—had never entered into the equation. Being on the road, with all those wasted hours running from town to town, from gig to gig, from crazy scene to crazy scene, there was no time or even the inclination to eat a proper meal. We lived on a steady diet of fast food, the tasteless sandwiches grabbed on the way out of town from an all-night drive-in or the spare bag of chips someone had abandoned in the car. These were the days before limos and MTV, when life on the road felt like a long forced march.

"The food came later," Ash said. He'd cooked as a kid, as I had, but nothing very serious. And his mother's culinary undertakings verged on the criminal. She could take a gorgeous piece of meat, a well-marbled ribeye, for example, and turn it into a missile-defense shield. "That's why I started cooking for myself; I figured I could make *anything* better than she did."

He taught himself to cook, but all he wanted was enough experience, a few imaginative recipes, so that his own family would never have to suffer the gastronomic misery of his childhood.

When he hit his thirties, however, the strategy went awry. He took a couple of cooking classes in the downtime, between tours promoting Rick Wakeman's *Gospel* album. "I was getting very adventurous, far from being just a home chef," he said. "My kids, who were little at the time, used to sit on highchairs and watch me stuff game birds with pancetta and prunes." His wife, Jackie, entered him in the *Observer's* Château Mouton-Rothschild contest for amateur cooks. Bob made a filleted four-rib of beef in a coriander sauce with mussels in snail butter—and won first prize. "I thought they were joking," he said.

Quite the contrary. The *Observer* sent him to Burgundy for a *stage* with cranky Claude Chambert, from whom he learned how to think like a chef. Then he parlayed the experience into apprenticeships at various upscale bistros until he became *chef de cuisine* at the Blythe Road Restaurant, which was on the cutting edge of London's culinary renaissance.

"I thrive on the mayhem in a restaurant kitchen," he said, while instructing me how to trim the breasts evenly so they were identical, as precise as petals. "It never stops—six or eight hours of absolute chaos. It's like rock 'n roll to me. There is a rhythm to it that you hook into and it takes over your body. The background music is solid shouting—not anger, just everyone shouting back and forth. And then, suddenly, it's all over and you down that beer in a flash."

I could see the manic intensity percolating in Bob when he cooked. He handled the knife like a trusty, beat-up Strat, punishing its grip the way your hands bite into a twelve-bar blues. His fingers looked like cocktail franks, stubby, hardly what you'd expect of a flash guitarist, but he used them with assuredness. When he cooked, it was without the graceful body language that my friend Sandy displayed at the stove. There was no nimbleness or finesse, no expression of formal training. His expertise—like that of his guitar playing, I am certain—was learned on the street.

But he was good, damned good, the kitchen equivalent of an outsider artist. I loved his whole approach, his sense for the rhythmic mix of bluff and guess that distinguishes sumptuous cooking. In love with all things flavorful, he worked with an unchecked passion that seemed genuine even now, after all those nights on the line feeding hundreds of impatient strangers.

I knew enough not to interrupt with questions as we pieced together a *cèpe* sauce, but I could not help throwing sidelong glances at his stubby fingers as he sliced through an onion. He slid the knife blade smoothly forward and down through the onion's slippery surface as opposed to my savage, choppy technique. His dark eyes twinkled as he caught me trying to imitate his moves.

"Here, try this," he said. By now my bad hand was throbbing, but he grabbed my arm from behind and guided it in a steady sawing motion weighted by a slight arc. "You want to slice *across* the onion, pressing only slightly, and let the knife carry you through the flesh. Chopping, which we'll do afterward, is an entirely different process."

While the sauce simmered, we began making a chicken stock that would evolve in stages over the next few days. I had always wanted to make my own stock, one that was infused with tons of rich chicken flavor, but I despaired of the fuss that went into it. Bob, in his offhand way, made it a painless affair. He used everything he could get his hands on for stock—the guinea-fowl carcasses, any old bones that were left on dinner plates, wings, necks, feet, unmentionables, whatever enriched its flavor. "I don't believe in *artisanal* stocks," he said, articulating the word the way George W. said *liberal*. "My purpose is to give it an honest, homemade taste, as opposed to something to admire as if it were a delicacy."

BOB ASH'S CHICKEN STOCK

Preheat the oven to 425 degrees.

Roast the carcasses of two chickens or any fowl until they are browned. Deglaze the roasting pan with a little white wine, scraping up the brown bits, and transfer everything to a bowl. Deglaze the pan a second time with water and throw that into the bowl as well.

Quarter 3 onions (with their skins on) and sauté in 2 tablespoons of vegetable oil, in a stockpot, along with 2 slim leeks, 2 carrots, and 2 stalks of celery, all sliced in 1/2-inch chunks. Throw in a handful of parsley stalks (minus the leaves) and 2 bay leaves. When the vegetables

are softened, add the carcasses and deglazing liquid and cover with
water (about 3 quarts).

Bring everything to a boil, cover, and simmer 2 to 3 hours, skimming
the fat from time to time with a spoon. Season with salt to taste.

Makes 2 quarts

"Tomorrow, we'll parse the bones in a colander, then strain everything
through a *chinoise* [a fine-mesh conical sieve on legs—that funnel-shaped
gizmo I'd seen in the sink] before putting the finished stock in the fridge,"
Bob said.

I managed to pinch a ladle of soup and tasted it. It was exactly as he'd
promised: not fancy, but honest and delicious, strong, well seasoned, redolent of roasted meat.

"Better than that canned stuff you use in the States?" he asked, smirking.

I admitted it was. He grinned and balanced a load of sizzling plates on
my arms like the pigeons on the tourists in St. Mark's Square.

"Let's rush these to table, lest our friends think we're jerking off in here."

Even money says it never crossed anyone's mind.

Dinner was a ridiculously happy affair. It was long and lazy outside on
the flagstone terrace, with a chorus of ribbonlike laughter accompanying
each amazing course. We ate well: thick slices of seared *foie gras* in a port
gelée, followed by the guinea fowl cooked to a rosy perfection and buried in
the decadent mushroom sauce. The cheese selection had grown even more
expansive since lunch. I picked at it sparingly, feeling a wave of protest rising within me but knowing too that I might never enjoy such a luxury again.
Afterward, guitars were dragged out, and Ash raced through what seemed
like the entire Dylan songbook, singing such forgotten gems as "Hollis
Brown" and "With God on Our Side." He played spot-on, with unflinching
easy brio though a little helter-skelter, with Paul strumming impishly behind.
I even joined in on a few numbers until my damaged hand gave out.

Across the room, Susie and Helen harmonized to the teasing refrain
of "I Shall Be Released." There was a palpable thrill in their performance:

". . . any day now, any day now. . . ." My voice, high and hard, burst through with all the hope the words intoned, but it was well past two in the morning and I was still hours from bed.

As always after late-night hi-jinks, there was a price to be paid. Ordinarily, in my life at home, it meant getting a monstrously early start to clean up the evidence, giving the dog an overdue spin around the block and my daughter her breakfast, answering urgent email, all while nursing the effects of precious little sleep. My dreams, as a result, were tumultuous, anxiety-ridden affairs. That night in Burgundy, I dreamed that I stood at the edge of a cliff, looking out over a knoll to a field of freshly plowed earth. Below, two lovers planting crops called up and asked me to choose: catnip or thyme. I was about to suggest nightshade when a waiter appeared at my side and, speaking French, demanded I pay their check.

I blinked twice at the clock on the bureau in my room. Impossible: it was well past nine a.m., which is the latest I'd slept, by many hours, in the previous eight years. I remember sighing, as if in resignation, but at breakfast I was overcome by this circumstance. This was the first time in recent memory that I had no one, other than myself, to worry about or take care of; no obligations, no responsibilities, no errands. The crises that strangled my well-being seemed an ocean away. By separating myself from them, I was regaining something, a private humanity that had been lost in the shuffle, although I ached for my daughter, who never strayed from my thoughts. The day felt dreamlike. It was the strangest of sensations, liberating, but in another respect also filling me with loneliness.

I marveled at my own soft response. I had never in my relationships felt dependent upon others, yet I thrived on the extravagant companionship that a good woman provided. I gleaned undeniable comfort from sharing my days, my work, my heart with someone who appreciated the way I functioned. Marriage, to that extent, had suited me. It established an intimacy I could sink into—the structure to carry on alone during the daily grind, knowing that through lovemaking, conversation, or just proximity my mate was always part of the configuration.

For the longest time, that had grounded my life and given it an exaggerated sense of serenity. But any marriage is a gamble, and I'd wagered a good deal on mine, expecting the odds to fall in our favor. When I spotted the bluff, it was already too late in the game.

All of this coalesced as I headed down to breakfast. It was hard being here alone, liberating, as I said, but also disorienting, disorienting as all hell.

Bob was impatient to get things under way. He had been puttering around the kitchen, pretending to labor over some sea bass, but our socializing was clearly gnawing at him. Underneath his smile was displeasure.

"Anybody want another cup of coffee before we start?" he asked. His eyes were sharp little darts offsetting the morning's chalky warmth.

No one dared to so much as lick his lips.

We began organizing lunch by checking on the progress of our two salmon preparations gestating in the fridge. Both the gravlax and the ceviche were doing what was expected of them. With hardly a hiccup, we started a leek-and-potato *dauphinoise* for dinner. I had never used a mandoline before. They were scary contraptions—like little guillotines, only deadlier and more accessible. Bob demonstrated how to use it before allowing each of us to slice a pile of potatoes into perfectly matched rounds. At first glance, there seemed to be nothing to it, even with my swollen hand, but I left pieces of shredded knuckles on the glistening blade. Ash shook his head at my startled, pained expression, and said, "Nice touch, mate . . . it'll thicken the sauce and help to bind it." He taught me how to do it safely, by holding the vegetable with a tea towel.

We also prepared a *tarte Tatin*, which I had made dozens of times at home, albeit with unspectacular results. I'm not sure where I got the recipe from, but the apples, though well caramelized, always disintegrated in the pan or just looked as though they'd been thrown haphazardly into the shell. And my pastry crust crumbled. The same thing happened when I tried it with pears. No matter how I made the tart, my guests oooohed and aaaahed, but that was only because it smelled so heavenly and they had never attempted anything as daring at home. Deep down, I thought they'd react the same way to burnt toast. This *tarte Tatin* had a kind of Frank Gehry symmetry to it, and the crust, mottled with butter, was delicious. The *pâte sucreé* fit over the tart as snugly as a Japanese condom, and as it began to cook, the butter pastry wilted over the apples so that the outline of each chunk protruded through the crust. It was the kind of *tarte Tatin* displayed on the counters at Fauchon—perfectly shaped, completely flawless, with only a thin glaze of brown syrup holding the whole crazy structure in place.

There were so many details that demanded our attention. A half-hour before lunch, we still hadn't begun the main course. Even so, Bob cautioned us against watching the clock. He proposed seared salmon on spinach in a lemon *beurre blanc*, a dish that took only a few minutes to prepare. It had an obscene amount of butter, what looked to be an entire block—Bob called it a "wodge"—swirled in at the last minute to thicken the sauce. When I let out an audible gasp, Ash responded with a line I'm sure he first heard during his early training in France: "Listen, if you're gonna make a butter sauce, it's gonna have to have butter in it."

I have to admit that I lapped up every last drop of it with a thick crust of bread. The very thought of it makes me queasy now, but it was luscious at the time. And I'll never forget how stunning the finished meal looked on the plate. Served on the terrace, with a sticky slice of *tarte Tatin* and a glass of Banyuls for dessert, lunch was one for the record book.

"Is it always like this?" I asked Susie while Paul and Roger cleaned up the kitchen. She and I had pulled two canvas chairs to the edge of a murky little pond outside the house.

"You mean the feeling that we are eating ourselves into an early grave? Apparently Bob thinks our bodies can withstand this kind of gluttony. Frankly, I feel like one of those geese the French force-feed to produce *foie gras*."

"The process is called *gavé*," I explained, "which is why, after dinner in Paris, you will often hear someone say, '*Je suis gavé*,' to describe their bloat."

We exchanged the kind of embarrassed laugh that people share after screaming out loud in a horror film.

"I guess it would be rude to ask for Pepto-Bismol?" I suggested.

"Rude—or plain risky," she said. "I think Bob would take it personally.

When I refused a dollop of whipped cream, you should have seen the look on his face. It was as if he'd been scolded."

As Susie and I sat in the late-afternoon sun, fending off the onset of a gluttonous coma, we developed an intimacy peculiar to people who meet while traveling abroad. At first we talked in pleasantries, but as time wore on, the conversation shifted toward my situation at home—from the emotional bruising left by the divorce to the ongoing tug-of-rope with Carolyn.

Susie too had her conflicts. "I have a friend," she said slowly, "who just told me, 'I'm leaving my husband.' I was shocked. They'd seemed so happy together, and after such a long marriage. 'I know,' my friend said, 'but I hate my work and I hate my boring life and I don't really have any passion left for my husband—and he's the only thing I can change immediately.'" Before continuing, she looked over her shoulder toward the open kitchen window where Paul, in a burst of energy, splashed playfully at the sink. She took a long, reflective sip from a *Kir* made with local Mâconnais wine. When she looked up again, tears had pooled in the corners of her eyes. "I can't tell you how sad a time this is in life. Most of us have raised our children, and now, suddenly, they are gone, either to their gap year or to college, and our husbands have their work. Here I am turning fifty, with nothing to do all day long. For twenty-two years, I did the housework, arranged everyone's life, did the cooking . . . and now that's all gone. So I have to reinvent my entire life, and I think it's very cruel."

"You sound as if, somewhere along the way, you should have taken a different turn in the road," I said.

"It's just the facts. I'm not complaining. Whereas, you . . ." She looked at me with a tact more meaningful than admonishing. ". . . you have the opportunity to begin all over again. Take it from me, my friend, don't look a gift horse in the mouth."

Susie recovered her gaiety during our dinner prep and seemed eager to cook. Sensing her initial pensiveness, Bob lightened the mood by streaking through three hard-hitting Jimmy Webb tunes on the piano: "P. F. Sloan," "Do What You Want to Do," and that old workhorse, "MacArthur Park." Roger made Bellinis, and we set to work on an appetizer that had been at the forefront of some discussion.

Earlier, we had visited a *fromagerie* in the Bourg-en-Bresse market. It was an incredible stall with the kind of selection that prompted Charles de Gaulle to wonder, "How can you run a country with four hundred cheeses?" Among other things, a Camembert *premier cru* had caught our eye, a slightly swollen little fellow with love handles bulging over the sides of a thin wooden box. Bob decided to buy one to bake in its container, but the cheesemonger knew some English, and when he heard the word *bake,* his eyes blazed and his weedy, hollow-cheeked face became ugly.

"Fuck him," Bob said sharply, eliminating any need for translation. "It's a modern European dish done at all the chicest restaurants, but the French absolutely deplore it. Tough shit. I'll show you what we're going to do."

Later, back at the house, he made a few knife slits in the Camembert and poured some Aligoté wine over the top so it seeped inside. Widening each slit with a finger, he stuffed in some fresh thyme, put the lid back on the box, and baked it at 425 degrees for a few minutes. "The box will burn," he said, "but you want to watch it so the cheese doesn't cook; it just bakes. Then we'll bring it to the table and dip bread in it."

When it was finished, I dug out a large, runny gouge and, after blowing on it to no good purpose, steered the whole mess into my mouth as best I could. It was hot, though not too heavy, with a nutty, pungent flavor complemented by the herbs. Needless to say, it was rich beyond belief. We all tried eating a few helpings to humor our tetchy chef, but when Helen saw him break the seal on another wooden box, she staggered comically toward the door and moaned, "Call the police! He's trying to kill us."

No one had to remind us that we were closing in on dinner. We polished off the final steps to several dishes we'd been working on from the beginning—the gravlax and the ceviche, followed by the meltingly tender duck *confit* on a bed of garlic mashed potatoes and more spinach, this time sautéed in butter with shallots and bacon. Yet another plate landed noisily on the crowded table, a long, deep-cratered platter heaped with limp and lightly charred slabs of grilled Mediterranean vegetables swimming in a Roman dressing.

Not surprisingly, our appetites sagged under the burden of lunch. Bob gave out first, pushing away his plate after a few sorry bites, and soon

each of us followed suit, good soldiers to the end. Without much difficulty, we talked him out of an intemperately rich dessert that had been
cooling on the windowsill.

It was all we could do just to haul ourselves onto the living-room
couches, where we anchored, helpless with dazed exhaustion, for another
round of music. Bob, to his credit, led us through an agreeable Lovin'
Spoonful medley, then popped off a few of those awful robust pub songs
such as "I'm Henry the Eighth I Am," which only Brits have the nerve to
sing. I couldn't help but dump on their unblushing exuberance. "Let's
hear it for 'Winchester Cathedral,'" I roared. Afterward, each one, in
turn, made me explain why Americans travel like Mongol warriors. They
offered fiery opinions on the Bush White House and European football.
It had been a long time since I had felt so relaxed discussing the issues. It
gave me a special feeling of warmth and contentment, sitting there with
seemingly uncomplicated, endearing people.

The next day, Ash drove us harder, doubling up recipes so that we were
preparing three or four entrées and as many appetizers at each meal. He
wasn't cruel by nature, but there was a slashing fury to his pace, and we
flew around that kitchen like a swarm of hornets.

I felt invigorated, really buzzed, and tried to match Bob's frantic pace.
Wanting to study him, yet afraid to slow down and be caught, I allowed
myself only brief glimpses while he orbited the cutting board, performing
those everyday rituals. It was reassuring the way he put his nose right on
the wood and gave it a few heavy huffs, sniffing it to make sure he wasn't
using one for pastry that had recently served for fish. His body expressed
confidence, his arms and hips moving like synchronized parts, eyes locked
in total concentration, with an unspoken awareness of the others working
around him. His hands, steady as a surgeon's, were everywhere at once.
No matter how hard I tried, it was impossible for me to imitate this. I had
the same instinctive moves but none of his poise. My fingers jerked with
indignant energy.

"Slow down, take it easy," he murmured, as I julienned a small head of
fennel. "You want every slice the same size so it cooks evenly. Now throw
that head in the bin and do another one, but do it right."

We baked for the rest of the morning, three different desserts. I immediately claimed the *crème brûlée* recipe for myself, leaving Helen to make biscotti and Susie the *mousse au chocolat*. I'd always wanted to make *crème brûlée*, and it turned out to be a lot easier than I'd expected—really no more than whisking together a custard, a *crème anglaise*, and cooking it, as Bob instructed, "just until it sets, so that it still wobbles." The cream would stiffen up during a brief spell in the fridge.

The tricky part was creating a good burnt crust with a baker's torch, and I lost most of the hair on my wrist trying to perfect this stunt.

As for biscotti, I usually gave mine to the dog. The ones I've eaten are about as interesting as the Zwiebachs that babies teethe on. If you have dined well, it seems mad to ruin such a memorable meal by serving a biscuit afterward that has been calcified beyond redemption. Dunking one in *vin santo* or a little *marc*, as custom dictates, certainly improves its flavor, but I'd just as soon enjoy the drink without all the sediment or the chance that I'm going to break a tooth in the process.

Of course, my intolerance for biscotti flew right out the window after tasting one of Helen's little beauties. The cookies were so good, so sweet and crusty and full of nuts and fruit that gave them a chewier consistency without losing the mandatory crunch. Now I long for biscotti to finish a perfect meal and serve them regularly, along with coffee, using Bob's simple recipe.

HEAVENLY BISCOTTI

1/4 cup each: yellow raisins, dried apricots, prunes	*1 cup all-purpose flour*
1/4 cup each: whole almonds, hazelnuts, pistachios	*1 cup superfine sugar*
	1 1/3 tsp. baking powder
zest of 1 lemon	*2 large eggs*

Preheat oven to 350 degrees. Chop the fruit coarsely, leaving the nuts whole, and combine with the lemon zest.

In a large bowl, combine the flour, sugar, and baking powder. Mix thoroughly. In another bowl, beat the eggs and stir into the flour, drop by drop, until it is still slightly dry and not quite holding together. (Withhold some of the egg if it begins to resemble pie crust; otherwise, it will be too wet.) Now beat in the fruit, nuts, and zest until it becomes heavy and sticky.

Turn out onto a floured surface, divide into 3 equal parts, and with floured hands roll each part into 9-inch sausage shapes, keeping the ends the same thickness. Place on silicone or parchment-lined baking sheets and bake 25 to 30 minutes, until firm and rolls are golden. Remove from oven and reduce heat to 275 degrees, allowing oven to cool for about 5 minutes. On a chopping board, slice the "logs" into 1/2-inch segments and return to oven, baking another 15 minutes.

    Makes about 2 dozen

The biscotti can be stored in a jar for several weeks, as long as it is not airtight. Lily loves them with a glass of cold milk, but even she has been known to dunk one, on the sly, into some tawny port.

We served them after dinner that night in what turned out to be our farewell banquet. There had been a debate about what to cook. We had bought a chicken at Bourg-en-Bresse, but Roger reminded us about three sea bass from the market for which we'd paid a whopping sixty-five euros. They demanded consideration, if for no other reason than that their freshness expires faster than a New York parking meter.

"Take a good look at these babies," Bob said, placing them dramatically on the counter. "Their eyes are still bright and dark, and the gills are nice and pink. Another day, and they'll look like Courtney Love." He lifted one to his face and gave it a few heavy huffs. "They have the smell of the sea on them, too, which is the best indicator of freshness. More important, it's time you learn how to fillet a fish. You have no business being in the kitchen without that bit of knowledge."

There were any number of reasons I didn't go to medical school, and gutting a fish reminded me of one in particular. Only a pervert enjoyed sticking his hand inside a slimy belly and pulling out innards as if they were garden weeds. There was a disc the size of a quarter covered in black ooze, which

I dropped faster than a scorpion. A handful of pasta-shaped organs were snipped from the cavity, and for a moment I thought I'd go the route of those rookie cops on *Law and Order* during their maiden visit to the morgue.

Cutting off the tail and fins was child's play by comparison. Bob had us make an incision along the backbone with the tip of a knife and run the blade the length of the fish on either side, pushing against the bone as a guide until the fillets came away clean. "Now trim them so they look elegant," he said. "You don't want to put jagged fillets on a plate." I looked down at the mess I'd made. Mine wouldn't have gotten past Mrs. Paul.

Next, we made a fish stock from the bones and a few vegetables, with white wine and lemon. I always thought fish *fumet* was a long, difficult affair, but according to Bob it would be done in twenty minutes flat. "Otherwise," he said, "you're making paste." And he was right. Less than half an hour later, we had a rich, aromatic stock as a base for the fennel cream sauce to accompany the bass.

The recipe called for us to cook the fillets simply, sautéing them skin side down for only a minute or so in a nonstick pan, while pressing down on the flesh with a tea towel to keep them from retracting. In another pan, we sautéed my julienned fennel, along with chopped shallots and garlic, in a knob of butter, then covered it with white wine and reduced the liquid to a syrup. When only a tablespoon or so of liquid was left in the pan, we covered it with fish stock and reduced it by half, before adding about a quarter-pint of heavy cream and a capful of Pernod to give it that anise sigh.

Had the sea bass known beforehand of the emulsion in which they'd be served, I assure you they would have fought to take the hook. The butter-and-cream sauce was as thick as cake frosting; the fennel was as sweet and fragrant as an Easter lily. Each bite left my mouth in a kind of gustatory shock.

The last piece of fish remained on my fork. I knew I had to swallow it but worried that once I did, there would be no evidence of perfection, nothing left to distinguish this dinner on this night. I stared at it with the pride of possession.

"You want me to wrap that for you?" Roger asked from his end of the table.

I winked facetiously at him and picked up my fork. While everyone watched, I let it sit on my tongue and then grinned with ecstasy to a round of rowdy applause. For a moment, I felt regret. But almost at once I realized what a special situation this was.

"Have you ever tasted anything better?" Helen asked me.

"Never. Not in all my days. This was the ultimate."

We talked until after two, finishing three bottles of wine that we all agreed were amazing. The wine had a residual impact, and I remember addressing each of my new friends with surprising affection, all of it sincere and gratefully reciprocated, and then each of us wandering upstairs, one by one, without acknowledging the fact that, for all we knew, this could very well be our last evening together.

Roger, who was last to stand up, stood by the light switch waiting for some indication that I was ready, but I merely shook my head and burrowed deeper into the chair. Eventually, the room filled with moonlight.

I remained behind, sitting peacefully in the dark for ten, maybe fifteen minutes, until the soft palpitation of footsteps in the upstairs rooms faded away. In the enveloping silence, a sense of nostalgia seized me as I closed my eyes to the endless perspective of night. I felt exuberant, soothed by the wine, relaxed. A tremendous promise had been carved for me out of the night. Everything else had fallen into place: the food, the people, the magic of Burgundy. Funny how these things happened, I mused. The combination of elements had come together in perfect harmony.

Robert Ash had shown himself to be a man who discreetly craved perfection, the ideal model for an aspiring chef like me. He had good insight and a pitch-perfect palate, an uneducated instinct for flavors and the right touch with food. More than anything, he had the patience to convey all of this to us in a way that made perfect sense. There are skills and techniques—secrets—he taught us that I would use for the rest of my life. I had to hand it to him. I hadn't expected it would be that way, but his passion for teaching defined him. He'd done an extraordinary job, the work of a *chef-patron*.

It was just as Roger had promised: He was the real deal.

Chapter Two

BEAUNE AND THE LUBERON

S oon after I arrived in Beaune, after the stay at Rue du Lac, it became clear that great food and great companionship wouldn't always present themselves so easily. For the better part of a week, I had cooked the kind of fancy-ass recipes prepared in the most celebrated European kitchens. I'd had my hand held, my head patted, and my stomach filled by a man who was amused by my glaring lack of finesse. Robert Ash, to his credit, loved the whole absurdity of teaching a dilettante how to cook. He insisted that it gave him great satisfaction, although it was no different, I suppose, from training a dog to fetch. In

any case, his pleasure seemed genuine. And when he dropped me off at
the train station in Mâcon, there was a look of triumph in his eyes.

There would be no such fuzzy reception in Beaune, the capital of the
Côte D'Or wine region in Burgundy. A friend from Louis Jadot, the great
wine *negociant,* arranged for me to have a *stage* with the chef at Jardin des
Remparts, but when I arrived at his door, he fixed me with a ferocious
stare and demanded to know where I had cooked.

"Well," I said, smiling feebly, in a manner meant to disarm while appealing to his dormant generous instinct, "just my own kitchen, really."

He stood blocking the entrance to the restaurant, pretending not to
understand a word of my broken French. His eyes were squinched into
obscure crescents, very dark and stony under the pleated toque.

"I've come to learn," I said, making a kind of idiotic whisking gesture.
Just in case he'd forgotten, I mentioned our mutual friend from Jadot.

At the reference, an eyebrow shot skyward. Ah, yes, it seemed to say, I
must have a word with that . . . friend.

He bent very close to my face and lowered his voice to a near-whis-
per: "Just in case you were unaware, *M'sieur,* this happens to be a fine-
dining establishment. The day-care center is somewhere on the other
side of town."

Back at my hotel, I struggled to salvage the situation, working the
phone in a last-ditch attempt to locate a more agreeable sponsor. One
of the directors at Jadot knew of a restaurant on Place Malmedin that he
was certain would cooperate on such short notice. "The chef is an artist,"
he said, "but I must warn you that he is crazy."

As it turned out, I would only have the opportunity to substantiate half
of that assertion. The chef, a bearish, cleaver-wielding man right out of
Central Casting whom I was prepared to adore, chased me halfway up
the street, screaming, *"I will have no fucking American anywhere near my
kitchen!"*

Out of the corner of my eye, I saw the quick glint of his blade, somewhere just above my shoulder, and without hesitation I turned on the gas.
Luckily for me, the French smoke like fiends, so he eventually gave up
after hurling a few choice expletives my way.

The source of his anger was disturbing, and his fury was even more so. The fact that I was a novice and had no business being in his kitchen went without saying, but the anti-American business was an issue I hadn't anticipated. I was still living under the post–9/11 conception, however fleeting, that everyone in the world wanted to be an American. You have to wonder how I could have been so foolish. Six months earlier, the right-wing faction in Congress had blamed the French for not joining in the Iraq madness and decided that from then on, French fries should be known as freedom fries. (We'll show those French!) To make matters worse, they convinced their half-witted sympathizers to pour vintage Bordeaux down the toilet— and, just in case no one noticed, the press obliged by photographing the folly. This coincided with a campaign to discourage Americans from vacationing in France, while Bush and his merry band of flamethrowers never missed an opportunity to disparage French culture. Why didn't we just bomb Paris while we were at it?

Nothing had prepared me for the backlash. Everywhere I went, a cloud of estrangement hung in the atmosphere. The French usually were good enough not to raise the issue, but you could see shadows of it in their expressions. One thing was clear: Anyone who stood in the way of the brash American bully did so at a grave price. My experience in Beaune certainly underscored the estrangement.

Instead of bolting for friendlier territory, I spent the night in Beaune, determined to visit the Saturday-morning market, which was famously bountiful. There my love of air-cured sausage would be consummated. My plan was to wander along Place Carnot from stall to stall, tasting the paper-thin *tranches* of fennel, *cèpe*, duck, thyme, wine, or blood sausage, each studded with knots of fat that melted on the tongue. Despite a spike to my already lofty cholesterol, I wanted to try them all. The only drawback was the market's brief duration. "It is open from seven until eleven," advised a receptionist at my hotel, "but get there before nine, when the tourists invade, otherwise everything . . ." She kissed her fingers and snapped them in the air.

It had been almost twenty years since my last visit, but the moment I set foot inside the ramparts, I knew exactly where I was. Beaune is that type of intimate town, every street pulling you farther into its embrace. There are no boulevards, no skid rows or Chinatowns. The walls that rim the old medieval quarter seem to guard against the times.

Visitors are seduced by the town's enviable debt to the past. The uneven streets and doorways are full of history. The buildings lean against each other like disabled war heroes. At any moment, I expected to see musketeers with swords drawn bolting around a cobblestone corner and up one of the dim passageways that reach like tentacles through the *quartier*. Unfortunately, there are crowds and everyone has discovered the Nike brand. When Napoleon promised to drive the enemy beyond the frontier, he forgot this sorry sect. It is a shame there are no ordinances against those sneakers and nylon sweat suits that pour off the tour buses in a cloud of Obsession.

To their credit, all head straight to an eminently noble attraction. Unlike other whistlestops on the Côte d'Or, Beaune wasn't built around a single church. The focal point, just off the corner of Place de la Halle, is the awesome Hôtel-Dieu, which sits in a square facing the town's tourist center. The building, better known as the Hospice de Beaune, was founded in 1443 by Nicolas Rolin, chancellor to the duke of Burgundy, who viewed it as his ticket into heaven. If first impressions were enough, it would be easy to defend his gift of this charitable hospital complex. But generosity wasn't one of Rolin's virtues. He was a despot by trade, the kind of consummate villain France does so well, and the hospice was his hair shirt. Built as the last earthly stop for Beaune's desperate poor, it catered specifically to those whose land Rolin helped pillage after the Hundred Years' War. Even Louis XI couldn't hold his tongue upon hearing of the project, saying, "It was only fair that a man who made so many people poor during his life should create an asylum for them before his death."

Evilness aside, it doesn't diminish the terrible beauty of this architectural masterpiece. I sat in a café across the square, mesmerized by the immense arched timber roof on which a plague of pigeons sunbathed. There was nothing modest about its magnificent design. The signature of local artisans is registered by a play of intersecting diamond-shaped tiles painted in green, black, brown, and gold that shimmer like jewels in the Mediterranean sun.

"Someone had their *petit blanc* dosed with acid when that roof went up," said a woman sipping wine at the table across from me.

She was squinting up at the kaleidoscopic pattern, sunstruck, shading her forehead from the glare, and when she eventually glanced my way, the color of her eyes startled me. They were an astonishing pale gray streaked with green, as though they were the handiwork of a Flemish portrait artist. Framed by a mane of dark-brown gypsy hair, they gave off an eerie effect. She milked it, too: staring, smiling, smoking, serene.

"You have to wonder what they were thinking," I said, trying hard not to look away.

"It's an age-old story. Some guy at the local lumberyard suckered a contractor into taking a load of tiles off his hands."

"Hot off a boat from Mesopotamia," I said. "Except I don't think boats went to Mesopotamia."

Her eyes smiled at me as if they were powered by a hidden generator. "Actually, Mesopotamia was on the Dardanelles," she said, turning up the juice.

My luck, Olivia was a teacher from Illinois—a history teacher, to be exact—with more than a little knowledge of the Ottoman Empire. One of her great-uncles had even died at Gallipoli. With the summer off and her two kids in camp, she was weathering a recent divorce by hopscotching around Europe. A friend had joined her for most of the trip, but she was traveling solo for the final two weeks. In fact, she had just driven to Beaune from Rouen, which was a very long way off. "It was pretty bleak, but the time alone was essential," she said. "I'm just trying to figure out what the future holds."

It was a familiar refrain. There seemed to be hundreds of Americans all over this continent trying to resolve the same thing. Everywhere I went, there were attractive, middle-aged people either strolling or sitting alone in cafés with the weight of preoccupation on their faces. You could easily spot the ones getting over a broken relationship. They had pumped them-

selves up to expect an exhilarating recovery and had to work especially
hard to hide the loneliness and alienation. No matter how they perse-
vered, it was always a letdown. One night alone brought everything home
to roost.

Of course, in some small way I was guilty of this myself. Just a few
years earlier, I had been content, steady-on, untouched by upheaval. No
one prepared me for a change to the arrangement—to the extent that, at
forty or forty-five or fifty, I'd still be trying to figure out what the future
held. Relocating myself. It seemed inconceivable that I'd wake up one
day, in my fifties, to discover that things hadn't gone according to plan.
Now, suddenly, here I was, alone in Europe, giving the once-over to an
attractive stranger in the same leaky lifeboat.

I couldn't help but wonder what that said about us as a race.

"Only that we're human," Olivia said, over a salad of sliced smoked
magret studded with duck sausage and a tomato *concassé*. We had gravitated to dinner at La Cibollette, a little storefront bistro on the Rue de
Lorraine, in the shadow of what a neighborhood woman described as "our
own little Arc de Triomphe." "And that," Olivia continued, "unlike penguins, we don't mate for life."

That may be so, I thought, but there was fallout from such behavior.
There were consequences only now becoming apparent to me.

The restaurant was quaint in a way that seemed forced and unnatural.
The two small rooms were given a provincial polish: white plastered walls,
a selection of mismatched antiques, and low-slung ancient rafters that
came from a building much older than this one. The wooden floor was
heavily distressed, or, rather, made to look that way by a zealous deco-
rator. Otherwise, as far as I could tell, the place was a family affair; the
father cooked and his wife took orders, while their daughter served and
bused an extremely restless full house.

The tiny kitchen seemed to be working way over its head. We shared
plates of the daily Burgundian specials recommended by the girl—some
pan-roasted sweetbreads and slabs of seared quail marinated in a tart
balsamic glaze—followed by the chef's way of preparing Bresse chicken
stewed in a grainy mustard sauce, which came in a big clay casserole and

drew the kind of stares models get at a swimsuit competition. It was everything chicken should be, substantial and richly flavored but straightforward, without any pretension. And when the chef sent out a potato gratin
blistered by bacon fat and reeking of rosemary and garlic, it was hard to
argue with his process.

It felt good to eat a well-made meal that I hadn't prepared. The same
could be said about the company of a woman for whom I felt a strong
physical attraction. Olivia was smart, delightfully witty, and very much
on the make: a hothouse flower. The sexual aspect of that equation led us
directly back to her hotel, where we played a scene right out of the Single
Lover's Playbook.

All the time, walking back, we had been rehearsing our lines. We talked
politely about our itineraries and the difficulty of shipping wine back to
the States and how it might be fun to meet up in Nice later in the summer. But eventually we found ourselves facing each other, sighing awkwardly, followed by the requisite searching stares. My heart was beating
like a kettledrum. This was awkward for me. I had been a devoted family man—a devoted husband—with no designs on other women, much
less dating again. I was a mess. Olivia's next line, on cue, would be the
dependable: "Would you like to come up?" But as we lingered by the front
door, a slow artificial smile creased the corners of her mouth.

"Nothing is going to happen tonight, is it?" Olivia asked.

I shook my head sadly. "No, I'm afraid it's not," I admitted.

"I thought so. The realization occurred to me over coffee." She looked
down at the room key that dangled in her hand. "You're in love, aren't you?"

"Yes, I am," I said, wondering if a smile would be too much. "Chances
are that it's a one-way proposition, but as long as I've come this far with it,
I intend to see if it can work."

"Perhaps all you need is a better offer," she said suggestively. "A night
off might give you some clarity."

"Clarity would be good, if I didn't feel so much like Mickey Mouse,"
I said, watching confusion cloud her splendid smile. We stopped talk-
ing and sidestepped the doorway to allow another couple room to enter.
When they had passed, I leaned a hand against the wall and continued.

"When I was a kid, there was a famous cartoon in which Mickey was faced with an ethical dilemma. I don't remember exactly what it was, but in any case, an angelic Goofy popped up over his shoulder, reminding Mickey to do the right thing. Then a moment later, he popped up over Mickey's other shoulder, only this time he had horns and was carrying a trident. 'Go on,' he'd say, 'take her upstairs. What are you waiting for, you chump?'"

Olivia nodded, laughing. "I actually remember that one." She folded her arms across her chest; in the process, a hand casually brushed against mine and, momentarily flushed, I pulled away. "So which Goofy shows up here tonight?"

"The virtuous one, I'm afraid." I put a hand out, which felt strange. "This has been a lovely evening. You were great company."

I walked listlessly back to my hotel, neither satisfied nor disappointed. The sky was awash in glossy light, giving me no cover. On both sides of the street, the café terraces were full of loud, ebullient tourists who scarcely glanced my way. I felt profoundly alone. The electricity between Olivia and me had been real, and I had no doubt that a night with her would have been memorable, free of all the tensions that exist between longtime lovers. But in a way, I was relieved by the outcome. Desire was thrilling, as anyone knows, but it could be conquered. For inspiration, I pounced on the computer for a message from Carolyn, but none was waiting for me. An automated email, however, alerted me that her plane was in the air.

The next morning, I hit the market early, as the vendors were still unpacking their carts. It was exactly as I had heard: an embarrassment of sausage intermingled with freshly farmed vegetables and the usual African leather bazaar. I was in heaven. Everywhere I looked, there were lengths of gnarled, air-cured *saucissons* hanging from hooks. The taste of sausage, for me, was still a little exotic. When I was growing up, my mother had kept a kosher house, which meant that pork and all its derivatives were banned from our mouths. Of course, once I left for college everything changed. Tasting *cassoulet* was similar to discovering the Catholic nursing school; every sinful impulse in my body came rushing to the surface. I couldn't keep my hands off *porchetta* stuffed with thyme and softened garlic. My pizzas got buried under mountains of sweet fennel sausage. I especially craved the *saucisson de ménage,* coarsely ground, hand-chopped pork, loaded with diced fatback and whole peppercorns, and often seasoned with brandy. If I could have figured out a way to eat it with Rice Krispies, I wouldn't have wasted a moment deliberating. Friends said I was making up for lost time, and perhaps they were right, but by mid-morning in Beaune, I was suffering from a serious sausage overdose.

I laid the blame squarely on a swarthy, hatchet-faced man in overalls pressing samples of his sausages on anyone who gave him a second look. He was working the crowd exuberantly, like a used-furniture salesman, finishing with one customer while reeling in two others. By my third time at the bar, he recognized me for the freeloader I was. Slicing open a new block of duck sausage, he skipped me when offering a taste. I was going to have to buy something in order to remain in the loop.

"Je voudrais . . . ," I hesitated, uncertain what to select.

He sashayed over and got right into my face. *"Votre choix, M'sieur?"* Staring menacingly at me, he pointed the tip of his knife blade somewhere south of my belt, where a variety of sausages lounged on a wooden board.

Wordlessly, I pointed to the rosette, the no-frills crude sausage favored by the local peasantry, and I could tell by his eyes that he was pleased. It was like someone ordering a drink at a serious coffee roaster's shop and passing over the hazelnut and cappuccino for a cup of the house blend: "Just black." A minuscule piece of the rosette was very dear—twelve euros. I quickly bought a baguette and a nectarine and sat on a nearby bench devouring my swag.

I ate like an indulgent child. The meat, as I had expected, was anything but crude. It was simple and savory, exactly what I'd craved. But after a while, it got to a point where I couldn't put another bite in my mouth. The pork was ridiculously rich, but there was something else, something incidental to sausage affecting my appetite.

Absentmindedly, I gazed at the cobblestone square across the way, suspended in ancient history, just as the gods had left it. Figures, formless, moved in and out of the frame. It took a few minutes until I brought it into focus. Olivia was seated in the café, wearing a lime green sweater over black leggings, her face turned into the sun. She was pointing at the roof of the Hospice de Beaune. Her other hand slid across the table to where a man with shallow eyes sat smoking a meerschaum pipe. I could almost read her lips, painted today a soft shade of plum, looking varnished, as if rubbed with lip gloss. *Someone had their* petit blanc *dosed with acid when that roof went up*, they seemed to be saying.

I knew the rest of the script almost by heart.

***

An invitation to the cooking school in Maussane came through my friend Julie in St.-Rémy, who knew a woman who gave semiprivate classes in her own kitchen. Madame's reputation was that of a grumpy virtuoso, a no-nonsense teacher with the warm-and-fuzzy quotient of Imelda Marcos. "She's not going to give you a big hug or anything," Julie said, which did not deter me from applying for a place. The opportunity to cook with an expert in a private home in Provence seemed too valuable to pass up.

We'd exchanged a number of emails until she was satisfied I was serious. Later, upon my arrival, I learned that the Internet helped her to weed out undesirables, the ones she regarded as soccer moms and *Hausfraus*. "I communicate quite a bit with anyone interested in cooking here, to get an idea of who they are," she told me, "so if I don't like the feel of them, I simply say I'm fully booked." Somehow, I managed to slip through her shit-detector. There weren't any weeklong sessions scheduled that month, but if I showed up on a Sunday, as instructed, there would be time for me to cook with a couple from California arriving later that night. "You are welcome to stay here for a few days," the woman said, which was extremely gracious. "I have a charming farmhouse in the country that you will find agreeable."

I already knew that Provençal food agreed with me—*la cuisine du soleil*, with its emphasis on fresh ingredients such as olives, tomatoes, anchovies, zucchini, and lots, I mean *lots*, of garlic. I couldn't wait to wade into the classics: *bouillabaisse, brandade, aïoli, daube, tapenade, ratatouille, pissaladière . . .* the lineup was tantalizing.

The drive from Avignon—right into the midday sun—was hair-raising, over the rough, steep Alpilles plotted with enough switchbacks to give a fellow whiplash. Every time I swung around one of those treacherous corners, I said a silent prayer, hoping the law of averages would preserve me from another French lunatic determined to pass on a blind curve. I relied on blind faith and worked the gears like a joystick in a daredevil arcade game.

Up and down I went, keeping to the road's narrow shoulder, which was the only thing that separated me from a sheer plunge down the slope into the deep canyon. The vegetation was almost like a prairie, covered with bramble and random boulders of limestone that had lodged in the valley floor. You could see the heat rise from between the rocks, which is why the locals referred to it as the *Val d'Enfer*. On either side, a veiny weave of roads was etched into the parched countryside. It looked empty and forbidding, not at all reminiscent of the light that had inspired Van Gogh.

Off to the right, the ruins of the village of Les Baux clung unsteadily to the jagged sweep of cliff, as pale and illusory as a desert mirage, and beyond it, where the landscape leveled out into terraced rows of grapevines, the first shy glimpse of Maussane peeked through the trees. It acted like a sedative after the nerve-racking trip. I cranked down the car windows until they were flush with the frame, letting the dry breeze air out the fear, and fixed my mind on a few days from now, when I would once more be with Carolyn, in Nice.

Her absence was more profound right now because there was no doubt in my mind that Carolyn would have loved Maussane. It was a dozy little Luberon village about the length of a sigh, with some lovely matchbox shops, a few cafés, and an unerring sense of romance. A row of tall plane trees lined the main drag. Their branches fanned out overhead, forming a thick green shade that gave the town, from one end to the other, a deep, tunnellike appearance. Wisteria hung from trellises above the doorways, and baskets on either side were nested with freshly cut stems of lavender. Their sweetness, combined with the sultry gust of open-door aromas, gave the place its own identifiable scent.

It took more time than I'd expected to make my way through tiny Maussane. On Sundays, after lunch, the street was an obstacle course, forcing my car to a vigilant crawl. Traffic flow, just past the Place Langier de Monblan in the heart of town, was a matter of feet and inches as opposed to blocks, but no one appeared to be in a rush or compelled by the sudden standstill to flip the finger at a fellow sufferer, as I might have done in New York. Every now and then, of course, a cyclist could push motorists to the brink, an epidemic everywhere that summer. They hogged the roads with an infuriating sense that they were somehow entitled to the right of way because of their noble preoccupation. But even in Maussane, they fell victim to the throng of dizzy tourists. Happy drifters tided along the crumbling sidewalks, zigzagging lazily from one gallery to the next in a kind of aimless procession, and at any moment a sightseer, lost in a convenient trance, might wander into traffic as if it would detour obediently around him.

Just when I feared that my cool would give out, the congestion dissolved into a jaw-dropping expanse of vineyards and olive trees interspersed with the occasional villa, and within a few minutes I arrived at the gates to Moulin de P____.

From where I parked, it was hard to see what kind of place this was. Madame, looking slightly perturbed, greeted me in the driveway as if I were a handyman or some kind of vagrant. Without an ounce of subtlety, she gave me the once-over, pricing my sport coat, sizing up my car, examining my bloated suitcase, all in an effort to place me on her social scale. Her eyes studied my face, which I kept discreetly impersonal. I honestly didn't know what to make of her. In all fairness, she wasn't at all what I had expected. She was the kind of handsome woman you see on the Upper East Side of Manhattan, well put together with a high aristocratic polish that took some serious money. If I had to guess, I'd say she was in her late fifties, dressed casually but with considerable flair and conscious of the statement it made, as though she were promoting the new line at Sak's or Bergdorf's.

Madame, as I learned, didn't run a cooking school per se. From time to time, as it so happened, people would write to inquire about taking classes with her, at which point she might *invite* them to cook *with* her, for which she charged a fabulous sum. It was a capricious kind of arrangement, scheduled for whenever the situation suited her, otherwise I got the impression that she didn't cook much at all. She was the eldest daughter of an international coffee tycoon who had moved often around the globe, dragging her through Indonesian rain forests and a succession of French finishing schools. There was always plenty of time to kill in strange institutionalized kitchens, where she watched the action like a spectator on a film set.

"I'm pretty much an instinctive cook," she said, without a trace of apology, "and the guests have to keep up with me. When I'm ready to go, we're ready to go. There's no shuffling of feet, no coffee break, no potty time." Because of her no-nonsense style, Madame was careful about who enrolled in her classes. Couples were fine, even though husbands usually got bored after a day or two and puttered around the house like zombies. But she absolutely refused to take three single women, because they never could agree on anything.

"Once, I had three housewives from Florida. Two of them bonded, and I came downstairs to find the third crying her eyes out in the laundry room because the others went to dinner and left her here. And I don't take any children between the ages of six and sixteen. Americans get very comfortable here and go out and leave their kids. It's okay if you're running an orphanage, but the next time that happens, I'm putting them up for adoption."

Everyone who seemed undesirable was referred to Patricia Wells, whose name Madame uttered with cranky disdain. There had been more than a lot of buzz that summer about Wells's new cooking school with its fancy location, a hilltop retreat outside Vaison-la-Romaine, and well-known instructor. "I mean, *the woman doesn't cook!*" Madame cried, her eyes flashing like sparklers. "If anything, she's a critic and she wasn't even that when she started writing her columns. Now, she's got this so-called cooking school that starts at $4,000 a week, and on top of that you have to find your own place to stay."

On the way to my room, on the second floor at the back of the house, my head kept rotating, trying to take it all in. Somewhere along the way, I had been sold a colossal bill of goods. The "charming farmhouse in the country" was a spectacular 12,000-square-foot old mill, once a badly scarred beauty with enough of its rock-ribbed skeleton intact to suggest onetime grandeur. Madame placed its origin around the late 1600s, and over the years it had languished in frightful disrepair. The agent who sold the place to her thought she'd taken a white elephant off his hands. At the time, the roof was completely caved in, the crumbling walls were useless. No doors or windows remained, and the interior was overrun with wild fig trees and blackberry brambles.

But money—lots of money—had turned it into a veritable palace. No expense had been spared in the house's miraculous renovation, which had taken more than ten years and an infusion of talent from the best French artisans. The rooms were huge, rather like what you'd expect to see on a Hollywood soundstage; they were filled from top to bottom with museum-quality antiques. Madame's husband, a poor big-city boy from the Midwest who had made a fortune in Internet technology, was an incorrigible collector who hoarded anything that amused him, like someone afraid of losing his shirt in the next downturn.

"Get a load of this," he said, steering me toward a glass-paneled bookcase in the dining-room hallway. "We have the entire collection of Michelin guides, dating back to the very first one, including the 1945 paperback wartime edition." They also had every issue of *Gourmet* and the complete *National Geographic* series bound in hand-stamped calfskin. Several good etchings from the European modernist movement hung in well-lit frames. And somewhere, hidden, I presumed, in a vast temperature-controlled cellar, were the hundreds, perhaps thousands, of bottles of important wine he'd been buying at auction.

In the kitchen, which was astonishingly spacious, treasures filled every inch of wall space: five rare cast-iron stoves, a display case with more than a hundred antique molds, shelves jammed with precious crockery, unusual antique pitchers, hundreds of cookbooks, and, on one wall, the framed, signed menus from each of the Michelin three-star restaurants, as well as every important restaurant on the Continent.

Madame and her husband reveled in the blessings of wealth, which they had bequeathed in a fashion to their spoiled daughter. According to their description, she was a gorgeous thirty-five-year-old ex-model, and ex-everything else, who had spent a year or two on a sitcom, jilted a well-heeled fiancé before dumping a French pop star, and now killed time in the Miami Beach scene, painting and going to parties. "She's living the life of a girl who has very rich parents," her father said, with something less than approval. "You never know, you two might hit it off."

There wasn't a chance of that, I thought, imagining the kind of nightmare she would be. Curiously, there wasn't a photo of her anywhere in sight, not that that would have convinced me otherwise. The last person I needed in my life was a professional heartbreaker. She was expected to turn up midweek with a likeminded girlfriend from the States, and I made a mental note to leave before their arrival.

Anyway, what I was looking forward to, in my usual fashion, was dinner. Madame had prepared an informal meal to welcome her new guests. It was a kind of strategy on her part to see how we'd interact. I was more than curious about her cuisine, of course, wondering if perhaps it would measure up to my expectations. I needed a lift after Beaune, something to offset the sour weekend, like an antacid, like an act of kindness.

By the time we were halfway through dinner, however, I knew my hopes were in the crapper. The food was ghastly, a fricassee of local rabbit in a mild cream sauce with fat bosky morels and the kind of garden herbs that required a machete to cut. On looks alone, it would have won the Miss Congeniality award. It smelled heavenly, as if someone had scattered sage and thyme around the room, but it was overcooked and absolutely bland, as was the wild rice served alongside it. I stared forlornly at the plate, feeling my appetite ebb away after the first bite.

"This is *exactly* the kind of dish I want to learn how to make," Doug cried, licking every scrap of meat off the bones like a Mandinka warrior.

Doug and his wife, Didi, were veterans of Moulin de P_____. They'd come here for three summers running, so that Doug could cook with Madame, mastering her Provençal recipes before trying them out on his friends back in a California 'burb, where he was renowned for throwing lavish dinner parties. To what extent he was talented, I never fully learned. He certainly talked a good game. He recalled specific meals he'd made the way friends of mine reminisced about an important ballgame. His over-the-top descriptions left no doubt in my mind that Doug enjoyed food.

He was quite a big man, bulky and broad-boned like an overfed Lab, but he moved with surprising grace. He was good with his hands as well, but there was something about the way he held a knife that made him seem dangerous. His eyes also made me nervous, drifting off some-where midsentence, as if he were unable to focus for very long on any one thing.

But all that mattered, for the moment, was that Doug had come to cook. From what I could tell, there was nothing more pressing on his mind. He spoke animatedly and with passion about his culinary exploits *chez* Madame, although I got the impression that he was a handful in the kitchen. Every now and then, Madame would roll her eyes and grimace when he rhapsodized about a dish they'd made in the past. After listen-ing to him recount their chocolate soufflé fiasco, she shivered with all the starch of an Ibsen matriarch and muttered, "It's a wonder you didn't burn the house down." It was endearing, though, because they seemed genu-inely to enjoy each other. I looked forward to sharing the stove with such a gung-ho guy. But I couldn't help wondering about Didi's involvement.

Madame seemed to imply that Didi had the kitchen instincts of a houseplant. If past experience was any indication, Didi wouldn't touch so much as a teaspoon. She parked herself at the counter, paging through magazines, not really reading them but looking at the pictures and ads, which allowed her to maintain a running dialogue during the lessons.

"She never shuts up!" Madame warned me, which turned out to be a remarkable understatement. Since walking through the door, Didi had kept up an endless yap-yap-yap in a tiny Valley Girl voice that finished each sentence a decibel higher than where it began, and with a question mark tagged onto the end of it. It was a funny kind of chatter, as if David Mamet had written it for Lindsay Lohan, running on and on with segues that defied all logic. Madame was amused by it at first and occasionally prompted her, subject by subject, but usually it was a one-woman show, with useless stories about *Survivor* and her niece and designing clothes for cats and how to cheat at Monopoly . . . anything that crossed her mind.

In no time, it drove Madame mad. Madame even began smoking again after a few months on the wagon, but nothing galled her as much as the woman's eating habits.

As we all sat down that first night, Madame's husband made a rather grand presentation by opening a bottle of rare white Burgundy covered in a fine layer of cellar dust. It was one of those Napoleonic wines that never come up for sale, let alone get served as an aperitif. Over our chorus of *oooohs* and *aaaahs*, Didi chimed, "I'll have a *Coke*? No, no, make it a *Diet* Coke? Yes, a Diet Coke, and with *ice*? I love ice. You know, if it's not cold enough, you might put some *ice* in that wine?"

"Oh, I forgot to buy the Coke," Madame said with scathing dryness. "How about a glass of water, dear? I'll be happy to put some ice in *that* for you."

But any beanball glanced right off Didi, who simply plowed straight ahead the way a sedan moves through an automatic carwash.

"I don't *eat* rabbit?" she said, wrinkling up her nose as the casserole passed in front of her.

Madame tensed a bit but otherwise seemed undaunted. "There's a delicious cauliflower purée and plenty of summer squash on the stove."

"I'm not really a *vegetable* girl?" Didi said.

"Do me a favor," Madame said, while topping off Doug's glass, "remind me to pick up some Cocoa Puffs for your wife."

As it turned out, cereal and soda would have done nicely all around. Madame's food, to put it bluntly, was a bit of a snow job. It was flat and unimaginative, which wasn't really her fault because the recipes, for the most part, were lifted straight out of magazines. I should have guessed as much after our first goofy lesson.

We discussed the menu that morning on our way to the market. "How about if we grill some fish with olive oil and herbs?" Doug suggested.

"Fish is good," I agreed, "but we're in Provence, you know. I'd hate to waste the time grilling. Is there any way we could give it a local twist?"

Madame knew just the thing. *Bourride,* a type of rustic fish soup using the catch of the day, was a Provençal specialty, one you could find on the menu of almost every corner bistro. I'd had it in Paris a few times, usually made with monkfish—or *lotte*, as the French call it—and wondered how anything so spiritually uplifting could originate in a soup pot. There was no argument from any of us about learning to make a respectable *bourride,* or the opportunity to pair it with a tomato *granité* and, for dessert, *coeur à la crème.*

When we got back, Doug and I began preparing the *granité*, with Madame dictating the recipe step-by-step from a brand-new cookbook. "This just came in the mail," she said, folding back the spine with a sickening crunch. When I asked if she'd tried the recipe before, the warm notes drained out of her voice as she said, "We're going to try it together, if it's all right with you."

Out of the corner of my eye, I saw Doug slip her a little Siamese smile and felt the cold, sharp pang of betrayal. My reaction seemed silly, considering I hardly knew this guy, but it seemed that we were teammates and therefore bound together in a sort of sympathy that necessitated our pulling for each other. I hadn't bargained for any competitive nonsense, and there didn't seem any point in promoting a rivalry. Suddenly, I got a bitter taste in my mouth, and when they decided to take a break for lunch, I went back to my room instead of sitting there and feeling even lonelier in their company.

It was a sultry afternoon, sticky with humidity, typical of the Luberon, which is landlocked and somewhat immune from breezes. From my window, there were olive trees as far as the eye could see, and their branches sagged, almost groaning, from the burden of ripe *picholine, verdunc,* and *gros ânes* (or "big jackasses"), which are the size of young figs. A dense crown of leaves shaded the room from sunlight, for which I was grateful. I splashed some cool water on my face and rather gingerly lifted the lid of my laptop as if opening a treasure chest.

I stared at the status line in the email from Carolyn for some time before clicking on it. The memo said, "Dear Bob," and without even opening it, I knew what the message held. *Dear Bob.* . . . She'd had a change of heart, as I'd expected, and would not be meeting me in Nice—or anywhere else. "I know we would have had a wonderful time together in

France, but I just don't think it would be fair to either of us. My life is going in a different direction from yours. . . ."

I didn't even bother reading the rest of it. A different direction . . . after all this time together, she couldn't even tell me in person. Somehow I knew that I was probably better off. Lately, friends had urged me to move on, to save myself. Apparently they had known something I didn't.

Even so, I was brokenhearted, utterly brokenhearted. I sat down hard, as the hopes I'd been safeguarding emptied out of me. There was a pounding in my chest I could not eliminate. Where was my trusty coat of emotional armor? Carolyn had been my lover and my muse and a large part of my dreams, so the wave of nausea curling through my stomach was altogether well earned.

I sat on the edge of the bed for a long while. If anything, I felt resentment, the resentment a man might feel toward his boss, his ex—someone who has driven him to his worst. Resentment was an unsteady state of mind for me, but I felt a strong pull of survival. After a long time—I'm not sure how long—I ran out of sorrows to dwell on, and I forced myself to think about France. France was too spiritual and beautiful for resentment to prevail, I told myself. I tried to shift my mood from the flash of anger, glancing over images and memories of France so irrationally dear to me.

No one, I tried to convince myself, was going to ruin my adventure. I had hoped the trip would be a way to have fun with Carolyn, perhaps more. Now it would become something else, something more difficult. I decided I'd have to throw myself even more completely into something that I could still feel passionate about, the embrace of the kitchen—in part to heal from this cataclysm, to rescue myself. I would strive to create something sublime. The experiences ahead would have to help me to put Carolyn out of my thoughts. I didn't know whether that would be enough to take my mind off of loneliness. I knew I might wind up dragging my sorry ass home with a repertoire of fussy recipes and nowhere to serve them but the bowl of Wink, my faithful dog. Unless he'd dumped me by now, too. All I could think to do was to plunge ahead. I'd rescued disasters in the kitchen before. It was time to improvise.

Sometime later, after a respectable period of self-pity, I went down to join the work on the dinner. Nothing was said about my disappearance or the fact that I walked through the lesson without saying ten words to anybody. I was not about to share my personal life with this crew. Insensitive fools, I thought furiously. You should notice, you should see how hurt I'm feeling. . . .

The dinner did little to distract me. The *bourride* was nothing more than an improvised fish stew, the same one I made at home, with cod, shrimp, squid, scallops, and some sautéed vegetables in a water base that begged for character. Madame dismissed as "absolutely useless" my glum suggestion that we make a *fumet* to intensify the flavor. Not surprisingly, it tasted pretty bland out of the pot. It needed salt, of course, which was one of Bob Ash's golden rules, but Madame looked at me sharply when I attempted to add more than a pinch.

"I don't love much salt in anything," she said.

When her back was turned, I defiantly began adding salt . . . and adding salt . . . and more salt, trying to bring the stock around. I might have been preparing the tub for a muscle soak. After everything had steeped for a while, I asked Madame to taste it. "See," she said, "it's getting there on its own."

When no one was looking, I also put in a few grinds of pepper.

Her "secret ingredient," as if I couldn't have guessed, was a half-liter of cream added just before serving to give the stew some depth, but even that couldn't rescue it from the dead. It was as far from a *bourride* as chili was from *pot-au-feu*.

I managed to stumble through the next day. The same disappointment happened that night, with an herb-stuffed leg of lamb that we cooked in a sea-salt crust. It was an eye-catching preparation that was all the rage in Paris. A lot of it was pure spectacle, of course, in the way that it was presented at the table. It arrived straight out of the oven looking like an igloo, which was then cracked open with great flourish, using a hammer and chisel.

The tricky part was forming a shell with enough salt. We used four and a half pounds of it, mixed with some egg white to give it a *papier-mâché*–like consistency. It is important that the roast be completely encased to keep it moist. But after an hour in the oven, I noticed that the shell was cracking.

"It's ruined," Madame declared, blaming the failure on Doug and me. She felt we should have monitored the cooking more carefully, charging in like vigilant Zamboni drivers to spot-repair the surface. But even if we had, it wouldn't have made much difference. The meat was overcooked, tasteless, and tough, like my mother's brisket. (Sorry, Mom.)

I found it disturbing that such a presumably well-respected cook chose to teach so carelessly, and I was disappointed by the results. I had expected more of an effort, if not a higher degree of creativity. The whole setup lacked a kind of eloquence. From what I could gather, Madame had no formal training as a cook. For her, this was a hobby, not an expression of art.

"She's a facilitator," Doug agreed, when I expressed my concerns. We were sitting on the patio, working our way through a bottle of extremely flinty Sancerre, while muting our voices to a conspiratorial whisper. Above us, a cough sounded from an open bedroom window. "She provides the house, an incredible kitchen, and fresh ingredients, and she shares her favorite recipes."

"If you ask me, some basic instruction wouldn't hurt."

Doug contemplated me coldly: "Man, you are one sorry fucker." He didn't know the half of it. "Just take a look around. This is an incredible place, and we get to come here—no, we're *privileged* to come here and learn how to make very special food. What more do you want?"

"I'd like it to taste good, for starters. And I'd love a little advice, a little how-and-why. So far, I haven't heard anything that broadens my understanding of cooking." I glanced up at the window, sensing an unseen presence hovering. My voice became so faint that I hoped Doug could read lips. "Were you there when she made the salad for our lunch? I asked Madame to show me a dressing, but she said, 'Oh, I just shake up some olive oil and vinegar in a little plastic container, and that does it.' Hell, I could have done as much with a Good Seasons bottle."

Doug shrugged, reluctant to agree. "Then you should propose another

option instead of griping about it," he said. "Why don't you look through
her recipe file on the kitchen counter. Maybe you'll find something in
there that will make you happy."

I wasn't optimistic, but there was nothing else I could think of that
would salvage the situation, or at the very least upgrade it from disaster
to shipwreck.

A half-hour later, after paging through dozens of recipes, all familiar enough to suggest they had appeared in cookbooks I owned, I com-
piled a short list of candidates that seemed unusual, challenging, . . . and
authentic. A mushroom *"tarte Tatin"* sounded especially promising. When
I asked Madame about it, she looked curiously at me, as if I had somehow
read her mind. Grinning, she led me to the refrigerator, taking my wrist
the way a mother does with a child. She took out a shopping bag, which
balanced awkwardly on the counter. She looked at me again, for effect,
before tearing the bag open. A cascade of wild mushrooms spilled across
the counter like diamonds.

The delight on my face amused Madame, who held up various specimens to the light. The *cèpes* alone looked big enough to topple tenpins,
the chanterelles were as leathery as a Coach bag, the *girolles* and *porcini*
meaty enough to grill. I had never seen such perfectly plump, bronze-col-
ored mushrooms. It seemed a pity to slice them, and I think I said as much
to Madame, although she assured me the result would be worth it. Doug
gave me the eye, which was his way of telling me to keep my mouth shut.

Apparently he never employed a similar tactic on his wife, or it didn't
work. As we brushed some residual dirt from the mushrooms, Didi stood
over my shoulder, examining the quality of my work. "There are a few
smudges on that one?" she said, poking at a chanterelle with her finger.
Wordlessly, I picked up the culprit and burnished its silky surface, grit-
ting my teeth as a safety measure against the escape of a vivid obscenity.
"There's some stuff on that one, *too?"*

"I'm not done with that one yet," I snapped, unable to conceal my
displeasure.

Didi didn't miss a beat. "Oh, don't mind me. I always stand behind
Doug and watch over things, kind of like his quality-*control* guy?"

"Then maybe Doug can benefit from your help, but I can't cook that way."

"But that's my *job?*" she insisted.

"Not here it isn't, sister. Unless you're going to cook, you have to stand on the other side of the counter, where you are out of the way. Just over there."

Instead, she tiptoed a few feet east to where her husband was working and stood flush against his back, massaging his shoulders. Pouting. Giving me—the *eye*.

Madame, who had followed the action with enthusiasm, put down her chef's knife and said, "We have a few good videos for you to watch, Didi. Come with me. I think there's a copy of *Pretty in Pink* in the parlor."

After they had gone, Doug and I began assembling the ingredients for the tart, whose recipe, I was told, came from a famous restaurant outside of Aix. It was a rich, jammy concoction of mushrooms, shallots, walnuts, garlic, and parsley, all of which were sautéed in sweet butter and then baked under an impossibly light layer of puff pastry. I doubt that a famous restaurant would have resorted to commercial puff pastry. Ours was store-bought and, to my eyes, every bit as elegant when it emerged from the oven.

Vegetable tarts are always a good side dish, given the minimal number of ingredients and the relatively short time needed to prepare one. When I was younger, with limited skills and less respectful toward the marriage of taste and texture, I became infatuated with churning out crude zucchini tarts, which were baked in a fluted metal pan lined with pastry, a *schmear* of Dijon mustard, mozzarella, and plenty of garlic. It was pretty to look at, and tasty enough, but it had all the consistency of a Ray's Pizza.

This version coaxed as much flavor as possible out of every ingredient and was capable of bringing an unemotional man to tears. In fact, crying would have been an improvement over the near-silence that permeated the kitchen. Muzzling Didi had just about eliminated the last good vibes that remained. I didn't dare bring it up to Doug, who crouched low over his cutting board in stony sufferance, tight-lipped. His body language was empty of grace. Several boxes shoved aside, their lids strewn across the counter, separated our workstations. He had thrown up a barrier between us, daring me to cross, and it was hard because of the utensils we shared and our common goal. But somehow we managed to cooperate on this beauty:

TATIN *aux* CÈPES

2 lb. assorted wild mushrooms, wiped clean
3 large shallots, minced
large knob (2 Tbl.) of sweet butter
salt and pepper
1/4 cup parsley, stems removed

3 cloves garlic
1/3 cup finely ground walnuts
walnut oil
10 oz. puff pastry
1 egg yolk

Preheat the oven to 375 degrees.

Slice the mushrooms thinly and sauté in a skillet with the shallots until golden in a couple of tablespoons of melted butter. If there is any accumulated liquid, reduce until mushroom liquid has cooked away, then season well with salt and pepper, and arrange the mushrooms along the bottom of a buttered 9-inch tart dish (not one with a removable bottom).

Finely chop the parsley and garlic together (this is called a persillade) and sprinkle over the mushrooms. Afterward, sprinkle with the ground walnuts, then drizzle a little walnut oil over the mixture.

Carefully lay one sheet of puff pastry over the top, tucking it under around the edges. Brush with the beaten egg yolk and bake 20 to 30 minutes, until the pastry is golden. Run a knife around the edges to loosen any pastry that might have become stuck to the sides. Carefully invert the tart onto a serving dish. Serve warm, with walnut oil drizzled over the top.

Serves 6

Madame had done little more than provide the recipe and offer about as much real help as you'd expect from a backseat driver, but she had been redeemed by the outcome. The first bites from the near-perfect tart made us gasp. The dense slurry of shallots, caramelized by the butter, married perfectly with the mushrooms, whose meaty heft buried the pastry underneath two inches of sweetness. We were all, including Madame, a bit stunned. Even Doug, clutching an oozing slice in his fist, looked up from his plate, grinning, and gave me an exuberant thumbs-up.

The bounce was short-lived.

The tipping point came at dessert. After we finished the main course, Madame pulled out printed directions for a chocolate soufflé and asked for our input. Doug and I looked at her in panic. Soufflés, as a rule, are an exact science, their nuances guarded like the atomic launch code, and no one fucks with the recipe. Duels have been fought over less. To make matters worse, I happened to know that Doug prided himself on being something of a soufflémaster, a distinction earned during some perilous moments on previous stints in Madame's kitchen.

He said, "Let's try it with strawberries. That should be enough of a challenge for everyone."

Almost perversely, he reminisced about soufflé experiments that had ended in soggy disasters. Several were just trashed, and I could tell by his condescending manner that he didn't think I was up to it.

"You need to concentrate; it takes plenty of finesse," Doug told me. "On the nights when I prepare a soufflé for friends, I don't even drink wine."

I had already consumed half a bottle of Côtes du Rhône, and he knew it. Nevertheless, I was determined to pull off a perfect soufflé—and then serve it to his wife. Madame had already made a soufflé base, the *appareil*, which was needed to draw out excess moisture when adding fruit or a liqueur. By the time I was ready to use it, the base was already cool, but its formula, as I learned later, was a pretty straightforward affair:

SWEET SOUFFLÉ BASE

4 Tbl. sugar	1 Tbl. unsalted butter
3/4 cup milk	1/4 tsp. vanilla extract
3 Tbl. pastry flour	

Sprinkle 2 tablespoons of the sugar over 1/2 cup of the milk and bring it to a boil in a medium saucepan.

Combine the other 2 tablespoons of the sugar and the flour in a medium bowl. Whisk in the remaining 1/4 cup of milk. Gradually whisk in the boiled milk and return the mixture to the saucepan. Cook over medium-high heat until it boils. Continue to boil 1 1/2 minutes, whisking constantly as it becomes thick, then remove the pan from the heat.

Immediately strain the mixture through a fine sieve into a bowl, using a spatula to press out any lumps of flour that may remain. Stir in the butter and the vanilla.

Cover the surface with plastic wrap (the wrap must touch the surface of the base to prevent a film from forming on top), and cool at room temperature. Refrigerate until needed.

The rest of the preparation required some fancy footwork. Madame gave us her version of the tao of soufflés: Sift this, beat that, whisk here, fold there, hold your breath, click your ruby slippers three times. It was like a religious rite. She thought it would be helpful if Doug and I worked individually, making separate soufflés, since the finished product would reflect our creative imprints. If you asked me, it would have been preferable ordering one off the Internet. I wanted to cook something I had the chance of pulling off, not split the atom.

Doug washed his hands like an obstetrician preparing to deliver triplets. "Are the eggs room temperature?" he asked, holding his palms out so Nurse Didi could dry them.

"Oh, please. Let's get these babies moving," I grumbled.

My spirits lifted somewhat as we separated the eggs and beat the whites with a pinch of salt into frothy peaks. A half-cup of sugar sifted slowly into the mix brought out a high gloss and forced them to ribbon outward like angel's wings. Eventually, the peaks stiffened like hair gel. Watching the beaters whir through the mousse conveyed the impression that the air's power was unlimited, and if the process continued for long, it might be possible to balance a stack of books on top without the peaks caving in. I became mesmerized by it—so much so that before long I had meringue.

"You need to start over," Madame said, above the din of machinery.

"It seems like such a waste."

"It has to be done. The egg whites need to be soft peaks, otherwise the oven's heat won't expand the air bubbles in the froth. That's what gives the soufflé its lovely lightness and makes it rise." Madame reached over and tipped my batter into the trash. "This time, stop beating as soon as the whites mount."

I felt my cheek flush under the discipline. Across the counter, Doug acknowledged the scene with a slight smile. This stuck in my craw as I wiped out the bowl and began separating a new set of eggs. Given the chance, I would have jacked his hand mixer into overdrive.

This time I was more attentive while beating the eggs, beginning at a fairly slow speed, as one would a serious walk, and gradually working up a full head of steam. When the slime developed its own fine froth, I let the salt slide from my fingers and watched as the magic happened: peaks rose from the foamy depths. As I added the sugar, the peaks took on that special glow and started to stand at attention, at which point I put on the brakes.

No one, I was certain, had ever produced stiffer, softer peaks. They looked like shaving lather, and I fought the urge to slap some on my cheeks.

Without waiting for Madame's approval, I whisked a teaspoon of strawberry jam into the soufflé base, followed by a cup of fat berries that had been stemmed and hulled and diced, then a splash of vanilla. Now came the tricky part: stirring a third or so of the egg whites into the base to lighten it and then quickly folding in the rest so that everything barely combined. I remembered what Sandy D'Amato had once told me, that the secret to a soufflé was its structure, finding the right balance between flavor and texture. "The more egg whites you have, the less flavor you get," he said. "If the soufflé is stable—really rich and strongly flavored—you can add the egg whites and it will still be delicious." That was why chocolate complemented the recipe so well; it thickened the egg whites without sacrificing taste, whereas with Grand Marnier, you often tasted only the egg whites. "It's easy to make a soufflé, then split it open and pour *crème anglaise* in the middle," he added, "but all you'll really taste is the *crème anglaise*. A real soufflé should be able to stand on its own."

I stirred another tablespoon or two of jam into my base, for good measure. As gently as a midwife, I helped the entire quivering mass slide into a well-buttered ramekin, then I set it on a trivet like fine sculpture.

I glanced over at Doug, who had arrived at the same procedural point but was whipping the mixture like a jockey down the home stretch. I suggested he might want to fold in the whites a little more gently.

"I've done this a dozen times," he insisted, fixing me with dagger eyes.

My shrug said, "Have it your way," but the words stuck in my throat.

"No! No! *No!*" a voice broke in from the other side of the room. Madame emerged all atwitter from behind cupboard doors. I thought she was coming straight at me, arms flailing, but she elbowed past, grabbing the whisk out of Doug's hands. "You've got *soup!* You *idiot!*"

I worried that she might rap his knuckles. Instead, she turned her back and shuddered, poking clumsily at the sticky mess without looking up, until Doug skulked from the room.

"Are the eggs room temperature? I've done this a dozen times." The evil Goofy was chanting in my ear.

For a moment I felt vindicated, until I realized that Madame's honor rested in my hands. She looked blank-faced at my soufflé and nodded almost imperceptibly at the masterpiece. Carrying it the way one would a newborn, or a live grenade, I placed it gingerly in the oven at 425 degrees.

How long we stood there I cannot recall, but it was a considerable length of time, maybe twenty minutes or more, and neither of us said a word. For my part, I had retreated into some private place, pushing everything else far away. Only now, these months later, can I remember how I spent that time. My mind spun through the succession of myriad slip-ups that had marred the last week. Beaune was a washout, from every point of view. And Madame—well, she had hardly lived up to the expectations I had had for a mentor in Provence. Compared to Bob Ash, this experience was strictly improvisational, although perhaps the soufflé would, to some extent, exonerate her. Of course, my cooking mates from California might have thought otherwise, but they were an unpleasant pair. And just in case I hadn't suffered enough, I'd been dumped by my girlfriend, and by email, at that.

"Maybe when the soufflé comes out, I can put my head in there for a while," I thought, not realizing at the time that I had said it out loud.

"You'll do nothing of the sort," a voice said crossly. I blinked a few times and Madame looked at me tactfully, with an uneasiness I had never seen in her before. Worry seemed to rise off her in little wispy vapors, like rain on hot asphalt. Perhaps it was a maternal instinct, or something as close to warmth as she could muster. I must have looked doomed, because as I tried to laugh it off, she reached out and threw her arms around me. It was as awkward a hug as I'd ever experienced in my life, much like one at my college graduation, when my physics teacher kissed me. Madame had a dishtowel in her hand, and afterward she held it out to me as a way of indicating that the moment had passed.

Obediently, I reached into the oven and took out my soufflé. Her eyes followed my face, which I kept as deadpan as possible.

"I think," Madame said significantly, "you have just conquered Everest, my friend."

For a second her face seized with pride, before settling into a professional mask. There was only so much she would show me, even though I knew I had pleased her in a vague and complicated way.

I set the dish carefully on the counter and stepped back to admire my handiwork. It was about as beautiful a result as I had ever managed to produce. The spongy crust, delicate and swollen, rose above the rim of the crenellated tureen and puffed out in a beautiful fawn-colored crown that was jeweled with bits of strawberries, like the hat of a high priest. I gently laid a finger on the center, unable to control my excitement. It trembled under my touch, and I knew it would be creamy, like an omelet, with what French chefs call a *babouse*, just a slobbering. A crack appeared in the surface, releasing a mist of aromatic heat.

"Quick," said Madame, "we have to eat it before it falls."

She called the others and insisted they come to the table, which I didn't think was such a good idea. To their credit, seemingly unruffled by the set-back, they smiled at my picture-perfect soufflé. I felt sorry for Doug and told him it was beginner's luck; that I didn't have the nerve to make one for dinner guests, as he had done. I started to say something else to bolster his ego, but Madame interrupted, reminding us that every cook had a souf-flé disaster or three—or eight—on his resumé. It came with the territory. Then I saw Doug look at Didi, rolling his eyes toward me. Or was I imagin-ing it? I couldn't help myself. I felt an intense antagonism toward him.

I glared at the two of them until I got their full attention. My eyes screwed into tiny points. I drew myself up, ready to give them a piece of my mind. But I held back, managing, in a brief moment of clarity, to rec-ognize the absurdity of two grown men getting into a dick-measuring con-test over who could produce the pouffier soufflé.

Madame looked cautiously between us and pushed helpings of the soufflé in three directions at once, mumbling, "Maybe this will brighten things up."

It sounded absurd, considering all the tension in the room, that I burst out laughing, a strange sound that must have seemed menacing the way it rumbled on too long.

As a way of ignoring my behavior, Madame, Doug, and Didi began eating. They put their heads down and attacked that soufflé, more out of necessity than desire, knowing they'd eventually have to render a favor-able opinion. It smelled sinfully delicious, but I didn't touch my fork. Nor did I wait around for forthcoming compliments.

While the others were absorbed, I got up and wandered out to the courtyard, where the air was moist and heavy with hibiscus. I couldn't believe I was letting such a petty dispute throw me. It didn't seem to matter who it was—my ex-wife, a lover, some two-day acquaintance in a cooking class—I couldn't seem to cope right now with anyone who turned from ally to antagonist.

Gratefully, I inhaled the liberating night. Across the road, the vine-yards appeared infinite, their cornrows camouflaged in the moonlight like armies at night. Even in the darkness the view was something to admire.

Squinting, I followed the trajectory of a path between the vines that seemed to beckon halfway up the hillside, then disappear in blackness, leading, as I imagined, to the edge of the universe. I stared harder, hoping to pick up its outline. Then I began to run.

⁂

Lunch the next day was like a scene out of a Pinter play. We had spent the morning wandering the local market in Tarascon, a particular favorite of the town's heavy concentration of North Africans and therefore flush with the kinds of spices considered exotic even by French standards. Tarascon shared nothing with the expanse of markets in Lyon or Bresse. The crowds were congested, unruly. The cramped stalls, teeming with immigrants, competed with traffic rolling through the main square, masking clouds of exhaust fumes with saffron and cumin.

Eventually, the fumes prevailed. Our only hope was to go toward the river, where the air would refresh our spirits, or at least our vitality. Directly across the Rhône, in the port town of Beaucaire, we found a shabby little lunch joint, Au Nord au Sud, that served *moules frites* twenty different ways. We settled at a table on the riverbank terrace.

While we waited for our food under the broiling noon sun, no one exchanged a word. The menu was discussed, orders were placed, but aside from that, we had nothing left to say to each other. Even Didi found it prudent to turn off the chatter. A carafe of rosé was poured in silence.

To stem the awkwardness, I excused myself and meandered around back, to the kitchen. It was nothing more than a hole-in-the-wall, a squalid little room at the base of an old office building, where two shirtless African men sweated over a commotion of steaming pots. Their skin was slick and shiny and very black—not shades of brown like most Americans but darker, like ebony that had been polished to a high gloss. How they managed to last more than a few minutes in that brutal, foul heat was a miracle. Everywhere there wasn't steam or grease or garbage, there were mussels. They were piled in huge burlap sacks against the wall and under the counter and on plastic oil drums and on shelves. Broken shells, prob-ably days old, were strewn across the floor.

The smell came at me hard and I reeled back. I must have gagged, because it drew their attention. One of the men looked up and grinned, his teeth as large as piano keys. "How ya doin', boss?" he said in broken English.

On a filthy cutting board, he chopped a fugue of carrots, celery, and onions, sweeping them with the back of a hand into an old iron casserole. A fistful of *lardons* hit the pot with a sizzle, followed by minced garlic and hot-pepper flakes. Mussels went in next, along with a chopped tomato and a few olives. The man was in a groove, on cruise control. There was a stylish mechanical efficiency in the motion of his huge hands: finding the salt, then enough white wine to cover the contents, stirring, grinding pep-per, adding butter, more butter, more, tilting the pot just enough to coat everything, before blessing it with a clutch of parsley. He plunked a cover on the casserole and turned up the flame.

For a moment, I felt hungry. There are few things more satisfying than a bowl of mussels steamed in a simple wine broth, and a side of crisp fries. If they are fresh—that is, if the mussels have been harvested in cold, clear water and cleaned properly and not overcooked—they will taste like the sea. Otherwise, they smell fishy and become as chewy as rubber. There seems to be no middle ground. I've known people who can eat several pounds at a clip, then hit a bad one and be off mussels for years. But if they are fresh, as I have said, and cooked in a savory broth, the combina-tion of flavors is unbeatable.

I'm a sucker for *moules frites*. Lily and I eat them whenever we're stuck for a dinner idea. We'll go through my entire range of recipes without finding anything that catches our eye, until, suddenly, Lily's face will light up and she'll say, "Hey, Dad, what about *moules frites?*" and we'll break out laughing at the obvious. It's also the perfect lunch, light enough but sub-stantial, especially in France, where the preparation is as sure a thing as terminal bureaucracy. If only my curiosity hadn't intruded. . . .

The cook stepped back and steadied himself against a wall, wiping a swash of perspiration from his face with the back of an arm. He hiked up his pants and flashed that brilliant grin.

"How ya doin', boss?"

I muttered, *"Pas mal,"* and almost meant it. He had put the dish together with such seamless effort; it was really quite beautiful to watch. And instructive. I would prepare mussels for my daughter in this exact manner once I got home. But the kitchen, if you could even call it that, was an unholy mess, and I doubted that anything from it would make its way down my throat.

A few minutes later, Doug wolfed down his mussels, proclaiming them the best he'd ever eaten. Then he helped himself to my share, which lay untouched in the casserole. I complained of the heat and the effects of Tarascon's exhaust fumes, but the vivid backstage business had been enough to kill my appetite.

Faithful to Madame's agenda, we discussed dinner during the long ride back. There was some debate about making an herb-crusted pork roast that I'd seen in a magazine on her desk, but it didn't seem like much of a challenge to me. It would not be anything I would ever make again, either. The *ratatouille* would be all right . . . the usual eggplant, zucchini, and tomatoes blended with capers and *herbes de Provence*, but nothing unexpected, nothing out of the ordinary.

I was frustrated but said nothing to the others. It must have been on my face, though. For the last few days, a general malaise had developed in which I more or less sleepwalked through Madame's cooking classes. I showed no enthusiasm whatsoever for the recipes that were presented. Aside from the soufflé and the mushroom tart, the lessons had been a waste of my time. And that must have irritated the hell out of Doug, who was psyched up for each lesson.

"Oh, look what the *mistral* blew in!" Madame cried, as the car turned into her driveway.

We pulled up to the guest cottage. On the front steps, two women in short little skirts were sitting with their long legs stretched out and bottles of Champagne waving in their fidgety hands. For all I could tell, they might have been outside a dance club in South Beach. Drinking straight from the bottles and chatting as if they were the only two people on the scene, they ignored us as we got out of the car. The glossy blonde, of course, was Madame's daughter. She was an unnaturally thin woman, with too much makeup around her raccoon eyes. The introductions were awkward; neither girl bothered to acknowledge any of us, even as outstretched hands were offered. They may have been too tired, or too drunk, or too ill-mannered—it didn't matter. Madame promised them an outstanding dinner, courtesy of her two "prize students," which I assumed meant Doug and me, but they weren't interested. On the patio lay the remains of our gorgeous platter of cheeses that had been gouged and ripped apart, as if animals had gotten to it; a knife had been stood upright in a sorry little *chevre*.

I stared at the scene and tried not to laugh. It was sad and vulgar and entirely out of context. I tried not to look at Madame, who was twitching with delight. This very proper woman, who otherwise might have assassinated someone for even *thinking* about such behavior, had turned into Supermom, all giggly and desperate to please. It was an amazing transformation. I hoped my face revealed nothing, but it would crack like a New Orleans levee if I stayed there another minute.

On the way to my room, I bumped into Doug and Didi. They were off in a corner of the parlor, heads close together, and I had a damned good idea what they were talking about. As I passed, they looked up and shook their heads grimly. I nodded once and winked.

Upstairs, I took a shower, scrubbing myself very hard. Then I opened my suitcase and packed in a slow, methodical way. Earlier, I had laid the groundwork for a hasty escape. I had no regrets about leaving early; it seemed pointless to spend any more time in Madame's kitchen. And now Doug would have the limelight to himself.

As I loaded the bags into the trunk of my car, it began to rain. Across the yard, on the patio, I noticed the two girls had disappeared but the contents of their suitcases lay in a heap by the door. When I went back inside to say my good-byes, no one seemed surprised that I was leaving. Doug shook my hand as if he were sorry to see me go, and for all I knew, that may have been the case. But he was on his own from now on. And Madame could go back to being the kind of cooking teacher he needed.

As I backed out of the driveway, Didi burst through the front door and

ran toward the car with a newspaper over he dow and pressed a tiny piece of paper into n

"If you're ever out our *way,* this is how yo leaned in the car to give me a peck on the ch

I drove slowly through the village and up in over the pass, I rolled down the windows, lett me. The rain had chased the afternoon heat, smell. The effect was dreamlike, invigorating: before descending into St.-Rémy, I stopped back into the valley, stretched out flat like a gi cloud had settled over Maussane, blocking it The piece of paper Didi had given me was still mation was written in big rounded script, with a each *i* in her name. Wasn't that just like her, I th

Then I folded the paper into a tiny square and the glove compartment, where it presumably rem

Chapter Three

THE MEDITERRANEAN

This was the summer few Americans traveled to France. Even though the U.S. economy was pumping along, there had been the knee-jerk backlash, a reaction against Chirac's failure to support the Iraq War. At least, that was how the sorry merchants described it to anyone who would listen. And nowhere, it seemed, was this more evident than in Nice. Everywhere you went, but especially on the Promenade des Anglais, where beachcombers locked arms and herded ritually along the boardwalk overlooking the Mediterranean, there was none of the strident English that usually pierced the hush of surf.

For some businesses, it spelled instant doom. Several long-established shops that depended on the seasonal dollar had posted CLOSING signs by mid-August, unable to sustain the lingering crunch. The restaurants suffered most of all. They refused to cut a single corner that would give in to the slump, even though on many nights they were empty. The open-air cafés and brasseries were full of Germans who sat like statues in the sun, drinking Löwenbräus and eating pizzas, taking advantage of the Allied retreat. But the serious restaurants, the *gastronomiques*, which the skinflint Germans avoided like cultural diversity, struggled against all odds to survive.

I had come to Nice ostensibly to cook. It had been high on my list of destinations because the food here was as close to everyday cooking as one could hope to find: full of razzmatazz and pretty without being fussy. The spectacular variety of Mediterranean fish was prodigious: *saint-pierre*, *mérou* (grouper), *rascasses* (scorpion fish), sea bass, *dourade*, *langoustes* (spiny lobsters), *lotte* (monkfish), *rouget* (red mullet), and my beloved *moules*. I also needed to stare out at the sea for a while, to clear my head, and I was determined to learn how to make something fabulous. That would do the trick. It would signify a new start. The thought alone gave me inspiration. A new recipe . . . for everything.

I had been promised a private session with Bruno Söhn, the chef at the glossy new Palais de la Méditerranée hotel, which held the enviable position of standing dead center on the Promenade. You could tell by its high-rise peacockry that the Palais signaled a new direction for Nice, much the way Caesar's Palace once transformed the blocky Las Vegas skyline. Even the stately Hotel Negresco was beginning to show its age. But after only nine months, the Palais was still finding its legs. Word had it that its restaurant, Le Padouk, was either trying too hard or not trying hard enough, depending on the source. "Nobody goes there," my friend Lanie, who lives in Nice, reported, but when I arrived, on a lovely Saturday evening well after ten, the dining room was packed with smiling faces.

Of course, the Promenade was notorious for places like that, flashy and expensive and indifferent toward food. There was always plenty of attitude, along with very pretty people who didn't mind being abused. But Le Padouk had Bruno Söhn, a safeguard against such pretension.

I had heard of Söhn through the grapevine, when he was scarfing up
Michelin stars like Cheerios. He received two stars *twice* before he was
thirty-five, certainly an incredible feat, but he'd also bounced around a
lot, from Alsace, where he was born, to Strasbourg, Paris, Hong Kong,
and several kitchens on the Côte d'Azur.

"Learning, always learning," he said, when we were finally introduced
the next day.

It was in the midst of lunch prep at the back of Le Padouk's sleek
kitchen, and cooks were flying around like pool balls after the break.
Despite the mad swirl, Söhn was perfectly calm and seemed unflustered
by my sudden appearance, inflicted on him by the hotel press officer.

He smiled indulgently at me and said, "We'll eat first," when I asked if
I could cook with him. Before I could confess that I'd already had lunch,
he had seated me at a table on the *terrasse* above the hotel's Art Deco
entrance, which offered the same unending view of the Mediterranean
that Jacques Cousteau must have enjoyed. It was a massive, corporate-
looking veranda whose magnitude made everyone on it feel small and
lost. There were Homeric stone pilasters left from the hotel's previous
incarnation and only a handful of small tables set to reflect the chef's
exquisite taste. Terns glided overhead, held motionless against the breeze,
and every so often one of them nose-dived, flying reconnaissance above a
waiter's outstretched tray.

It was supposed to be a simple lunch—"Just a salad," Söhn had promised—but there was a need for him to show off his food a bit, so it wasn't
that simple and it wasn't just a salad. In fact, the bowl in which this "salad"
arrived could have nicely accommodated a sleeping child, maybe twins.

"You've got to be kidding!" I muttered as it was set down in front of me.
I poked at it with my fork, to the waiter's bug-eyed consternation.

"Chef Söhn created this especially for you," he said with emphasis,
reminding me gently that the salad wasn't to be treated like a . . . salad.

There were too many ingredients to count, all arranged in a very specific way, all balanced perfectly like an edible Stonehenge: coco beans,
calamari, blanched almonds, *cèpes*, green and yellow squash. In the grand
tradition of European modernism, this salad expressed the chef's vision,

his take on composition and texture. And that is when it dawned on me: the salad was art.

"What happens when I dig into this?" I asked, admiring its architecture.

"You turn into ugly American," Söhn said, as he joined me, amused. He reached across the table with a fork and toppled the whole spectacular mess. "There. Just in case you got cold feet."

I was taken aback when he admitted to being only forty. He looked my age, with sallow skin and a good spreading girth, owing perhaps to a life spent mostly packed away in steamy kitchens. It always amazed me how many chefs gave up everything to cook. It was like the priesthood, in a way; once the calling struck, you devoted yourself entirely to food. Only recently had I learned firsthand the extent of that commitment, the punishing path taken by anyone who hoped to, one day, run his or her own show. It was a long, lonely excursion, beginning around the age of fourteen, when an aspirant left home to apprentice at a restaurant. In several of the kitchens I'd visited, there was always a corps of young *commis*, as they were called, performing the menial but essential tasks—peeling vegetables, measuring ingredients, kneading dough, assisting in all phases of prep—while studying the cooks working around them, always studying, watching the cooks' hands, their instincts, picking up pointers like clues to the greater goal. They worked long, hard shifts, often eighteen-hour days, broken only by spells sacked out in a dorm room, usually above the kitchen.

Bruno Söhn wasn't any different from other chefs I'd encountered. His entire adolescence passed in apprenticeship to a cook at a small restaurant in Strasbourg, where, because there were no Michelin stars, let alone any other employees, he had to learn how to do everything, from ironing tablecloths to breadmaking to tricky port-wine reductions. "We worked long into the night," he recalled, "doing very classic food, *tournedos Rossini* Escoffier-style, things like that."

He stopped talking suddenly, staring slit-eyed at two waiters who were auctioning food to a handsome foursome at a nearby table. We could read the waiters' lips as they held plates up to view: *"L'onglet?" "Le pigeonneau?"*

Restaurants of this caliber had to know who ordered what. I felt sorry but said nothing to Söhn, who seemed to take the miscue in stride. "This is the problem here in Nice," he sighed, wiping his mouth with the corner of a napkin. "The food, in general, is not very good, and the service, in particular, is awful. The city doesn't support *gastronomique* food."

"But certainly the Negresco is as good as they come," I said, trying to sound casual about his competition just down the street. Anyway, it seemed unfair to compare his new enterprise to a long-revered kitchen famous for turning out Alain Ducasse, Dominique le Stanc, and Alain Llorca.

A curious look crossed Söhn's face.

"Ah, it is a shame," he said, in a somewhat hollow voice. "Even a citadel like the Negresco suffers. They have a new chef, another new chef, the third one this year."

Later someone told me about an ongoing turf war between Le Padouk and the Negresco. They'd been raiding each other's staffs, to no one's benefit. Now both restaurants apparently were on shaky ground with the kind of clients who enjoyed following each battle of the local food war.

"But you will see how my food is conceived," he said confidently. "We will make something very special together later this afternoon, something I have been experimenting with for the menu."

Over the next hour, Söhn opened bottle after bottle of amazing white Burgundy brought up from the hotel's cellar. There must have been six or eight standouts on the table—Corton, Ladoix, Montrachet, the heavy hitters—and in the hot noon sun the alcohol slowly took possession of my body.

Perhaps as a result of the wine, I went directly to my room and placed a call to Carolyn. We had been exchanging some emails, but she didn't sound as happy to hear my voice as that last glass of Rully had led me to hope. After an hour, with a lot of fencing back and forth, an outside chance developed that she would meet me in Paris. She didn't say no, but she didn't say yes, either. She was "thinking and deciding"; I would have to be patient.

I was pretty much a wreck when I showed up for cooking in the kitchen of the Palais de la Méditerranée. I straightened myself up in a mirror over a small sink. Fortunately, Chef Söhn was preoccupied with collecting the ingredients for my instruction.

He had laid out six or seven small bowls that contained zucchini flowers, *niçoise* olives, purple teardrop shallots, marjoram, and a few other unblemished goodies that he had picked up that morning at the Saleya Market. After washing a few of the zucchini flowers, he settled on a tall stool at the counter with a bottle of cold Rully.

"This is for us," he said, pouring wine into a glass that he offered me with a small bow. "And this," he said, waving a hand over the bowls, "is for our soup."

If I experienced any kind of disappointment, I didn't let it show. It seemed like such a long way to come to learn to make soup. But, of course, chefs like Bruno Söhn don't make ordinary soup, certainly not the kind I'd been used to serving, and he had been working on a recipe intended to get a mouth-filling, emotional response from the very first spoonful.

"A meal should be full of such moments," he said, "and it should begin right away."

He planned to send up the fireworks through an explosion of herbs, spices, and flavors that, combined with several textures, turn a soup into culinary upheaval.

"Look here," he said, taking me by a sleeve to the walk-in refrigerator in the corner. He removed a dish with a white puddinglike blob that had the look and consistency of sour cream. He gazed at it with a longing that was almost obscene. "It is a fresh goat cheese that I will use for a zucchini cream to go into the soup. I got it from a woman at the market who ladles it out from a red tin she keeps under the counter, for special customers." He also produced a *crème fraîche* that had traveled from a friend's farm in Normandy. "It comes 900 miles for just half a teaspoon in the soup. You can't imagine what it costs!"

Soup, he explained, demanded as much attention as any other course on the menu. This wasn't going to be an easy recipe to prepare, but the result, he assured me, was well worth the effort.

ZUCCHINI SOUP MÉDITERRANÉE

1/2 med. onion, sliced finely
2 shallots, sliced finely
1 clove garlic, minced
olive oil
5 small zucchini (about 1 lb.)
2 cups chicken stock
1 zucchini (only the skin,
    removed in strips with a
    vegetable peeler, blanched
    for 2 minutes, drained,
    and restored in ice water)
1 Tbl. crème fraîche

1 small piece zucchini (about
    3 1/2 in. long) cooked in
    salted water for 5 minutes,
    restored in ice water, then
    crushed with a fork along
    with salt, pepper, and 1
    Tbl. olive oil. Reserve.
4 zucchini flowers
5 oz. fresh goat cheese
Kosher salt and freshly
    ground black pepper
12 small niçoise olives
1 sprig fresh marjoram

In a saucepan, sauté over medium heat the onions, shallots, and garlic in 3 tablespoons of olive oil until soft, but without browning (about 5 minutes).

Slice the 5 zucchini into 1/2-inch slices (not too thinly, otherwise their color changes while cooking). Add to the onion-shallot mixture and cook just until it loses its firmness, being careful not to let it brown. Add a little salt and cook 2 minutes more at a very low simmer.

Add the chicken stock and bring to a vigorous boil; reduce heat and simmer 10 to 15 minutes or until zucchini are tender. Add salt and pepper to taste.

Place a bowl capable of holding the soup into a larger bowl filled with ice, burying the bowl in the ice as deeply as possible. Place the blanched zucchini skin in a blender, add half the soup, and purée until skin is incorporated. Add to the bowl buried in ice. Purée the rest of the stock, add the crème fraîche, and blend at a high speed until it turns a gorgeous shade of green. Add it to the soup already in the iced bowl. Stir thoroughly and cool, correcting the seasoning in the process. (This much can be prepared up to a day in advance and kept in the refrigerator.)

Using a mandoline, slice the small piece of zucchini lengthwise and thinly. Coat each with olive oil, salt lightly, and allow to stand 5 minutes to soften. Curl each piece of zucchini in a circle and set aside.

Slice zucchini flowers in half, lengthwise, keeping the pistil intact in one half (discard other half).

To assemble and present the soup: In individual bowls, place a ladleful or two of soup (not a lot is necessary). Float a dollop (about 1/2 tablespoon) of fresh goat cheese in the middle. Dot with 1/2 teaspoon of the reserved crushed-zucchini mixture. Add a flower. Surround the cheese and the flower with three evenly spaced niçoise olives (they should float on the surface). Garnish with zucchini curls. Place a tiny leaf of marjoram between each olive and, finally, a drop of olive oil in an available space, as a signature.

Serves 4

First, Chef Söhn demonstrated his version of the sauté process, melting down a pile of sharp, toothy onions with a slug of the local olive oil and sweating them until the fingernail slices abandoned their structure, becoming almost fleshy, sweet. He sliced the zucchini with precision so that every piece was identical in thickness, each round flying off the mandoline in petal-perfect symmetry. He coated his fingers with a fine spray of oil and teased billowy curls from the paper-thin zucchini peels, adding more oil as necessary to give them a springy gloss. We made several batches until I blended the creamy emulsion to just the desired shade.

"You have to wait for the perfect shade of green to appear," said Söhn, who had watched the blender as closely and patiently as a birder atop Mount Hood. When the liquid had reached a hue that reminded me of lime-flavored saltwater taffy, he swatted at the switch with a violent backhand.

I was astounded at how beautiful the soup was when it arrived at the table. It was a magnificent presentation, with the use of color almost as crucial as texture and taste.

It was just as he'd promised: a mouthful of anarchy, all flavor and thunder. The sweetness of the zucchini provided the perfect balance to the lactic tang of the cheese and the smoky acidity of the onions, overwhelming my palate with a concentration of freshly picked vegetables.

I had made an ocean's worth of hearty soups in my time, but nothing that resembled this one. It was like some fever dream of French inspiration—creamy yet distinct, sweetly earthy, exotic, seductive, an experience that made you appreciate each spoonful as opposed to sloshing down a bowlful from my mm-mm-good repertoire. There was no way I would ever have arrived at this by myself; no cookbook recipe can convey the various techniques it takes to pull off such a lovely dish. This was a paean to the effectiveness of cooking schools, yet it became abundantly clear that Le Padouk was not set up for that purpose.

While I ate my bowl of soup, a snowballing bustle surrounded us. The dinner hour was approaching and already calls for room service had begun piling up by the stove. I could feel the exasperated stares of the kitchen staff awaiting their marching orders, willing me to disappear. Clearly, my cooking lesson had disturbed their set routines. The chef, to his credit, either didn't notice or refused to acknowledge them. There was a mounting tension among the cooks, who gathered in a corner of the room and eyed him the way Cassius and his posse eyed Caesar on the ides of March. One came very close to us, and for a moment I thought he was going to be rude. By the time the silver serving carts were wheeled inside, some stammering and sputtering erupted, requiring the chef to look their way.

"They are like children," said Söhn, with a sly smile of admission, "and they need their master's attention. It seems unimaginable, doesn't it, for a kitchen of this size? You'd think it would run like clockwork—a *salade*, an omelet, a steak. . . ." He shook his head and shrugged. "Maybe I should put you to work making the soup."

"As long as you have a can opener and a hotline to Progresso, I'm your man," I said.

"Yes, well, you need to practice what I taught you, but there is hope. There is hope."

By the time I got off the stool, everything was almost right again in the kitchen. The chef bullied his way into the center of action and, almost magically, the problems seemed to sort themselves out. Every circus needs its ringmaster, I thought.

At eight o'clock, the tables on the *terrasse* were nearly full, as Le Padouk, to my surprise, continued to defy Nice's hard luck. Standing by the door, I saw in one easy glance that only two, perhaps three Americans were among the diners waiting to be served; the two men in matching navy-blue blazers rapturously sharing a slice of duck *pâté* were a dead certainty, and I had my suspicions about a single woman paging through a popular travel guide. Otherwise, it was a mixture of local French who hardly glanced at the *amuses-bouche* as they gobbled them like popcorn and swirled their wine glasses as instinctively as my daughter might a Coke.

All at once, waiters converged on the tables with white soup bowls piled up on their arms. They slid them off with a clatter in front of each person, who looked suspiciously into them, mouth puckered and amused. It was my zucchini soup, of course, dressed in blazing regalia, with a wing of bright yellow flower peeking above the rim.

Just wait until they taste it, I mused, almost grinning in triumph. Then, before a spoon was lifted, I turned and went upstairs to send an email, thinking there is hope. There is hope.

It was unfair to expect more from Bruno Söhn, in spite of his deliberate attempt to walk me through a few lessons. There were simply too many distractions and not enough space to teach cooking properly in a kitchen that serviced a high-rise hotel twenty-four hours a day.

Besides, I was expected at Moulin de Mougins, one of France's most famous restaurants, about half an hour's drive into the mansion-lined hills beyond Cannes. It was there, nearly twenty-five years earlier, that I had savored my first gastronomic meal, and I had vivid, exciting memories of sitting at a table full of seasoned travelers and trying not to act the uneducated naïf caught in a rapturous swoon as each strange and extraordinary dish was placed in front of me. The food was like nothing I had ever tasted:

fish I had never heard of; vegetables that looked nothing like their coun-
terparts in the A&P; parts of animals I never dreamed of putting in my
mouth, much less celebrating as delicacies. There were sorbets made from
herbs and sauces doused with liqueurs and waiters who served us with the
kind of obsequiousness that I had only ever encountered at a wake.

The restaurant had been the jewel of Roger Vergé back then, and his
name was as synonymous with haute cuisine as a *truite au bleu*. Vergé was
a legend, and something of a legendary character. He was a very charming man, almost princely, and he carried himself with the confidence of
his great name. I remember seeing him drift through the dining room,
sipping intermittently from a snifter of Cognac, and greeting people I was
told were ambassadors and barons and famous French actors, all of whom
took his hand in theirs as if he were the Pope. There was an internation-
ally beloved entertainer sitting at my table, and when Vergé stopped to
say hello to him, they made several jokes about my inexperience that sent
an embarrassed flush across my face.

With eyes cast downward, I muttered a few *formidables* and *incroyables*—
all the appropriate *ables* I could think of—assuring His Holiness that the
meal I'd just eaten had changed my life.

"You have only to think of my food as a different kind of cheeseburger,"
Vergé said gently, "otherwise the entire experience will be *pretentieux*.

It seemed only fitting that my cooking odyssey should bring me back
this way. I had often dreamed of studying at the master's elbow. But Vergé
had recently retired, selling the restaurant to Alain Llorca, a disciple of
the great Alain Ducasse and a rising star on the international food scene.
To anyone traveling within fifty miles of the place, it would have been
impossible not to know of this. Llorca's name, announcing the transition, was plastered on roadside billboards usually earmarked for the new
Gérard Depardieu film. They were everywhere that summer, and it was
major news. The French considered Llorca, only thirty-six years old, indecently young to own such a shrine. It was a high-wire act for him, and
naturally the usual cynics were gathering in expectation of a spectacular
fall. In any case, expectations ran high that something consequential was
in the works.

At the very least, I expected a well-planned program. Moulin de Mougins belonged to the Relais et Châteaux network of establishments that offered short cooking weeks with the world's greatest chefs. For quite a reasonable fee, anyone with an interest in fine food could sign up for a session, which usually rewarded you with a seat for a memorable lunch or dinner. The only drawback, as I'd learned, was that the truly great chefs, the virtuosos, had a reputation to protect, so hands-on cooking was practically nonexistent. I'd experienced this in Lyon on another occasion with the amiable Pierre Orsi, who refused to let me touch so much as a napkin in his eponymous restaurant. He dressed me in his personal chef's jacket, instructed me on the proper way to wear an apron, then stashed me in a corner of the kitchen for three days, where his *pâtissier* put on a show.

Unfortunately, the same fate was to befall me in the kitchen at Mougins.

Alain Llorca was unlike any of the other chefs I'd met so far. He was, of course, younger than any of them and reasonably tall and handsome, but there was something imperious about the way he moved, something that seemed dark and almost frightening, as if he might suddenly reach out and, for no reason, slap me. It was his face. There was a roughness to it—not vulgar or unrefined, but threatening. He wore his long, dark hair slicked back like a movie star, not a strand out of place; and he dressed in tapered slacks and a rumpled linen shirt that hung loosely off his shoulders and seemed much more stylish than the attire found in other kitchens. The whole mystique was in place. He exuded the star quality that the place demanded.

The scowl on his face seemed to confirm that my presence was a huge headache, and before I could assure him otherwise, I was banished to the *pâtisserie*.

There were six of us in the station. Most of the others were young enough to be fighting acne, and they had a thick, pallid look, moving cumbersomely in identical gray-checked slacks and broad shoes like inmates at a reformatory. The prep work was absorbing, with all the measurements it entailed, and the staff seldom spoke to one another. Perhaps it was considered bad form. The line of cooks, who were clawing their way up the chain of command, treated them as inferiors. To the cooks, dessert was merely an afterthought. But once the meal service was over, the team whipped into action and demonstrated an artistry that expressed all the precision and meticulousness of world-class architects.

They built multitiered *crème brûlée* peach melbas mounded with mint lychee sorbet on sponge fingers as well as frozen nougat mousses atop a coffee macaroon surrounded by a moat of frothy Amaretto cream. Sticky praline cream churros were served in sealed Mason jars like a Joseph Cornell box. There was something called an Ivory Tower, which was a sculptured lime compote paired with passion-fruit cream, dried orange chips, and cocoa butter, and an ice cream sandwich the size of a softball on a bed of finely sifted coffee.

I spent a few hours doing nothing but dodging the others, who rushed huge bowls of mascarpone and *crème anglaise* this way and that across the aisle, like nurses in an emergency ward. I got high just watching in a kind of sugar-coated daze. The head *pâtissier*, J. M., a rail-thin man with shoulder-length hair and a monkish demeanor, would throw me a shy smile every so often, as if he understood my despair, but for the most part I stared across the wide kitchen to where the cooks buckled and weaved over sizzling hot stoves and longed for an invitation into their exclusive club.

Eventually, I could control myself no longer. During lunch, while Alain Llorca was out mingling with the guests, I stole into the main kitchen and cozied up to one of the cooks from Brittany who was hunched over a dozen or so steaming white bowls.

"*Qu'est-ce que c'est, M'sieur?*" I asked, leading with my nose into the cooking province.

"It's potatoes," he answered in perfect English.

Didier had served an apprenticeship in Washington, DC, where, as luck would have it, he developed a fondness for Americans. Unfortunately, those feelings didn't seem to extend to me. He knew I wasn't supposed to be anywhere around there, and he dreaded the wrath of Llorca, who had terrorized his staff, verbally and otherwise, throughout the frenetic lunch service.

He cast several meaningful looks over his shoulder and looked at me warily, trying to calculate the degree of havoc I might bring upon him.

Despite all that, he seemed to recognize my eagerness. All the time, I kept up a chirpy little exchange, asking about his worldly experience, laying it on thick, until I had coaxed the entire recipe out of him—a wonderful potato gratin in a slushy langoustine sauce that was served in individual bowls accompanying most of the restaurant's entrées.

POTATO GRATIN LANGOUSTINE

3 onions, sliced finely	3 cloves of finely minced
2 Tbl. olive oil	garlic
sugar	1 Tbl. thyme, minced
2 lb. red new potatoes	2 cups langoustine or chicken
salt	stock

Preheat oven to 325 degrees.

Make a confit of the onions by sautéing them in the oil until nicely browned. (It is expedient to sprinkle a little sugar over them to assist in the caramelization.)

Peel the potatoes and slice them to a thickness of about 1/8 inch, using a mandoline (or, very carefully, with a knife). Season potatoes lightly with salt. Layer potatoes in the bottoms of individual ovenproof chili bowls, or ramekins. Place 1 tablespoon of the onion confit in the center, then place a layer of potato slices around the confit, overlapping them as you would for a tart. Sprinkle with garlic and season with salt and thyme. Cover with the stock and bake 30 to 40 minutes, until they are fork-tender and a gentle crust forms on the top.

8 individual servings

As we finished a run-through of the recipe, Didier suddenly grabbed me by the shoulder and forced me to the floor, onto my hands and knees. When I tried to get up, he held my head down with a stunning grip, until I realized that he was hiding me. Alain Llorca had returned to the kitchen and was livid, hopping mad. With fifty clients still at tables, the food wasn't coming out of the kitchen fast enough. My presence no doubt would inflame the situation. Fortunately for me, his attention was diverted by a gaggle of waiters standing idly by a drinks cart along the wall.

"*Merde!*" he screamed, slamming the peppermill baton in his hand against a counter, snapping it in two. A glass rattled invisibly among the pots. Through half-closed eyes, he singled out his headwaiter from among the tuxedoes and fired off a rocket of vitriol. They stood nose-to-nose, barking at each other, the waiter refusing to back away.

"I've been doing this for fourteen years," he growled at Llorca.

"Then do it better!" he screamed.

I glanced up. Didier's eyes pulsed with fear. They were absolutely black. His free hand was jerking the metal spoon against the rims of soup bowls like Lionel Hampton at the Copacabana. I was trapped. There was no other way out, and it wouldn't be long before Llorca discovered me cowering there like a small-time burglar. I should just stand up straight and walk out as though nothing at all were wrong, I thought. Better yet, I should try to see if I could squeeze myself into a cupboard under the counter. But I didn't—too afraid to move.

Above me, the master's apron blurred swiftly past my nose on his way to check something sizzling in a Dutch oven. A familiar "*putain!*" echoed in the vicinity. Whatever was cooking had roasted dry and hijacked Llorca's attention. He called out a young Japanese cook and began screaming at him, banging a ladle against the cast-iron pot to orchestrate his objections.

Didier gave me a persuasive little shove and I practically somersaulted backwards, uprighting myself and scrabbling with my hands along the slick tile floor. As I spidered past each station, the presiding cook would look down and chuckle at my contortions, until there was a conspicuous ripple of choked laughter along the line. I knew that if Llorca caught on, there would be serious consequences. I gauged the distance to the *pâtisserie*: ten feet, maybe twelve. These kitchens were too damned big, and the heat from the stoves was unrelenting.

Suddenly, Llorca stormed out to the dining room. Not taking any chances, I practically vaulted a barrel of flour to reach the *pâtisserie* unscathed. The entire dessert crew was waiting for me, practically wetting themselves with laughter. They'd followed the entire action sequence with great amusement, even placing odds on the outcome. Most, I learned afterward, were disappointed by my escape.

"That was a close call," J. M. said, with an odd little smile, as I returned to my station, brushing off my pants.

He seemed like a sweet guy, and I hated disappointing him by sucking up to the chefs. It went without saying that he had no use for me in the *pâtisserie*. He'd gotten stuck babysitting me, yet he'd been kind enough to let me stand there while his team flew about making his intricate recipes.

"Sorry about that; it won't happen again," I said. "Guess my ass would have wound up in the soup."

J. M. nodded. "At the very least. Trust me, I have some experience with the chef."

I could only begin to imagine what that meant. Most chefs guarded their relationship with a talented *pâtissier*, few of whom were creative enough to complement this level of food. They formed complex, almost inseparable bonds but also had love-hate affairs, usually pinned to the intensity of the spotlight on the chef and the acclaim for his food. Naturally, the greater the glare, the less emphasis on dessert, which often touched off some kind of ego implosion. Llorca and J. M. had a mutual understanding, an unusual kind of communication conducted entirely through eye contact, nothing more. A suggestive glance across the kitchen would earn back a well-pronounced nod, followed by a sequence of events resulting from it. It was like sign language. Since arriving at the restaurant, I hadn't seen them exchange more than two words, yet they were always on the same wavelength.

"Is the chef a good man?" I asked, wondering where this might lead.

"I hope so," said J. M., moving aside the strap of his apron to reveal the lavender stitching of his last name, which happened to be the same as the chef's.

"Ah, you're his brother," I said, unable to suppress a sheepish smile.

"It's about time you figured that out. Lucky for you, you didn't say what you were thinking," he said, grinning.

I let that one go; a denial would be disingenuous, and what I was thinking must have been all over my face. Later, I learned that Jean-Michel and Alain had cooked together since their childhood in Cannes. In fact, they were raised in the same small room, along with an older brother who went nowhere near the kitchen. The younger brothers apprenticed out before they were sixteen, on the condition that they never be separated. They were a novelty act in a way: one a superstar chef, the other his equivalent with desserts. They had run their own show for nearly a decade now, much of it at the Negresco in Nice; for the last eight months, they'd been in Mougins, attempting to stake their claim. It was beginning to occur to J. M., however, that they'd bitten off more than they could chew. The restaurant was consuming them, he said. Too many hours, more than they'd ever dreamed, and the responsibilities were brutal. There had been several backhanded reviews, too many comparisons to Vergé. Tensions were strong enough to expose a strain in the brothers' relationship. In an unguarded moment, J. M. confided that maybe, after twenty years, it was time they go their separate ways.

I felt a congeniality arise, as he'd meant it to happen.

"Look, I have to take care of something for a few minutes," he said abruptly. "So I would appreciate it if you would help out in the *pâtisserie.*"

For an hour, while the dessert orders came flying in—all fifty at once—I measured out huge vats of sugar and glucose, the latter a particularly loathsome task that went to the lowest slave on the staff. (The restaurant's fifteen-year-old apprentice was delighted by my presence.) It entailed prying open a plastic tub and scooping out a clear, gluey syrup that was difficult to maneuver onto the metric scale. To get it there, the scoop had to pass over my shoes, a pair of brand-new nubucks, which soon glistened with scabs of sugar. Every time I took a step, I had to pry my sole off the floor. You could hear me coming from across the room: *squranch-squranch-squranch!*

"Try slipping past Alain now," J. M. said upon his return, awarding me a discreet look of triumph.

It is embarrassing to admit that at first I wasn't capable of scooping the sorbet without shaping it into a snowman. (If they had handed me a few raisins, I could have made eyes, a nose, and a mouth.) J. M. stared at my sad effort and then gave me one of those looks that convey the per-

fect mix of amusement and pathos. There wasn't a restaurant in France
that served sorbet like that, not even the Go-Go Café in Arles, where
Americans lined up for banana splits and milk shakes. Sorbet always
appeared in *quenelles*, elegant oblong petals formed by scraping a large
tablespoon along the surface of the ice until it was filled, and then holding the back of the spoon in your palm for just a moment or two, which
warmed it enough to release the sorbet.

The real chefs—and that meant just about anyone with a French
mother who routinely cooked at home—don't even palm the spoon but
simply keep passing the *quenelles* back and forth between two tablespoons
until little footballs drop neatly to the plate. I watched J. M. windmill off a
few with nimble ease and then practiced it during some spare time, developing a nice little delivery that eventually passed muster.

Later, J. M. assigned me to the prep for his *biscuit Savarin*, a spongy
finger cookie that was the foundation for *sorbet citron vert vanille avec sauce
pamplemousse*, one of his showcase desserts. "It's simple—just follow the
directions," he said, handing me his King J. M. version of the Bible, a dog-
eared and battered notebook with all his prized personal dessert formulas
handwritten inside.

Of course, they were in French, and worse—a kind of shorthand
French, making it almost impossible to decipher.

"What is this measurement?" I asked Stéphane DeWitt, his imperturbable *sous-chef,* turning the notebook right side up to face him.

"It's the phone number for one of J. M.'s women," he said without
missing a beat. "Begin on the line just below it."

The principle was like any other for cookies, making a pastry of eggs
and sugar, but because the recipe was restaurant-size, which is to say enormous, the amount of each ingredient seemed ridiculous. With an effort
that took more nerve than finesse, I measured out 14 ounces of egg yolk
(about nine eggs) and then cracked another dozen eggs into the same
bowl. Afterward, I rummaged through several cupboards until I found 26
ounces of almond powder and 2 1/2 ounces of cream powder and combined them with 30 ounces of sugar, balancing each amount exactly on
the metric scale as I'd heard drug dealers did it.

Thankfully, Bob Ash had showed me the proper way to scrape out the seeds of a vanilla bean—by pressing down the dull side of a knife and running it along the entire surface of the bean to flatten the pod, which made the seeds easier to extract after slicing open the pod lengthwise. The recipe required the pulp from three Indian beauties. Then I zested four lemons and five oranges. All the ingredients were stirred in the industrial-size mixer until very well combined and then stored overnight in the refrigerator for the following day's lunch.

By the time the kitchen broke from lunch service, after the last coffee was served, I was exhausted. Just after three, and still shaking hands with guests, Alain Llorca was awaiting me in the reception area.

"What did you think?" he asked in fractured English, which I had been warned was less than serviceable.

"It was a wild scene in the kitchen," I said, wavering my hand, "a real roller-coaster ride."

"*Oui,*" he said, bulging his eyes in that comical French way. "You come back tonight for evening service." A command, as opposed to an invitation. "Now, go upstairs . . ." Searching for the right word, he put his head in his hands to illustrate a nap: ". . . and have a little fuck."

Actually, I got fucked twice, without taking off a stitch of clothing.

An email was waiting from Carolyn: "There is no reason for me to join you. . . . I never considered you my soulmate. . . . Enjoy your little adventure. . . ."

Little?

In any case, she was ending our relationship. Again (in case I hadn't gotten the message the other three times). That settled things for good. An hour passed, then two. I had done a real number on myself, sitting in that delicate little room above the restaurant. Outside, the staff began to return for the start of dinner service. Not for me, though. I couldn't face the thought of it tonight. I was hurting too much. And, anyway, the Llorca brothers wouldn't miss me. Instead, I called my friend Lanie in Nice and asked her to meet me for dinner.

As I pulled out of the parking lot of Moulin de Mougins, it was beginning to drizzle. Even so, I rolled down the windows of my tiny Renault and inhaled the damp, earthy highball. Air . . . I needed it in the worst possible way. The lights had just come on over Cannes, a gorgeous twinkling nightscape, and the drive down the *autoroute* would provide a welcome distraction.

Just as I settled onto the road, a car came up fast behind me. It attempted to pass but couldn't, pulling back at the last second because of a truck barreling down in the opposite direction. Instead, the car tried to pass me on the right, except that no lane existed there, only a soft gravel shoulder. Fishtailing in the gravel, the car hit me from the right and bumped me into the path of the oncoming truck. I don't remember the impact, only one thought: It figures.

My car was a wreck. Somehow, incredibly, I managed to walk away without a scratch. The instigators, an elderly French couple from nearby Le Cannet, insisted I wait for the police to arrive. They were indignant about the accident, as if I had caused it myself. Creeps. I called Lanie to explain why I wouldn't be arriving in Nice anytime soon and replayed the whole nightmare for her.

"Just tell me one thing," she said, interrupting my tale. "The people who hit you—were they American or French?"

"French," I answered, "the worst of the species."

"Then I'm afraid the accident was your fault, my friend."

She probably didn't understand. They hit me after trying to pass me *on the shoulder.* There were no two ways about it, I insisted; the fault was entirely theirs.

"You'll see," Lanie said, and I absolutely detested the note of levity in her voice.

The police arrived soon afterward and conducted a makeshift investigation. The French couple, standing by their barely scuffed Mégane, kept pointing at me, stabbing fingers, as if they'd just identified a serial rapist. When it was my turn to explain, I showed the cops a clear set of tire tracks in the gravel. As far as I was concerned, it was an open-and-shut case.

"Let me see your license, please," the taller of the two policemen said.

While he examined it, I could see the word *American* forming on his lips: "*M'sieur,* this is definitely your fault."

There was nothing I could say or do to change his mind. When the insurance investigator turned up the following afternoon, he handed me a bill for $4,200. An additional charge would be forwarded, he explained, as soon as the owners of the Mégane filed for damages.

With a mean case of French (in)justice fresh in my mind, I was in no mood to spend another day meting out flour and sugar in the Moulin de Mougins *pâtisserie.* I had come all this way to learn how to cook, not to lackey, not to drudge, not to observe, and I said as much to Llorca's lovely assistant, Hélène. "Perhaps the chef would be willing to take me aside and teach me one of his preparations?" I suggested.

"Perhaps. I will ask him," she said. But it was the same closed look I had seen on the policeman's face.

To her credit, I was placed in the "Alain Llorca Cooking School," which was held a few mornings each week in the restaurant's glass-enclosed sun lounge. It became apparent, instantly, that the course was something of a misnomer: no Alain Llorca, no cooking school to speak of. It was a *demonstration* given by Eric Howard, the *sous-chef,* and what I came to discover was a real "lady's affair." My sticky shoes fell well below the standard of their Chanel pumps as I sat in a row of lovely brocaded chairs with six housewives from the area. We received our own special notebooks, each stamped with "La Cuisine du Soleil," and a chic Lucite clipboard to write on, if we pleased. Fine silverware was at our disposal to taste the various dishes from the class. The food was served on bone china, and a uniformed waiter stood at attention by the door with chilled bottles of rosé for us to sip, while Chef Howard went through the motions.

It was a bit of a disorganized demo, which was more than partly my fault, because I kept interrupting the chef, demanding specific measurements for each ingredient in the recipe. And it was a good thing I did, because the dish he made was a brilliant take on tabouli, involving zucchini, mint, and a boiled egg, that I have revisited often in my kitchen. It never fails to impress.

TABOULI WITH ZUCCHINI, MINT, AND BOILED EGG

3 tomatoes	3/4 cup chives, chopped finely
1 lb. medium-grain instant couscous	1/2 cup parsley, chopped finely
1/4 cup olive oil	1/3 cup mint, chopped finely
salt and white pepper	2 shallots, diced finely
4 eggs	1 large lemon, juiced
2 medium zucchini	

Bring to a boil a pot of water large enough to cover the tomatoes. Score the tomatoes, blanch them for 30 seconds, and revive them in an ice-water bath. Then peel and quarter the tomatoes, removing the pulp and seeds with a finger. Set aside.

In a medium bowl, cover the couscous with the olive oil and refrigerate 2 to 3 hours. (The coolness allows the grains to expand and open.)

Bring a highly salted quart of water to a boil, then pour it over the couscous, just combining it, not mixing. Season lightly with salt and pepper, then cover with plastic wrap and allow to stand 15 minutes. Fluff couscous with a fork.

Meanwhile, bring a pot of water to a boil, add the eggs, and boil rapidly for 5 minutes. Immediately place the eggs in ice water to stop the cooking.

Peel the zucchini and cut them in half lengthwise, removing the skin and some of the pulp; julienne into 2-inch sticks. Then dice finely (a mirepoix). Dice the tomatoes in the same manner and combine with the zucchini. Add the chives, parsley, mint, and shallots.

Fluff the couscous, add some more olive oil to freshen, and salt well. Add all the vegetables to the couscous and combine, then add the lemon juice. Correct the seasoning. Refrigerate until ready to use.

Peel the eggs under cool water—they are undercooked and fragile. Carefully slice a little white off the top of each egg and invert it so that it stands up in an individual small serving bowl. Surround with tabouli and juices.

Serves 4

There were several other recipes in the demonstration, but they were overly complicated, using techniques that required years of service to the Lord and ingredients that were mostly unavailable in the States. For *daube* cannelloni, the veal-intestine skins seemed like an especially difficult purchase; the butcher at my local Stop & Shop has a hard enough time differentiating between chuck and round. In any case, my classmates weren't visibly disappointed. From what I could tell, they never intended to prepare any of the recipes at home. This was merely a pleasant way for them to pass the morning, a pause in the daily grind with the help of several glasses of rosé. When Alain Llorca swept in at the end of the class, you'd have thought Tom Jones had arrived the way they encircled him, ooohing and aaahing, touching his hand, stroking his hair, flashing their eyes. I wouldn't have been surprised if one of them had thrown her underwear and room key at him.

"You learn something today?" he asked me, when the ladies had finally departed.

"Yes," I said, clumsily clutching a sheaf of notes while shaking hands, "I did, although not everything I learned pertained to food, if you know what I mean," thinking of his success at coddling the ladies.

He threw me a dark, searching stare, too dark, it seemed, to fathom my intent. Then all at once a smile of wry indulgence spread across his face.

"Yes, we—all of us must have our needs met, *n'est-ce pas?*" he said in better English than I would have expected.

Try as I might, I couldn't stop myself from laughing. Everyone, including the most extraordinary chef, was entitled to his own version of hands-on cooking.

As for me, untouched by love or anyone else, I was happy simply to steal off to my room, no longer willing to compete for anyone's attention, but rather to rest and, if the chance arose, to have a little fuck.

Chapter Four

LA MAISON AVEC LA PÉNICHE

When the train pulled into the station at Agen it was still dark. I had spent all night curled up in a *couchette* from Nice, under conditions that reminded me of troop transports chronicled in World War II films. It was a down-market affair. There were five other men, all strangers, sharing my quarters, each stacked on a wooden platform, three to a side, like bodies in a morgue, so that by the time we reached the West, the place smelled like a damp gym sock.

I had been reading *Night Soldiers,* one of Alan Furst's atmospheric spy novels, and suddenly it seemed as if I'd been thrust into the story. My instructions were explicit: to find the sole taxi parked at the curb. The driver, Etienne, would be asleep. Wake him up, I was told; he would be expecting me. Then give him this instruction: "Please take me to Brax, Château Camont, *juste après le village, sur le canal, en face des trois couronnes.*" If he was at all hesitant, I was to remind him it was *la maison avec la péniche.*

To borrow from Furst, nothing here was what it seemed. The streets were empty, shrouded in patchy fog. Nothing stirred, aside from the growl of the retreating train. It was only by chance that I located the taxi, revealed by a momentary strand of light. The tide of secrecy that rippled through the streets made me tense and watchful. Of course, if Furst had written the scene, Etienne would be a woman and we would wind up in the tub together in the next chapter. As it happened, my driver, under his cap, had the face of Ernest Borgnine, and our clandestine exchange was acknowledged with a guttural *"Oui."*

I couldn't see a thing through the shifting darkness, only fragments of landscape as we sped off into the countryside. *La France profonde:* no real landmarks, no bread crumbs to mark my way. There was a web of narrow roads, one dissolving into the next, and before too long we were cruising through miles of shuttered farms that seemed shunned by civilization. I could smell the river, the Garonne, somewhere nearby—the moisture was so constant and strong—and knew we were close to the cluster of villages on its banks. Nevertheless, it was disconcerting, at five-thirty in the morning, to be this removed from humanity.

Of course, no one forced me into this strange scenario. The prize was a few days under the tutelage of Kate Hill, one of the unsurpassed virtuosos of Gascon cuisine. Hill had spent years here, exploring the distinctive kitchens of southwestern France, eager to promote its classic dishes and traditions. From duck *confit* to *cassoulet*, Gascon cuisine is food for hearty appetites, richly flavored with duck fat. A cookbook of Hill's, *A Culinary Journey in Gascony*, had pride of place on my shelf, although the ongoing experiments with it, like most of my cooking, lacked the essential magic. Her *foie gras au torchon* had challenged me until I threw in the towel. And a *magret* flambéed in a splash of Armagnac was good, nothing more. I couldn't quite swing it, despite a faithful preparation. I seldom opened the book anymore without reflecting that the cook who wrote it had some kind of pact with the place and its food that was either unavailable to or beyond me. It must take something very special, I thought, maybe genetic. Whatever it was, Kate Hill had the wherewithal to capture the magic on a plate.

"There isn't a duck alive that hasn't prayed for her demise," said a friend who had urged me to put her school on my itinerary.

It wasn't as easy as it sounded. There were a few references to her cooking program on the Internet, though all seemingly out of date. A notice posted on her website was even more enigmatic: "NOTHING OFFERED THIS SEASON."

"She just seemed to drop out of the picture," I was told by Karen Herbst, who runs The International Kitchen, an agency that represents some of the best cooking schools in Europe. "I used to send people there, but I felt like she got distracted, just lost her enthusiasm for organizing programs, which is a shame, because when it comes to teaching cooking, Kate is practically beloved."

A flurry of emails and phone calls eventually produced a response: "Come if you wish. I can give you a few days at the end of September. There is a room here you will find quite comfortable."

One of the things that attracted me most was the idea of a visit to western France. I had often been drawn here, like most Americans who make the pilgrimage to Bordeaux, and traveled extensively when I was younger and more impressionable, in search of the noble *châteaux:* Margaux, Pavie, Cheval Blanc, d'Yquem, La Tour, Haut Brion, the litany of names like rock stars on my lips. I had been back a few times recently, but without the same enthusiasm. The names still had that sizzle, though they no longer offered intimacy, having bequeathed their lovely assets as commodities to very rich men.

I have, however, felt a spiritual tie here that eluded me elsewhere. Perhaps it is because of its resemblance to the area where I was born in Pennsylvania, a buckling of farms and scenic villages in a forgotten corner of civilization. Agen was close enough to Bordeaux and Toulouse to spend the afternoon wandering around either of them, but remote enough so as not to attract significant crowds of tourists. There were none of the whistle-stops on your typical swing through a designated region, no cave drawings, few notable ruins, none of the glittery churches in which to stop just long enough to take in an all-important fresco before heading off to the next artistic highlight noted in the guidebook.

Visitors came here to shed their skins, to wander unobstructed, seeking immunity from the clutter of choices, to relax, to reflect, to eat. If they were moving around fast, they might stop for a platter of oysters fished that morning out of Arcachon Bay; if they managed to strike a more soothing pace, maybe a fork-tender duck *confit* or a *cassoulet* simmering with flageolets. Those home-cooked dishes give the region its cachet, and the agricultural bounty—the endless miles of farms, orchards, and vineyards—distinguishes its character.

I'd heard all sorts of rumors about Kate Hill, an American cook living alone on a barge in the middle of nowhere. An American woman, no less, pushing the anomaly to its limit. "She's running away from a broken heart . . . ," one version went. ". . . from the pressures of success . . . from a family fortune. . . ." "She's a misfit . . . a gypsy . . . Jim Morrison. . . ." They got wickedly silly. Her colleague, Susan Loomis, warned me to get serious about the work. "Kate cooks as if every day is her last one on earth, and it's a race against the clock to turn out the entire Gascon repertoire," Loomis said. "You are going to work until your head will spin, but I doubt you'll meet a gentler soul anywhere in Europe."

I was not sure, as I made my way to Camont, that I was going to learn all that much. After the last few outings, my opinion of cooking schools had diminished.

"*Les trois couronnes, M'sieur,*" Etienne said, pointing at a billboard where three crowns floated above a neighboring orchard's bill of particulars.

Before I could respond, he jerked the steering wheel to the right, and the car shot off the road onto a dirt track that seemed to plunge downward through an opening in the trees. The car hurtled through a thick salt mist. On all sides, tall sea grass rustled and slapped at the windshield. "*Arrrgh!*" I grabbed for something with which to brace my jerking body as we dipped into the last hollow before another modest rise. Suddenly, when I was certain the end was nigh, the Renault braked to a stop just inside a little gravel turnaround.

"*Camont, M'sieur.*"

In the clearing, I could just make out the outline of an ancient stone farmhouse, the mist rising around it like a showgirl's slip. The half-light revealed a lovely crumbling limestone façade, worn by centuries of volatile weather, with a miniature turret off to the side and a curtain of ivy spilling over the red-tiled roof. Several tall potted plants stood on opposite sides of a blue doorway just beyond a lavender hedge. At one corner of the yard stood the *potager*, a vegetable garden whose neat rows pointed to a modest Puritan sense of how much the land would return. A trail, no more than a footpath worn into deep grass, splintered off in several different directions, where I assumed other gardens lay hidden beyond the surrounding brush.

Across the yard, almost like a mirage, was the *péniche*—the barge. It seemed like a prop at first, as if someone had moored it there and left it to rust, the French version of a hillbilly car cemetery. The vessel was larger than most canal barges I'd seen, a sixty-five-ton Dutch *tjalk*, with a long, flat white cabin, its hull painted a deep turquoise, and the wheelhouse, blocky and high-crowned, trimmed in teak. Next to the door, painted in a bold, greeting-card scrawl, was its name: the *Julia Hoyt*.

I smiled at it, feeling relieved, delighted, and touched by this poignant artifact transported from another kingdom. Behind the absurdly situated boat I imagined a philosophy, a lifestyle.

It wasn't until I took a few steps toward the prow that I saw the canal, a narrow little channel, low at the moment, cut into the soft green woods. A manmade tributary of the Garonne, it stretched in either direction for seventy-five miles. On either side of its banks, a gravel footpath traced the trench and continued through backyards and along hedges and fences, past twenty-one locks, stringing together the nineteen villages like plastic beads.

I sat down on a garden bench to take it all in. Darkness still clung to the landscape like a lace shawl. Nothing moved in the house, on the barge, in

the water, and the solitude was like a dream, unsteady, an enchanted stillness. For all I knew, this could be anyone's house. I might be trespassing,
soon to be confronted by some angry farmer in a housecoat and slippers,
threatening to call the police. French police: *your fault, M'sieur.*

The cool air drew tight around my shoulders, so I fished a jeans jacket
from my suitcase and shrugged into it. Dawn was not far off. Eventually,
someone would appear and find me sitting here, their imprudent garden
statue.

Not more than twenty minutes passed before a light went on in the
wheelhouse. A gangplank fell out of the doorway like a dragon's tongue,
and a woman leaned, silent and smiling, in the open frame. A black dog
slid past her legs and bounded straight for me.

"Don't mind Dupont," she called out gaily. "He's in charge of passport
control."

"I've got contraband," I confessed, holding a rumpled plastic bag above
my head. It contained some chocolate truffles I'd brought as a house gift
from Nice.

"In that case, you have to hand it over to the proper authorities. *C'est
moi.*"

Kate Hill shuffled down from the boat and across a rose-arbor bridge,
her soft face full of welcome, and pulled back comically when she saw my
tower of baggage. "Are you leaving on a world cruise?" she wondered.

She was a tall woman, about my age or perhaps a little older. Her body
seemed to fit my idea of someone who drove river barges, hearty and
broad-shouldered, though trim in every other sort of way. She wore her
hair short, in a spiky shag with a blotchy henna tint to it, and held back by
a bandanna knotted at the top of her head. Her face was a good one, too,
not classically beautiful, but pleasant and lived-in, with an outdoor blush
to it, like windburn. There was nothing precious about her, nor about
her personality, which was outgoing, even a bit horsy, and just Bohemian
enough to pull the rest of it together. Carolyn would have referred to her,
condescendingly, as a *character*.

Kate made coffee for me in the house, which had its own oddball story.

It had caught her eye fourteen years earlier when she had been sailing down the canal. The building was an eighteenth-century relic, nothing but a wreck, with a fireplace the size of downtown Cincinnati. It might have been unlivable, she remembered thinking at the time, but you could cook your ass off in that hearth. There was a list of dishes she'd been dying to master, a veritable smorgasbord of duck and rabbit viscera. Meanwhile, there were two acres of incredibly fertile ground buried under the weeds and thicket, the soil covered with a dazzling coat of wildflowers that varied with the seasons. And it was situated directly on the canal.

All day long, a blur of faces strolled along both sides of the banks, stopping always to wave or to rest their feet from the unforeseen miles they'd walked. Shepherds used the path each morning and again just before twilight, herding their flocks to a sloping green meadow just beyond the canal.

"I couldn't resist," she said. "All my life I'd literally been floating from one place to the next. Here, within one scrap of land, was everything I had been searching for: the romance of the soil, the mystery of the water, the soulfulness of the food. It had the right stuff to hold me. It was my Shangri-la."

The kitchen alone was worth dropping anchor for. It looked like something in which cavemen might have grilled a mastodon leg, renovated by Martha Stewart. The walls were sun-washed river stone, very simply adorned, with a few unmatched cabinets and flea-market shelving. A disfigured refectory worktable occupied the whole center of the room. There was a stove, of course, but Kate's primary cooking source was the fireplace, where roasts and tarts came out crisped by the coals. It was a cook's kitchen, basic, but with real style. In fact, Rick Stein, the British TV food personality, had just finished shooting a segment there. I couldn't wait to get my hands on everything in the room.

During a walk along the canal, with its long, looping bends, Kate and I came to an agreement. We'd stuff as much of the Gascon cooking experience as we could into three days, visiting the markets and farms so that I could see where everything came from, while making the most essential recipes, the ones that defined the region, except for *cassoulet,* which

would have kept us from doing much else. The Saturday-morning market was in Nerac, where we would buy most of what we needed. She had
invited friends for Sunday dinner and expected me to collaborate on every
dish we prepared.

"I'll teach you as much as I can, all my *trucs*," she sighed, sketching
out an approximate schedule. "You're not going to learn a whole world of
cooking here in two or three days, but what you will get is a consciousness
about what we have here and how to apply it to food—the Gascon sensi-
bility, which contributes to the cooking, the rusticity, the honesty."

Kate had adopted that lifestyle as her own, studying the conditions
that defined its specific personality: the soil, the weather, the seasonal
harvests that dictate the regional cuisine. "This valley is the most fertile in
all of France, with a climate very similar to that of northern California,"
she said, explaining how major flooding several times a century subjected
the Garonne estuaries to the overflowing of its banks, depositing rich layers of soil with which to nourish the crops. "It's the *terroir* that's the secret
to Gascon cooking."

The *terroir*. The farmers of western France uttered that word with exaggerated reverence. The *terroir*—the *earth*, its sense of place, and the char-
acteristics it imposes on its output. Its essence. Hearing it expressed as
a postulate was like listening to rabbis justify ancient doctrine: *because
it is written*. The Bordeaux oenologists, especially, worked the term to
death. "Got *terroir*?" It hadn't come to that . . . yet. Still, the *terroir* gov-
erned everything that eventually reached the family table. That is why in
Gascony, where the soil is tilled by farmers who measure weeks in nutri-
ents and seasons in crop yield, every ray of sunshine and hit of fertilizer
can seem as important as a breath. As a result, Gascony provided most of
the produce to all of Western Europe.

We walked the perimeter of Kate's next-door neighbor's land, where
they farmed about a hundred acres of kiwis, apples, plums, berries, and
pears, as well as green vegetables and roughage, the cabbages and lettuce.
Adjoining them was a cattle rancher, and beyond him a hog farmer. Kate
got invited to their homes, saw how people cooked for their families using

the food they produced "in a rustic, simple way," and it drove her into the kitchen to master the Gascon specialties.

We sorted out a few menus over lunch at the Café de la Paix, an old hotel in the poky village of Bruch. A young woman had bought the place and turned it into a kind of working man's pub. The food was nothing to write home about—you ate whatever they put in front of you—but, after all, that wasn't why the place was jammed at noon. It was jammed because of Sandrine, an insanely sexy French pixie with a battleship of a body and a French attitude to match, so that you knew she ran the joint. She swept through the ugly bourgeois parlor like Miss Kitty in the *Gunsmoke* saloon, drawing everyone's eyes in her wake. And when she leaned across the table to slam a bowl of soup down in front of Kate, I had to struggle to keep my hands in my lap.

I was heartened by this twitchy attraction to Sandrine. On top of everything else, she came with her own legend. "She was raised here and went away to school," Kate said. "Somewhere along the way she got married, but she came back with a daughter and no husband. So every guy in this place wants to fill that vacancy. You, too, pal—I can tell by the weaselly look on your face."

It was determined that I would reserve my passion for the cooking on our agenda, which began almost immediately upon our return to Camont. While we were gone, Kate's assistant, Andy Losh, a pale, slight, bearded man with ghostly eyes, had staged the kitchen for the upcoming dinner menu. Several cutting boards were laid out with a selection of knives at each side. A variety of vegetables picked straight from the garden lay gathered on the counter, next to an uncorked Côte de Gascon, the thin, white local wine that hadn't been *traffiqué,* as the French say, with sulfites or sugar. It was a safe bet that we would run through the bottle before our entrée hit the oven. Dupont folded himself on a pillow next to the fireplace and hardly gave us a second look.

"This is the first thing I learned how to cook here," Kate said, pulling a freshly killed rabbit out of a bag in the refrigerator.

Uh-oh, I thought, looks like the family pet.

"I'm going to show you how to cut it up, then we are going to fricassee it in a prune sauce, which we'll serve over polenta."

Without any fuss, she lopped off the head, and I felt my gorge rise. I put my hands firmly on the counter and leaned all my weight against them, steadying myself. Chicken, I told myself . . . looks exactly like chicken.

She pushed the cutting board across to me and signified a knife with her chin. "Let's take off the hind quarters next," she said, like a medical-school instructor.

Chicken . . . chicken . . . chicken. . . .

I lifted one of the legs and made an incision close to the bone, pulling it toward me gently as the knife sliced through the connecting tissue and cartilage. The next leg came away with the same degree of ease. My handiwork was first-rate, and I preened a bit . . . until I realized exactly what I'd done. For some strange reason, the front legs got short shrift. We'd use them to flavor the sauce, along with the rib cage, but they weren't considered the noble pieces that wound up on the plates. Instead, we concentrated on the saddle, which we hacked into three equal sections, then seasoned and dusted them with flour before putting the meat aside to rest.

The remainder of the preparation was similar to a *coq au vin*. We browned a chopped onion, some shallots, a couple of cloves of garlic, and a handful of *lardons* in an obscenely large spoonful of duck fat, bringing it along slowly to guard against burning, until the vegetables were nicely caramelized. Then we moved everything to the side of the casserole in order to brown the rabbit pieces lightly, just enough to get the meat juices into the pan.

Kate had me peel and cut carrots and celery into large chunks. They went into the casserole, along with a chubby *bouquet garni*, a bottle of sturdy red wine (minus two glasses for the cooks), and two leeks chopped into half-inch rounds.

"Here is the best part of the recipe," she said, reaching for a glass canister on a high shelf behind her, near the lights. It was two-thirds full with a dark-amber liquid, and I could see a dozen or more shriveled black walnut-size orbs floating in it. If these were bunny organs, let me assure you, I was on the next train out of Agen. "Try this," she said, plucking one out and steering it toward my mouth.

There are defining moments in one's culinary education that set the course for everything that follows: making vinaigrette, preparing risotto, bringing a steak to a perfect medium-rare. I'd survived oysters and sweetbreads in my time, developed a fondness for escargots. There wasn't anything in the manual about swallowing bunny eyes or testicles or whatever slimy grotesquerie was pinched between Kate's fingers. I took a deep breath, convinced that I might be able to do this quickly, without thinking, although I was equally certain that deep down I could not. Even the chicken mantra wasn't going to bail me out this time. I was going to be sick.

There was a look of dreamy expectation on Kate's lips. But she laughed suddenly, harshly, like someone coming late to a joke. "Don't tell me, you thought these were. . . . ? *A-ha-ha!* You thought I would. . . ."

"I don't know what you're talking about," I said, holding an innocent stare.

"Oh, that's a good one." She continued chuckling at my obvious discomfort. "Look, you don't have to worry about eating anything against your wishes. And, anyway, I wouldn't do that to you on the first day."

In spite of her assurances, I still gave that black thing a long, hard stare.

"Here's looking at you, kid," I said finally, taking her offering like Communion, in one chomp.

I don't know what I'd been expecting, but it certainly wasn't the upshot. My mouth filled with an alcoholic burst of ripe fruit that set off every taste bud I owned, like a package of Chinese firecrackers. It was so unexpected I had to laugh. A concentrated sweetness emerged from the alcohol and seeped over and around my tongue. There was a faintly toasty aftertaste, but it softened, with a fine finish.

"Prunes steeped in Armagnac," Kate said, ending my speculation. "No cook here is ever without a supply."

Making them, I discovered, was a cinch.

PRUNES IN ARMAGNAC

1 lb. pitted prunes   *1/2 cup sugar*
water to cover   *Armagnac or brandy*

Boil enough water in a saucepan to cover the prunes. Add the prunes and immediately turn off the heat. Let the prunes sit in the water 10 minutes, just long enough to plump (rehydrate) them. Drain, reserving the liquid, and store the prunes in a Ziploc bag until cool.

Make a simple light syrup by boiling the sugar and the reserved water. Place the prunes in a jar and add enough syrup to fill the jar halfway up the fruit. Top with Armagnac or brandy. The prunes can be stored this way for months—or years. Use as needed.

No fewer than a dozen prunes went into the casserole. Then we brought everything to a good rolling boil before covering the pot and simmering it slowly, as long as an hour and a half, giving the protein a chance to bond so that the meat became tender.

I'd eaten rabbit before only out of courtesy, for reasons not worth mentioning. Buying one was problematic enough, but here in Agen and all along the Gascon valley, they dangled in store windows, as common as Christmas lights. The sight took some getting used to, especially the floppy ears and fur. Perhaps there was a windup switch in the rear, or a place for the puppeteer's hand? The odds were good that an invitation to dinner anywhere within the area might lead to a tangy rabbit stew.

Our *lapin aux pruneaux* was, in a word, amazing. It was thick and rich, with a jammy, old-fashioned flavor that let the vegetables exert their influence without being overly persuasive. Kate's polenta, moistened by the sweet meaty juices that collected on the plate, served as a slightly chewy counterpoint to the fricassee.

Dessert was simple but delicious, and very satisfying after such a rich, wintry meal. Kate merely put a slab of ripe *Tomme*, the ubiquitous cheese from the Savoie, on a plate along with a spoonful of fig jam, nothing else.

It was perfect, just a mouthful of the cheese accented by the fruit. I especially loved the jam, which Kate had made earlier in the week—enough for six jars.

FIG JAM

3 1/2 lb. fresh Black Mission figs	1 vanilla bean
2 lb. sugar	1/2 tsp. ground cinnamon
1/3 cup water	juice of a small lemon

Rinse and dry the figs and remove any stems. (If the skin is very thick, you can partially peel it back without bruising the membranes.)

Combine the sugar with 1/3 cup of water and heat in a medium saucepan, stirring frequently, until sugar dissolves. Bring to a boil and let syrup cook until it reaches 210 degrees on a sugar thermometer, then remove pan from stove. Scrape seeds from the vanilla bean and add to the sugar solution, along with the cinnamon. Add the lemon juice and combine well.

Add the figs one by one, gently sliding each into the pan. Cook 1 hour at a slow simmer, skimming frequently, just until the figs are translucent. Remove from heat.

Remove the figs from the syrup with a slotted spoon and place in prepared jam jars, distributing them equally. (If you prefer a more blended jam, as opposed to a fig confit, break up the figs with an immersion blender.) Return the syrup to a boil and pour it over the fruit in the jars. Refrigerate and use within a week. For longer storage, refer to one of the many published guides for the proper procedure for canning.

Makes about 3 small jars

Probably the most intense cooking I did was with Kate Hill at Camont. She and I scavenged the market in Nerac the next morning, after breakfast in her crowded little kitchen, having decided that for all our compatibility at the stove, the greatest gift was that we were on the same wavelength. A balance had been struck. It might have bored most amateur cooks like me to focus specifically on duck recipes, as we'd decided, but there were so few opportunities to cover that ground with the thoroughness it deserved.

The region around Nerac had become the focus of the British Invasion, those "heathen northerners," that began at the end of the last century. Every weekend brought new friends of friends of friends. Even the recalcitrant French had become accustomed to the phenomenon; over time, they encountered an alien neighbor or two whom it was agreed they would tolerate, maybe even invite for a meal. The settlement of streets directly off the central canal was referred to as Little London, and the Saturday-morning market served as the official meeting spot.

I suppose it was like an outpost of Portobello Road. Most of the itinerant weekenders walked into town along an access road over the bridge across the Baïse River, sweaters thrown just-so across squared shoulders. As they greeted fellow countrymen, the murmur of *cheerios* and *tas* resonated like the chorus of a Gilbert and Sullivan operetta.

Kate had misled me about the region's economy. Parking, not agriculture, seemed to be Nerac's most precious commodity, and the competition for a space on market day was as fierce as a local football match. The curbs had been filling up since the crack of dawn, with cars parked nose to nose and wedged into clearances not large enough for a scooter, while latecomers patrolled the fringes around the market with the vigilance of commandos.

Kate had her standby spot in an alley beside the church. We sailed in like VIPs and took a shortcut around the magnificent château that Henri IV had built for his mistress. The sovereign from Navarre, had left an imprint on the town. Despite centuries of siege, the castle remained impressive, its tower walls as sleek and beautiful as the day it was built. Just as constant, perhaps, was Henri's knavish reputation, which was still alive in Nerac. One of the king's teenage victims, depicted in a stone carving in the park, was full of desperation and innocence. "Here lies Fleurette ravaged by Henri IV," said an inscription beneath the prostrate figure. "She gave him her life; he didn't even give her one day."

We bought a whole fatted duck, along with ten legs, right off the bat. Then we found a box of nice-looking duck *crépinettes*, little finger-shaped cylinders of chopped duck meat mixed with prunes, Armagnac, and herbs, all bound with an egg and wrapped in caul fat. We planned to sauté these as an appetizer. According to Kate, it was traditional to serve a *crépinette* with fresh oysters, so we selected a dozen beauties from nearby Arcachon Bay. We also picked up a whole *foie gras* for a *terrine,* and tons of duck fat for our *confit.*

"The duck here comes from an economy of scale," Kate explained as we cruised the stalls, selecting reedy stems of rhubarb for several tarts. "These small farms had to feed their own families from the *basse-cour*—the barnyard. My neighbors, the Sabadinis, are a perfect example. They raise beef cattle and piglets for other producers, all handled rather crisply by the father and the son, while the mother and daughter take care of the small animals—the game hens and the rabbits. But the duck, unlike those small animals, could be put up and preserved for the whole year in its own fat."

Annette Sabadini preserved thirty-six to forty ducks at one time. Her ducklings were born in the spring; they free-ranged behind the barn through the summer, growing and developing, and often at the end of the year she would force-feed, to fatten (or *gavé*) them for two weeks, so that by December they would be ready.

"So here was a food crop that took very little care and provided a good, wholesome meal for the rest of the year, whether you made *confit* or *garbure* or *cassoulet.* All you had to do was to take out a duck leg from the preservative and be creative. Economy of scale. *Voilà!*"

Making duck *confit* was a two-day affair, so we intended to begin the preparation as soon as we got back.

The church carillon tolled twelve bells. Most of the farmers began to break down their stalls as the crowd dispersed for festive lunches in nearby cafés, with terraces that opened like steamboats onto the river. The flushed-faced Brits overran those places, and sometime before the first tray of food arrived, they launched a sing-along of those awful pub songs—"Mrs. Brown" and "Two Pints of Lager and a Packet of Crisps" and anything else that showed they were united and strong.

Kate, Andy Losh, and I headed toward the park with a basket full of market treasures and an unlabeled bottle of *vin de pays* for an impromptu picnic. Andy sliced up a rustic sausage (made from the Gascon black pig) that we had bought from an admirer of Kate's named Kakou, whose green T-shirt boasted: "Here we sell what we like." There were the fattest prunes I had ever seen and olives cured in sweet fennel oil and ripe, juicy peaches and several cheeses, including Salers, a sharp sheep-milk variety from the Massif Central whose two-inch crust was used to flavor soups. There was a baguette, too, as crusty and honest as they came, which we slathered with a chunky roasted artichoke tapenade. It was one of the most satisfying lunches I had eaten in France. After downing some wine, I reached into my pocket, unfolding a grease-stained paper, and offered to show Kate something that I had been wrestling with throughout the morning.

It was Bob Ash's version of duck *confit* that we had made at Rue du Lac a few weeks earlier, and I already knew, while she scanned it, the type of reaction it would elicit.

Kate looked up gently at me. "Well," she said, "this is meaningless to me, you understand. It is a recipe for a restaurant chef made to resemble *confit*, but the only thing familiar in it is the duck leg, nothing else I'm afraid."

I tried explaining that Bob's version respected the French basics and, if nothing else, coaxed as much flavor out of the duck as possible. It sounded good as I said it, but Kate shook her head with inflexibility.

"First of all, you'd be laughed out of Gascony," she said with sincere fervor. "I don't know why you'd use pork fat to make duck *confit*. It compromises the whole flavor. When you poach the duck, it has to be in its own fat. That's the essence of Gascon cooking: flavor on flavor on flavor. By 'confit-ing' the duck in its own fat, you are doubling the flavor. Your English chef just tweaked the flavor with a bay leaf, thyme, and some garlic. But the traditional way to make *confit* is with just salt and pepper. The duck delivers the flavor all by itself.

"And why would you put it in the oven for six hours when it takes forty-five minutes on the stove?" she demanded. "We don't do it for speed or economy, but to preserve the duck for the rest of the year."

I tried to argue on Bob Ash's behalf, for his honor, but Kate would have none of it.

"You'll see," she said with a dismissive wave, tabling further discussion of the subject.

Later I read, with some satisfaction, that an authentic *confit* could be simmered in duck, goose, or pork fat. A few ardent supporters of French cuisine admitted that, in a pinch, they even baked their duck legs in a slow oven, as Bob did. And no less an authority than Jacques Pépin offered a sharp one-hour abridgment. But, of course, these recipes were playing to palates attuned to white zinfandel and bottled mayonnaise. The essence of Gascon cooking didn't lie in the details; it was not a collection of recipes, not even a place, but the overall spirit: a cook's state of mind.

Everything I encountered there started to creep up on me: doubting, questioning, second-guessing. Who was the ultimate judge when it came to cooking a particular dish? Who was entitled to set restrictions concerning a preparation? At the moment, I was growing anxious about the oysters in Kate's market bag. They'd been stashed in there for several hours, indifferent to the blazing heat, and all the tales of toxic-shellfish emergencies started to shake my sense of well-being. It must have been obvious, my jumpy eyes darting toward the bag a dead giveaway, because Andy eventually pulled me aside and asked whether something was bothering me.

"We've got to get those oysters into the fridge," I whispered, "or at the very least on ice. Even then, I don't think they are going to make it."

"You can relax," he said with a good-natured laugh. "They are fresh and alive. We can leave them in the shed for three or four days without worrying about them."

Sure, I thought, but they're going to smell like dead squirrel.

I also worried about the eggs sitting on Kate's shelf since the morning I arrived, and the block of butter in her cupboard. The French know how to cook like nobody's business, I thought, but their habits, in regard to sanitary matters, reminded me of the reptile house at the Bronx Zoo. Hadn't these people read about salmonella? If Andy chose to eat an oyster that had been festering all week in a shed, my feeling was, "Good luck and good night, *M'sieur.*"

The show began in earnest when we arrived back at Camont. Kate was eager to get to work on the duck almost as soon as we climbed out of the car; there was so much she wanted to teach me in our remaining time together, and it seemed necessary, as each hour passed, to sacrifice another objective or two. A duck mousse with truffles and port wine was scratched, as were *graisserons*, the leftover scraps of *confit* that yield fabulous hors d'oeuvres. Still, from where I stood, we were primed for a veritable duck orgy.

"Here is what I propose," Kate said, as she and Andy prepared the *mise-en-place*. "We'll do the *découpage*, the cutting-up of the duck. Then we have an additional ten legs that need careful salting. After we finish that, it will be necessary to cut the fat and render it. Then, we'll cook the *magret* for tonight's dinner, and if time allows we'll devote some attention to *foie gras*."

It was decided that I would do the honors with the *découpage*, which was no small feat, considering that the duck was a hefty seven pounds. Kate instructed me on how to score it along both sides of the backbone, pulling away the meat with my left hand while the knife descended deeper along the bone. The difficult part wasn't in the surgery so much as it was leaving the outer skin intact. I removed the entire *manteau*, separating it gently from the ribcage, and then split it in half so that each portion contained a breast, a wing, and a leg. While the meat rested, we cut the excess skin into fine dice and rendered it in a pan over slow heat.

The word *scraps*, as I discovered, does not apply to a fatted duck. Everything served a purpose. Even the skin around the neck cavity received a special treatment—dredged with salt and pepper and tossed in a flaming-hot pan, where it crackled and jumped like popcorn.

"It's customary to nibble on the *gratons* while you make *confit*," Kate said, scooping them into a bowl once they were browned and curled like little chips. She sprinkled on more salt.

I looked at the fried fat with suspicion. "My internist is going to have a stroke if I put one of those in my mouth."

"Then let's not tell him."

She held out the bowl with playful readiness. Chicken . . . chicken . . .

chicken. . . . It wasn't working this time. The French could call them *gratons* or anything else and pass them off as a delicacy, but cracklings—for that is what they were—held no appeal for me. I lumped them in the same category as beef jerky and scrapple. Still, I had to admit they smelled absolutely heavenly, with just enough meat to suggest the smokiness of bacon, yet saturated with the aromatic succulence of duck. The Goofy with horns and a trident was hovering nearby, murmuring, "What are you waiting for, chump? The whole cholesterol business is a medical-establishment conspiracy. Go on. It won't kill you. Dig in. *Dig in!*"

Addiction isn't one of my vices. I'm not compulsive when it comes to drinking wine or Champagne, both of which I love, and I've never been tempted by online poker. Smoking repulses me. There is a particular type of candy that I crave more than once or twice a week. Other than that, there are few weaknesses from which I have to protect myself. But if I am ever sent to the Betty Ford Clinic, rest assured it will be for *gratons* dependency.

The first one melted on my tongue like a pat of superfatted butter, leaving an exquisitely salty sweetness in my mouth. The second and third sent me into a lightheaded swoon, and after that, there was no turning back. I'd been corrupted. I tore through the bowl of treats like a junkie. I couldn't get them into my mouth fast enough. I tried to be discreet, pacing myself, but it was a NASCAR-type pace, nearly two-fisted and certainly off-putting to any spectator. And when Kate turned her back, I snatched another handful, smoothing out the top layer so that she might not notice how many were gone. I fantasized knocking over a butcher shop and stealing a dozen duck skins.

I felt gratified and contented about my discovery, and I turned my back smugly on any thought of what the *gratons* might do to my arteries. Men shouldn't be slaves to their self-preservation, I decided. Life was too short. There was plenty of wiggle room in my diet.

I gorged myself guiltlessly while Kate salted the duck legs with a scant tablespoon per leg, pressing the granules into the meat and skin with just enough pressure so that they adhered. Afterward, we put them into a glass casserole large enough to hold all the legs in several layers, then turned them skin side down so that the skin formed a sort of cradle to hold the moisture in each piece. She draped a tea towel overtop before placing them in the fridge for an overnight maceration.

Kate stirred the rendered fat and turned down the flame on the stove. "Before we start dinner, let's do a quick *foie gras* preparation, shall we?" Why even cook it, I thought? I'll just slather it on my thighs.

Without waiting for an answer, she ducked into a pantry adjoining the kitchen, where rosy globes of fresh liver sat on the edge of a crude stone parson's sink. She had me sever the vein connecting the two lobes, gently pulling them apart and just coaxing the vein with the tip of a knife so that it would give itself up like the roots of a plant. The *foie gras* was smooth and creamy, with the consistency of modeling clay.

"We'll sear another one tomorrow afternoon, to go with a salad," Kate said, which suited me fine, because there were few foods I found more hedonistic than seared *foie gras,* and I had been eager to learn how to prepare it properly, without panic or undue awe.

The method she had in mind right now took absolutely no work at all. It was called *foie gras au torchon,* which meant literally duck liver served in a tea towel, where it "cooked" naturally in a little crust of salt and pepper while it hibernated in the freezer. I'm not sure about the specifics of the chemical process. To a secular mind, it didn't make any sense at all. There was no reference, other than to say the *foie gras* was as delicious and well-cooked as any I'd ever eaten. And the simple presentation was just as unassuming as they came.

FOIE GRAS *au* TORCHON

1 whole foie gras, deveined
1 1/2 tsp. sea salt
freshly ground black pepper
  to taste

1 tea towel
kitchen string
crusty bread, for toast pieces

Salt and pepper the insides of the lobes, then put them back together, making a presentable package. Spread out a standard-size tea towel,

salt and pepper the inside of the towel, then place the foie gras in the
towel and roll it up to form a nice oval shape much like a jelly roll. Tie
the ends in an attractive way, using kitchen string or ribbon. Place the
package in the freezer for 6 to 8 hours.

Defrost the towel and its contents in the refrigerator overnight and
bring to room temperature, making sure the liver doesn't get too warm
and melt. Open the towel, slice the foie gras, and serve it directly from
the towel, along with the pieces of toast. (After defrosting, it will keep in
the refrigerator for 4 or 5 days.)

Serves 6–8

Making it was a cinch. There wasn't much advance work necessary for
our dinner, either. The *magret* recipe promised to be a fairly straightforward sauté, with a tangy "double wine" reduction that Kate would walk
me through as we made it. In the meantime, I cornered Andy and asked
him to give me a lesson in opening the oysters, that is, if they hadn't
already turned to shit in the shed.

Incredibly, the oysters smelled as fresh as when we'd bought them, with
the breath of the sea still on the shells.

"Opening them is a breeze," Andy said, pulling out the kind of knife
that inmates whittle from spoons and call their "shiv." It had a stumpy
wooden handle that fit perfectly into his palm and about a three-inch
blade, punished by use. "You just have to be smarter than the oyster," he
said, "and the oyster is not very smart."

I watched the way Andy found the opening to the shell with his knife,
wiggling the blade deep into the crevice in the same way you force a spoonful of puréed asparagus into a baby's mouth. All the time, he kept twisting
it with his wrist to separate the top shell from the oyster, and finally cutting away the muscle until it settled with a little plop in the adjoining halfshell. It was like a wrestling match, with the satisfaction of knowing you
were going to win. Those suckers put up a good fight, too. I gave it a try,
fussing clumsily with the knife, and cracked a few shells in the process, an
outcome that might have been acceptable had I been opening bluepoints;
using Arcachon oysters was like practicing one's corkscrew technique on a

case of Château Petrus. Bits of shell floated conspicuously in the spoonful of brine around the muscle. I threw Andy an apologetic grimace, but he was busy slurping down an oyster with unmitigated gusto.

He studied the empty shell appreciatively. His eyes were large and captive.

"There's nothing like it for pure pleasure. *Volupté*, as the French call it, a bursting sensuality." He laughed at the pitch of his glibness. "You'll have to excuse me, I'm getting a little carried away."

"You're coming off an oyster high," I said, smiling. "I'm more than familiar with the symptoms."

I'd almost forgotten, until I slipped one of the oysters into my mouth. The incomparable taste immediately transported me to a skiff in Arcachon Bay. It had been almost twenty-five years since I climbed into its square stern with a handful of friends, on our way to a day tour of Cap Ferret. We had spent the cool, sentimental April morning conducting a barrel tasting in Bordeaux. None of us had had time to grab lunch before shoving off, and dinner, we'd been told, would come very late that evening. As we sailed past the monster dune, we moaned in harmony about our hunger.

"God, what I wouldn't give for a plate of oysters," said a buddy, eyeing a nearby trawler in the midst of pulling up its net.

Our captain, who spoke no English, understood the gist of what was said enough to give us a pitying shrug. He grabbed a misshapen metal-handled bucket and dipped it into the tide, letting it drag as we made sail across the bay, farther from the mainland. After a few minutes, he pulled it up and dumped the contents—eight or ten oysters—onto the deck.

"*Voilà!*" he said, grinning, showing a mouthful of gold.

His bounty caused a good deal of excitement on board, although a lot of good it did me. I had never put one of those slimy creatures into my mouth. Never would, I thought, if there was anything else fit to swallow. A little sushi every now and then was the extent of my flirtation with raw fish. As far as oysters went, there were those people who did and those who didn't, and I knew damned well on which side of the halfshell I stood.

A crowd pressed around the captain as he began to pry open the shells. He had the most intuitive hands I had ever seen, and he used them with the skill of a mechanic handling something he understood perfectly. I watched, silent and entranced, while he loosened each mollusk with a flick of the knife. I felt a sense of exclusion as my friends cupped these unexpected treats in their palms and snarfed them down. It was the same feeling I used to have in college when my friends passed a joint. The first few times it happened, I casually waved it away, until it became my idiosyncrasy not to smoke dope at all.

"You don't know what you are missing," said Harvey, a columnist for the *Globe,* chucking an empty oyster shell overboard.

"I imagine you're right," I said, letting out an irresolute sigh. "Feel like giving me a quick lesson on the proper etiquette?"

Harvey's eyes looked almost lascivious, as if he were turning on a virgin. "O-blah-dee, O-blah-dah," he cried, passing me an oyster with uplifted joy.

It is difficult to describe the anxiety attached to eating one's first oyster, just as it is difficult to describe the sensation of discovering its pure delight. Anyone who's been there knows exactly how I felt. The entire boatful of oyster-lovers watched me with drunken anticipation.

"Yes, I'm very familiar with the symptoms," I reassured Andy all those years later in Gascony, as I worked my way through opening the entire dozen oysters.

After the first few clunkers, I developed a nice little groove, wedging in the knife with a serious shove and delivering the *coup de grâce*: zip-zip-zip. My initial timidity had been tied to the odds-on chance that the knife would slip and rip a nifty gash through my hand, no small worry to anyone who prized his own flesh. But I solved that by using a dish towel to grip the oyster, giving me not only a better hold on the shell but also an inch or two of forgiveness.

The Arcachon oysters were meatier than those normally found on American menus, the Malpeques or Caraquets from Prince Edward Island and the Kumamotos from the Pacific, even brinier than the *spéciales* indigenous to Parisian bistros. For many, their density was prohibitive.

But they had an ethereal, sweet, buttery finish not unlike a fine sauterne. And they exploded with a flavor that identified a region all its own.

"Try a *tranche* of Kakou's sausage in between each oyster," Kate suggested.

Not surprisingly, it gave the oyster experience a whole other dimension, as when two volatile weather fronts meet over a valley. As I washed it down with a sharp-edged *floc de gascogne,* I imagined a typhoon blowing through the small parlor, decimating it with . . . *volupté.*

Dinner was a more temperate affair, with the *magret* a well-matched foil for the voluptuous oysters. Kate was as good as her word when it came to guiding me through the preparation, and we effortlessly produced the dish in no time at all.

MAGRET IN DOUBLE-WINE SAUCE

2 duck breasts, 3/4 lb. each	*2 Tbl. shallots, chopped*
salt and freshly ground	*1/2 cup red-wine vinegar*
pepper	*1/2 cup red currant jelly*
2 Tbl. unsalted butter	

Salt and pepper the duck breasts on both sides. Cover loosely with a tea towel and allow to stand 2 hours.

Place a scant tablespoon of butter in a saucepan over medium-low heat and sauté the shallots gently until they are translucent but not brown. Add the vinegar and the salt and pepper to taste, and reduce the liquid to half. (If the flavor is too intense, add 2 to 3 tablespoons of water while reducing.)

Add the red currant jelly, stirring until it is entirely melted, and turn off the heat until ready to serve the duck.

Sauté the magret in a dry, nonstick hot pan until the meat is medium-rare (about 6 minutes per side). Finish the sauce with the left-over tablespoon of butter. Slice, spoon sauce over the duck, and serve.

Serves 2

"I started cooking duck the moment I landed here, and I don't think I'd ever eaten it before," Kate said, as the breast smoked slightly in the hot butter. "As far as I knew, ducks swam in ponds."

"And devoured stale bread," I said. "Eating one seemed inhuman. The closest I came to duck was in the window of a Chinese restaurant. It looked diabolical the way they hung there like mistletoe. The work of heathens. You couldn't have convinced me to prepare one at home."

"What did we know? The great thing I discovered is that it's a rich meat, without being fatty or marbled like beef. Besides, it is very high in iron, and it's delicious. A little goes a long way."

The simplicity of the dish required an equally homespun accompaniment, so Kate showed me how to caramelize a mélange of white and sweet potato chunks in two tablespoons of duck fat (or lard) with a sprinkling of sugar, cooking them ever so slowly, so they formed a good crust without drying out. It took us about thirty or forty minutes of persistent cooking until the potatoes obeyed, but it was well worth the effort. The sweet potatoes tasted almost candied, and they balanced out the much blander whites, soaking up the fat and releasing their own earthy perfume.

Through all of the cooking, Kate was the eye of the hurricane, calm and comforting despite our apparent scramble to coordinate these recipes. She remained unruffled even when it seemed that things were swerving out of control, and as I watched her orchestrate the seemingly endless steps and maneuvers in an organized, matter-of-fact way, I began to draw on her relaxed pace to counterbalance my normally agitated approach. I let her instincts guide me. "Think . . . Bing Crosby," I remembered from early media training. The mantra here seemed more suited to a long, deep *ommmmm*. I let my body ease into it, let it overtake me, inhabit me. It felt almost like taking a Valium. Somehow, all my countertop anxiety got displaced, moved *over there*, where it couldn't touch me. I felt capable of doing any number of tasks without rushing them and being overcome by adrenaline, which had always been my downfall. I hooked right in to Kate's even-handed tempo. Her manner was mild and irresistible. Her motions were fluid, her hands nimble; they struck a nice, easy groove: Buddy Rich with the brushes.

Up to this point, Kate seemed invulnerable to me, mainly because it was so obvious that the world she inhabited suited her so well. She genuinely *loved* Gascony and seemed fulfilled by her role here, by the scope of the cooking, which she did with a kind of chastened amusement. She enjoyed having visitors, especially those who came as students, some of whom had talent, some only enthusiasm. Even the food writers, she said, had their own plodding charms. I envied her genial resilience, her freedom to plow through recipes and people in search of that harmony. She was free in a way that other people weren't. From what I could tell, she was perfectly content.

Still, there was something about Kate, a shadow within her, that I couldn't put my finger on. Perhaps it was the alienation, the price of living alone, on a barge, in a provincial corner of the world. An enchantment—or a mistake?

Perhaps it was too close to issues I was wrangling with. Where would everything leave me when I got back home? What was in store ahead? One option was for me to lead a lonely life dedicated to my art—my writing, my music, my cooking. Would that be enough to sustain me? I doubted it.

Over dinner, I prodded Kate about her passage to western France, which I assumed had an interesting and perhaps melancholy story attached. There was a hesitation, but only momentary, during which it seemed she was making up her mind whether to give me the standard CliffsNotes version or to reveal something else. Andy looked the other way; nothing puzzled him, there were no mysteries. The length of the indecision betrayed Kate's reticence; despite our developing camaraderie, perhaps I was nothing more than a stranger after all.

"I didn't leave the States to be an expatriate," she began, choosing her words with care. "But I had been in Africa for a year, traveling extensively, and I didn't want to return to the States so quickly that I would forget everything I saw on that continent." Instead, she drifted to Holland, joining its community of itinerants lost in the warp. Somewhere during that interval a boyfriend materialized. "We bought a barge together and sailed off with a lot of dreams. I don't really know what happened to him, but the dreams . . ." She smiled inwardly and laughed. "I've been sailing ever since, mostly around the Canal Latéral à la Garonne. And somewhere along the way, this became my home."

Kate shied from the ghosts. It was clearly an abridgment meant to keep me at a safe distance, which I accepted graciously, although her eyes clouded with memories. They stayed with her for a few minutes, intruding on her grin and producing a faint tremor, which, admirably, she did not try to hide. She sat at the table, folding and refolding her napkin and asking distractedly if I'd like more *magret* or if I was ready for dessert. I mumbled something about the dinner and being stuffed.

A transition was needed to move us away from the bone. I stepped up to the plate: "The cooking couldn't have been something you learned on the spot."

"Hardly," she said, with an appreciative smile. "I owe it all to the Skyline Truckstop Diner in Kingman, Arizona. My parents bought the place after my father retired from the navy, and I got a ready-made education serving my mother's food. She was Italian, so there was a touch of foreign influence, but my interest didn't peak until I arrived here. I was so close to the source and could see the food coming right out of the ground. I lost all connection to the restaurant aspect of food; it became a way for me to communicate with the earth and nature."

To make ends meet, she started European Culinary Adventures in 1991, at a time when only a handful of cooking schools catered to foreign travelers. There was Lorenza de Medici in Tuscany and Anne Willan at La Varenne, but few others, aside from Kate. She created a getaway that celebrated the cultural heritage of Gascony, evoking not only its food but also the atmosphere and splendor of the area.

Most people who came through were on holiday, not serious culinary students. They wanted to master a few recipes, but they also wanted to visit a winery and go into town and buy postcards and souvenirs. "You've got to cater to your constituency," Kate said, "so I combine it with a barge trip on the canal, which makes everything so beautiful and accessible. And the food we make is always something that can be reproduced back home, specialties of Gascony that will impress friends but without being so difficult or impractical."

It didn't matter that I probably wouldn't make the rabbit stew when I returned home. There were too many prejudices attached, although I knew my friend Craig would be game. I kept envisioning Friday-evening dinners at which my guests would eat *foie gras* from a tea towel while I hummed away in the kitchen, or popped a handful of *gratons* instead of cashews and olives. Not a week would pass when I wouldn't be shucking a bushel of oysters for astonished friends. As for the variations of duck, you could count on their reappearance once I learned where to shop for it. It was exactly the kind of honest cuisine—and secrets of great cooking—that I had been searching for since arriving in Europe.

"Impress friends," I said, laughing, delighted by the thought. "All right, you've caught me red-handed. Although it sounds as if you get something out of it for yourself."

She opened her mouth to say something but reconsidered. Awkwardly, she looked toward the floor, at her shoes; a skirt of dried mud clung to the soles. An uncomfortably long time passed without a response.

"I'm very happy where I am," she said. "I finally feel grounded. For someone who was born on an island and bounced around a lot and sailed for years, I finally have a home of my own. Food is only the catalyst, not the end product."

That may be so, but in a way, I thought she was emblematic of other chefs who have given themselves so completely to their art. The process was consuming, and few people felt more at home than Kate in the confines of a kitchen, a plodding, solitary existence where attention to details and hard work often deterred cooks from having anything that resembled a normal lifestyle. I admired her focus, her total immersion in the atmosphere and bounty of the Gascon countryside, the spiritual effect it had on her.

Be that as it may, Kate seemed fulfilled by the cooking. It was her craft, her art, an ongoing adventure. Her pursuit of a perfect recipe, the synergy between flavors and ingredients, reminded me of a scientist determined to explore all the variables. As a writer, always searching for the right combination of words to express myself, I understood the process. There was always another verbal recipe to tease out more flavor. Of course, the solitary component of it was essential.

Could I find that same kind of fulfillment in cooking? I didn't think so. For me, cooking for people was too important. I needed to share the food I prepared. I depended too much on the overall dining experience, a comfortable friendship at the table, hoping that my guests would be satisfied. The professional aspect eluded me.

I could echo her words—that food was the catalyst, not the end product. But we were talking about two different things.

Sunday morning, after a visit to the indoor market in Agen, we foraged through Kate's garden, cutting small bouquets of herbs for our lunch. Thyme and chives were the featured flavors on our menu. Some silky leek shoots went into our basket as an afterthought, along with fourteen plum tomatoes we intended to use for an informal soup.

"Let's also pick a few figs, just in case . . . ," Kate said.

"In case what?"

". . . we get hungry later tonight and crave a rustic tart." I watched her large, sure hands moving methodically, plucking fruit from the lower branches of a tree. "There are some good ones hiding around the bottom. We only need nine or ten figs."

It seemed ludicrous, considering the menu she had planned. We were finishing the duck *confit* to accompany the tomato soup, a salad with seared *foie gras,* Kate's trademark potato soufflé, and a selection of good cheeses, including a piece of Reblochon I could have smelled had I been in the next county.

As it turned out, Kate and I were very much alike. She couldn't resist inviting lunch guests. It was part of her makeup. She was hard-wired for generosity, and visitors gave her an audience, an opportunity to cook, to feed people, without having to explain all the dance steps. With Andy and me, she was always deconstructing the food as if it were part of a greater lesson, but with guests—that is, anyone who wasn't cooking or scribbling madly in notebooks—she was inclined to pull out all the stops.

It was a tradition, especially on Sundays, that friends drop by for an afternoon feast. Many of those who showed up regularly were neighbors, the farmers who had indoctrinated Kate into their customs, shared their recipes, and, over time, came to be regarded as her "adopted family." Others were a nomadic assortment of travelers passing through, or drifters on barges, or friends and friends of friends with summer houses near Agen and Toulouse. In any case, the day was set aside for the kind of blissful rendezvous that revolves around gardening, cooking, and eating, with enough food from Kate's kitchen to endow an emerging third-world country.

Before her friends the Hodges arrived, we fixed the duck legs, letting them come to room temperature, then we rendered five pounds of fat, enough to cover the casserole. Once the fat came to a boil, we wiped off the excess salt clinging to the legs before lowering them into the bubbling yellow ooze and brought the fat back to a burbling simmer. In forty-five minutes, as the meat began to pull away from the bone, the confit was nearly finished.

"We're only serving four legs for lunch," Kate reminded me, "which means we'll have about six left over to preserve."

The whole preserving business, I have to admit, was something of an anomaly to me. It brought up images of pinch-faced pioneer women with their hair up in buns, churning butter and tapping Bunyan-size maple trees.

"I don't know, Kate. It'd be a lot easier to go to Le Cirque, don't you think? This seems like an awfully big production for a bony duck leg."

"Why waste your time at Le Cirque? There's always your buddy Robert Ash. Or McDonald's." She stopped chopping the tomatoes to give me a look less of reprimand than disappointment. "All kidding aside, the *confit* is a farmhouse tradition, not a restaurant process. There are no shortcuts. You take your time preserving it, with love, in order to protect the character of the meat, so that when you take it down from a shelf two, five, or even fifteen months from now, it will have a moist, succulent tenderness that takes you back to the day it was cooked. It is impossible to appreciate what I am saying until one winter night when you are caught without dinner, and that jar of *confit* happens to catch your eye. To me, there is nothing as delicious. You'll see."

I continued to monitor the progress of the duck, feeling chastised. Every so often, I looked quickly over at Kate, wondering whether my attitude toward the *confit* had been too impertinent, that perhaps it might prompt another early exit, but she was blanching the tomatoes in a pot of water and whistling to herself.

Around noon the Hodges arrived, carrying a quart of Laphroaig, which made them instantly acceptable in spite of their tinny Lancashire accents. A good birdlike pair in their mid-to-late sixties, they lived on an old tobacco farm in Mont-Cuq, a tiny enclave of Brits in the hills on the other side of Agen. Cynthia, the chirpier of the two, recounted the events surrounding their recent retirement to France, insisting they had been just as happy living in the States, where Brian "did squiggles," which I assumed was tied in some way to math, but I later understood it to mean a kind of computer hieroglyphics.

"Oh," I said indiscreetly, realizing this was spywork of some sort.

Cynthia kept up a blistering dialogue about their peregrinations, while Brian sat there in a kind of stiff silence, with his legs stretched out and a tumbler of Scotch in his hand, staring off at a spot on the far wall, which must have gone toward solving a precarious programming glitch that none of us could comprehend.

The tradition on Sundays was for everyone to pitch in, with Andy and me doing most of the grunt work. Kate expected me to finish the *confit*, which amounted to nothing more than sautéing the legs in a knob or two of duck fat until the skin was nicely crisp, then turning down the heat and cooking the other side until the meat was warmed through. After I had finished and placed them in a warm oven for later, she sent Cynthia out to gather mesclun in the garden, and Andy to scavenge capers from a row of thorny bushes out back. Meanwhile, she rummaged through the refrigerator to locate the ingredients for the potato soufflé.

I sighed, recalling the soufflé debacle in Madame's kitchen, and ran it down for Kate, including a fairly good imitation of Doug and Didi.

"Of course, you'd have to boil me in duck fat to learn the identity of the cooking school. . . ."

"But I'm sure I could guess," she said, rattling off a few names. "Aha, I can tell by your expression that I hit one on the nose!"

She looked at me, gloating. I shook my head without acknowledging since she had failed to mention Madame's name.

"Those places are all alike," she said, "—like fancy finishing schools, except they never really prepare the students for reproducing a dish at home. You might as well read a cookbook and save your money." Kate pulled down a heavy earthenware bowl from a shelf. "Let's remedy your bad experience with a soufflé that always comes out great."

SOUFFLÉ *de* POMMES *de* TERRE

10 large potatoes with waxy skins	1/2 to 1/3 cup heavy cream
	pinch of nutmeg
5 large eggs, whites and yolks separated	salt and freshly ground pepper
5 Tbl. unsalted butter, softened	

Preheat the oven to 425 degrees.

Don't peel the potatoes, but if they are too large, cut them in half, trying to keep the chunks around the same size so that they cook evenly. Cook the potatoes in well-salted boiling water until they are fork tender, 15 to 20 minutes. Drain the potatoes in a colander and break them up a bit. Put the potatoes through a food mill or ricer. (The skins will stay behind and should be discarded.)

Whip the egg whites until they form soft but not stiff peaks, making sure they are not too dry. Set aside. Place 3 yolks in a large bowl, add the butter, cream, nutmeg, and salt and pepper. Combine, then add the potatoes, mixing gently with a wooden spoon. Taste and correct the seasoning, adding more cream or salt as necessary. Gently fold the egg whites into the potatoes all at once—gently, but making sure they are well incorporated.

Butter a porcelain or enameled metal casserole. Let the potatoes tumble gently into the casserole, being careful not to pack them in or tamp them down (peaks of potatoes are fine). Bake 25 minutes, until a golden-brown crust forms on the top of the potatoes. Serve at once.

Serves 8

Preparing the recipe, I hadn't the slightest expectation for success. If a strawberry soufflé failed to puff and rise like a hot-air balloon, it would be stupidity to hope for such a result from potatoes. The vision I had was of the *Hindenburg* over Lakehurst.

In the meantime, Kate deveined another fat orb of *foie gras* for the salad, which Cynthia had collected in her apron. This preparation required even less fuss than the *torchon* method. It was so quick, in fact, that we had to plate the salad in advance so it would arrive at the table before the liver disintegrated into Silly Putty.

"It's all in the timing," Kate said, heating a pan just until a drop of water jitterbugged across it. "Everything has to be perfect—the temperature, the seasoning, the length of time on the fire." She cut the liver into half-inch slices, sprinkling them with a fine dust of cornstarch to keep the delicate meat from scorching, and popped them in the pan until the fat they released broke a faint sizzle, a matter of a few seconds. Immediately, she flipped them over and then removed them after they'd barely touched the heat.

It seemed preposterous to believe anything could have cooked in less time than it took to sneeze, especially something as troubling as duck liver. I shuddered to think what kind of intestinal damage a raw hunk of it might cause. But both sides were perfectly seared, the liver trembled to the touch, and when a slice was pricked with the tip of a knife, its juices ran clear.

We rushed to the long table under Kate's grape arbor, where Dupont lay sunning himself on a stretch of flagstone. A bottle of Muscat de

Beaumes-de-Venise passed from hand to hand in order to tease the sweetness from the *foie gras,* and by the time it made the first circuit, the salad was already gone. It was the richest, most sensual salad I had ever eaten. My mouth was thick with honeyed fat from the liver, which had melted on my tongue like a pat of butter. Everyone had the same intense reaction. We nodded eagerly at each other, delirious with pleasure. The Brits were always amazed that an American could cook like a French farmer.

Of course, the duck *confit* was yet to come, and the potato soufflé neared completion. I sidled over to the oven and peeked into its dark yawn. Far be it from me to write a cooking tragedy here. That little bastard had puffed and risen like a contented adder. It smelled incredible, too, toasty and peasanty, with a slightly sour whiff of cream that flattered the overall fragrance.

The table conversation provided an aria for the food, which was lavish and delicious, and the *floc de gascogne* unburdened our souls. Even Brian, whose entire output was measured in words as opposed to sentences, fell victim to the magic spell. I noticed that his tongue loosened and he laughed hard, too hard, at his wife's pithy remarks. The day disappeared, and our inhibitions along with it. I remember how we complimented each other with surprising fervor, toasting every contribution to the meal, especially Kate's heroic effort, and how after our glasses were drained, more *floc* appeared, until the sun on my back and the lightness in my head conspired to carry me over a cliff.

I don't know how long I sat there without saying anything, or how strange it must have seemed, but I was surprised to find everyone laughing at a story Cynthia was telling about serving steak-and-kidney pie to a family of Gascon farmers. Suddenly, I felt very grateful. I wanted to lean across the table and hug her, as if she had purposefully covered for me. We fortified ourselves with cheese and strong coffee. It was criminal to allow heartache to intrude on such a day.

The Hodges left around five. As soon as their car disappeared from view, Kate and I finished preserving the leftover duck legs, sterilizing the tall, liter-size Mason jars, filling the capsules with *confit,* and cooking them in a bath of boiling water until the meat was tender. Then, around nine, right on schedule, we rolled out the dough for a couple of rustic fig tarts. The recipe was a simple one, using a sweet, free-form pastry crust that folded over itself, with two different undercoatings for the perfectly ripe fruit: Kate chose slices of fresh goat cheese for hers; I slathered chestnut purée on mine. In either case, it demonstrated how easy it was to bake something rustic and delicious in no time at all.

While it cooked, Andy kept running back to the barge, where he got updates on the Sunday football games back in the States. He seemed especially disheartened by the downfall of his beloved 49ers, although any reference to San Francisco sent him into a discernible gloom. When he was fifteen, his father had died suddenly and his closest brother committed suicide. Andy escaped to cooking school with every intention of becoming a chef, but following graduation he knew beyond a doubt that his future would be elsewhere—anywhere, in fact, but a restaurant—so he took off for France, where he had been working for Kate on and off for two years. He was headed back to the States in another month, perhaps to law school, but . . . he wasn't sure.

"Before you do anything," I said, "go check out Sandrine at the Café de la Paix. A woman like that might throw your life a pretty powerful curve."

He laughed, promising to write if anything developed on that front.

"You boys look hungry," Kate said, presenting a tray brimming with thick slices of Kakou's dry-cured sausages, a wedge of Manchego cheese, some shredded duck *confit,* and tall *Kirs Gascons,* those potent potions of *crème de mûre* and red wine, all of which we devoured with frightening gusto.

The amount of food we'd eaten was alarming. My belt was already a notch or two higher on the JumboTron. Andy looked as though he'd been *gavé*-ed like a duck. With stiff, distressed smiles on our faces, we grabbed slices from each of the steaming tarts, acting terror-stricken, positively bug-eyed, at the suggestion of *à la mode.*

Kate laughed appreciatively and just stared at us with a kind of maternal clumsiness, growing increasingly melancholy in the silence that ensued.

"You two better prepare yourselves for the good things that are headed your way," Kate said. She turned slightly and stared at her reflection in a mirror that hung just beyond the fireplace. I was about to say something, to thank her, but then I realized she had gone to the same place I'd been to earlier that afternoon.

Andy and I looked at each other. With a shy, affecting shrug, he got up and left the kitchen, Dupont padding faithfully a few steps behind. I waited for another minute or two. Kate never moved from her position, nor said a word, not even a sigh. The stillness of her body established a tension that was impossible to intrude upon. In fact, aside from the hush of my own shallow breathing, there was no other sound in the room, although for a moment I thought I could hear her heart beating.

I wasn't exactly surprised. In fact, I remember thinking at the time that we were all—Andy, Kate, and I—in some kind of weird emotional purgatory. I suddenly felt a strange camaraderie with them, as if a veil had been lifted.

Yes, we're all in this together, I thought. Without a word, I threw a muslin scarf around my neck and went outside, another shadow in the night, walking by moonlight along the canal as it flowed toward the Garonne.

Chapter Five

PARIS

No one has the right to be ambivalent about Paris. The city, as Elliot Paul wrote, was inexhaustible, as was its memory. But as the TGV sped northward past Chartres and then Versailles, my feelings about the visit were indefinite, if not mixed.

The night before, I called Lily to tell her how excited I was. I had three very different experiences penciled on my dance card: working in the kitchens of two of the city's most renowned restaurants, and taking an intimate class in someone's home. For the last few weeks, I'd been working my way through the minors; now I had a shot at the big leagues.

There is little I can add to the enchanted lore of Paris, other than to say that I go there every chance I get. The beauty and the romance seem fresh every time. It would be an understatement to say I've made twenty-five pilgrimages, the highlights so numerous they tend to melt into one another.

My memory, on the other hand, was very sharp about the last time I had been there. It was just a few months earlier, with Carolyn, whose only experience with the city had been a rainy one-night layover more than twenty years before, and we spent a week soaking it into our skins so that it might never wash off. And so an edginess overcame me as the train pressed across the city line.

There was also a hotel problem I hadn't anticipated. A friend had booked me into Le Meurice as a favor so I could work in the kitchen under its heralded chef. But the reservation was canceled at the last minute; the *prêt-à-porter* and auto shows were both in full swing, and every courtesy room was reclaimed for the bloat of latecomers. There wasn't a room in Paris, I was told, that hadn't been scooped up for conventioneers. In a pinch, Expedia came up with the All Suites Hotel Plazza St.-Antoine, which, as luck would have it, was situated on the Rue du Faubourg. The double zs in the name, of course, should have been a dead giveaway, but I was too relieved to have a room confirmed and figured it couldn't be that bad, considering the location. The hotel was on the same street as the Ritz, right by the Opera, and it had three stars next to its name: a little bauble among jewels.

It wasn't until I got into a taxi at Gare Montparnasse that I realized my Zirconian error. The driver wanted to know *which* Rue du Faubourg, as there were several in the city. It took him some time paging through a *Plan de Paris* to sort out the problem. The one I was looking for, we determined, happened to be the Rue du Faubourg *St.-Antoine*, a little detail Expedia forgot to mention. And where was the Rue du Faubourg St.-Antoine? If you are a New Yorker and you've ever been to Jackson Heights, you have a pretty good idea. It was in the eleventh arrondissement, which is about as far as you can go in Paris before you hit the next town. It's where trolls live under the bridge. I had been hoping to check out a few great bistros while in Paris, but the cuisine in my neigh-

borhood was limited to Indian, Turkish, Sudanese, and Bangladeshi. The
only decent possibility—and that was stretching the point—was called the
Extra Old Café. If ever a name said it all, this one did the trick.

The hotel was practical for a certain kind of tourist. There were many
American guests who had never before visited Paris and were seeing the
city in a day-and-a-half sweep. Others had decided that any place was
central, no matter where they stayed. And some viewed the all-Indian
staff as a way of not patronizing the French. In their view, the hotel wasn't
pretentious, it wasn't hoity-toity, it wasn't . . . *French*.

There was certainly nothing charming about the facilities. My room
was an ugly airless cell, cramped and tatty, with a badly stained carpet and
1950s dormitory bedspread, which I pulled off and stashed in the closet.
A bouquet of Eau de Lysol hung in the air. A sad little refrigerator stood
in a corner, and when I opened it the shelves were empty, except for a
plate of chicken bones under plastic wrap.

"Is this the mini-bar?" I asked a porter who helped with my bags.

A huge grin of acknowledgment lit up his face. If I wanted sanctuary, somewhere to unwind, he suggested a bar on the corner, across from
Place de la Nation.

I made a beeline for the place, which was filling up with people who
met there regularly. It was a little before five, what the French call *purgatory*: too early for dinner, too late for lunch. Groups of men were sitting
quietly at postage-stamp–size tables, drinking Campari and eating hand-
fuls of pistachios. From my seat near the door, I could watch the strange,
eclectic sideshow streaming from the *Métro*, a mix of swarthy North
Africans and Middle Easterners, along with thick sorts in corduroys and
clunky shoes, the backbone of working-class Paris. At the table next to
me, a stubby little man lit a cigar and sucked at it like a nursing calf.

He must have seen me wince. "If it bothers you, I will put it out," he
said, in perfect English.

"Pas de problem, M'sieur," I lied.

He smiled slit-eyed, as if he'd caught me with my pants down. "You can
speak English to me," he said. "I worked in New York for three years—
and loved it."

He was a garmento by the name of Maxim, which seemed rather grand for such a feral old man. His clothes, while not shabby, revealed a disdain for Seventh Avenue. They were dated, conventional-looking knockoffs worn with a flamboyance meant to camouflage their age. Already there were shiny streaks on the elbows of his sport coat where the fabric had worn thin. There was dark stubble on his cheeks where he had forgotten to shave, and a few raw patches where he hadn't forgotten. But in every hair on his finely combed head there was a reminder of style. He had an air of sorrowing endurance. The skin at his temples pulsed as he sucked that cigar.

He'd been waiting eagerly for someone with whom he could reminisce about New York. "I loved it," he repeated, "loved how aggressive it was. The people there would eat you rather than let you get the upper hand. In Paris, everyone is a pussy. No backbone here at all. The boss looks at you funny, you roll over. In New York, you tell him to go fuck himself. *Hah!*"

He broke into a few bars of "I Love New York" and polished off a stiff shot of whiskey.

"You obviously love Paris, too," I suggested.

"Paris has its interesting points." He relit the cigar and sent smoke signals into the air. "See that truck over there?" he asked, pointing to an idling Hertz van that advertised a day rate on its panel. "You take the *Métro* out to Porte de Vincennes and you'll see hundreds of them parked by the *bois*. It's like a little city. They are called *cabinettes*, and if you knock on any one of them, you'll find whatever you want: women, men, young girls or young boys, young girls *and* boys, transsexuals, Africans, Asians, chimpanzees, whatever your heart desires. I could take you out there and show you around."

"I don't think so," I said. "I've sworn off chimpanzees."

He fired off a too-loud guffaw. "I like you, Mr. New York. I'm even going to buy you another one of those sissy wines you are drinking. Or would you rather have something more manly?"

"No, a sissy wine would be fine. And I'm going to buy you another shot of those depth charges that will kill you before you're sixty."

"I'm already sixty," he said, grinning triumphantly.

I thought he was seventy but had opted for flattery. Jesus, sixty—he looked almost dead already.

We spent a few hours talking about the precarious world situation— American politics, which seemed to be every European's favorite subject at the moment; French politics, which Maxim considered as dull and toothless as his country; German politics, which intrigued him because the old Communist regime seemed to be on the upswing; and British politics, which he described by making little doglike whimpering sounds.

"America squandered so much goodwill," he said, between shots that were coming faster than automatic-weapon fire. "After nine-eleven, everyone wanted to be an American, even the Algerians that pester us like fleas. Even my mother-in-law, the French purist." He spat on the sidewalk in her honor. "Then, Bush invades Iraq and America is shit. Everywhere, not just in France, which you whip like a dog. All of Europe is disgusted. You should be ashamed."

He waited for me to defend my country and grew irritated when I refused. There was nothing I could say that would justify such a mess. It had been like that since I'd landed in Europe. Everyone I met wanted some kind of explanation. They weren't anti-American, as Maxim implied; rather, they were disappointed, embarrassed. They'd expected something better from Washington. America had been their last best hope.

Maxim's voice clawed. "What are you doing in Paris, Mr. America, scouting for the next invasion? Perhaps your president intends to ban French toast."

I explained that my dream was to learn the secrets of great cooking. "But even if I have good teachers in Paris, being stranded in this neighborhood won't help. There is no place to eat, no imaginative French food. My presence here is as contingent as that of the refugees. I feel like a gourmet adrift in Nebraska."

Maxim contemplated me impersonally over the rim of his glass. After a reflexive cough, he stood up abruptly, the glass light in his hand, while trying to remove a cell phone from his breast pocket with the other hand. In the jumble, he sloshed some whiskey on his lapel. "Wait here," he said, dabbing at it with a napkin. Then he stalked off toward the bar, presumably to freshen his drink.

I don't know why, my first night in Paris, I wasted time sitting there for another twenty minutes. At some point, I gave up thinking that Maxim would reappear. My thoughts had shifted to tomorrow, to a cooking class that sounded promising.

The hour was getting late, and by the time I shaved and showered for dinner and took the *Métro* to a decent bistro, it would be almost midnight, which was too complicated. Going back to the hotel was an even more depressing idea, but it seemed like the most sensible alternative. Perhaps I should grab a good salad somewhere nearby and then hit the sack. But as I got up to leave, Maxim corkscrewed his way through the crowded bar and motioned for me to stay put. He had called his wife, who just happened to have dinner waiting on the stove, more than enough to include a hungry guest from America, and if I didn't mind a little hike up five flights of stairs, he promised a meal, by God, I would never forget.

It was as lovely an invitation as anyone could expect, and it made me feel welcome and alive in the midst of this ugly but diverse neighborhood, knowing that a stranger had offered me a home-cooked meal. At the same time, I couldn't help remembering an episode of *Law and Order* in which an ostensible dinner guest wound up a corpse in a maniac's stairwell. I cut a sidelong glance at Maxim, who looked about as wholesome as Hannibal Lecter.

We walked a few blocks to a stately old Haussmann-era building with graffiti slashed across the front doors. There were flowers in the window boxes and enough lights in open windows to reveal a pattern of silhouettes though the curtained gaps. Competing strains of music helped to ease my fears. In all honesty, a fire-snorting beast couldn't have driven me from Maxim's flat. As we entered, I was hit with a blast of a richly scented braise so intense, so powerful, redolent of wood smoke, that my saliva began to run. Dogs don't drool as readily, I thought. I stood without moving, filling my lungs with the aphrodisiac, struggling to identify the source.

Maxim sniffed the air with his bulbous hound's nose. "Ah, a veal roast," he said, shrugging indifferently. "Eat some, just to be polite, even if it tastes like shit."

He said it deliberately, of course, to antagonize his wife, Solange, who sighed as if in resignation. She was a small, stooped, aristocratic woman with a European sense of order, whose vexed expression seemed compressed around long sufferance. I could tell that she was used to Maxim's blustering, which appeared to have no effect on her whatsoever, and she treated him with the kind of parental scorn lavished on a habitual mischief-maker. It wasn't clear whether she enjoyed this role or was simply inured to it. Even so, she must have been made of something very hard to endure such treatment.

Dismissing her dinner as "a veal roast" was like calling Krug's Clos du Mesnil a fizzy wine. It was a masterpiece . . . a tour de force. . . . If I'd been born with Cyrano's eloquence, I might have rattled off a litany of platitudes. But of words, I only had three: "This is incredible."

In all my travels, I had never been served such a meal. Even my friend Sandy's food was . . . different . . . refined. This was down-and-dirty, as if it had been dug out of the ground, and it reminded me of my Hungarian grandmother's goulash, honest old-country fare. There were grease stains branded on the pot, and bits of meat stuck to the side, and a certain smell, elusive and smoky, that went with something long simmered. It had the earmarks of home cooking all over it.

The veal seemed to float in a dense trough of rich brown stock infused with white wine, spices, and fresh herbs. It was surrounded by mounds of garlicky sautéed onions and sweet carrots. Meaty roasted *cèpes* the size of handballs filled another bowl, along with fork-smashed *boulangère* potatoes crisped with bits of bacon and caramelized onions.

I looked at Maxim to see if he appreciated the food, but it was impossible to tell. He was preoccupied, expounding fiery views on Jacques Chirac's economic indiscretions, and he ate like an animal, gums bared, teeth gnashing like a trench plow. His hands with their tobacco stains never stopped moving. Le Pen . . . the skinheads . . . the thirty-five-hour work week. . . . Every so often, Solange leaned over and, wordlessly, refilled his plate, but she might have been serving lime Jell-O for all his obliviousness.

Dinner stretched on into the early hours of morning, filled with conversation and bickering and tankards of wine. I was delighted by the situation and relieved to be traveling alone, to be able to interact, to be myself. There was something hideously appealing about these characters, Maxim and Solange. They had an unusual repellent charm. They were smart and wickedly cynical, with convoluted good humor, but infuriating, like cats. At times their behavior was difficult to parse. Was it cruel or harmless teasing? An act they replayed for strangers? Sitting with them made me appreciate the complexity of marriage, all of its demands and considerations, and the compromises that are made.

I was confused to have felt this way in front of strangers. But I was also very grateful for their hospitality, which had saved me from a night of certain loneliness and self-examination.

Around three o'clock, I felt my residual energy give out and asked for directions to the hotel. Maxim walked me back to the hotel entrance, and when we shook hands, he looked at me dolefully and said, "I wish we had stayed in New York. There was much less there for me to despise."

We said goodnight and good-bye, and I promised to call before I left Paris and give him an update about the cooking. Then he walked slowly along the pavement in the opposite direction, cutting as sorrowful a figure as anyone I had ever seen.

I grew more confused than ever. I have to do something, I thought, otherwise I'll wind up angry all the time, like Maxim. Being alone like this in Paris was far too anguishing. Much as I loved the city, all I wanted was to go home. I took the stairs up to my room and found myself back on my trusty Expedia home page. No Rue du Faubourg for me this time. It was the Plazza Hotel or nothing.

There wasn't enough time the next morning to finalize arrangements for a flight to New York. Arrangements require initiative; I needed resolution.

In the meantime, I'd already arranged to take a cooking class with Samira Hradsky, who offered intimate one-day seminars in her Paris flat. According to a brochure, she claimed to teach students how to whip out a five-course meal in a few hours' time, which seemed preposterous in a city where cooks struggled for months to perfect a simple *demi-glace*.

This sounded like a kitchen version of the poetry slam. I grew even more skeptical after a phone conversation with Chef Hradsky confirming my enrollment. "Meet me tomorrow morning at the stairs by the Argentine *Métro*," she said, with an air of cold-war intrigue. "I'll have a blue shopping cart and a cast on my left hand."

At the appointed hour, the four of us waiting there, all strangers— Penny and Howie from Vermont, and Stephanie from California—converged on a woman with a cast, who subsequently threatened to call the police. Fortunately, Samira came along a few minutes later to defuse the situation. An exotic, dark-haired woman as high-strung as a Pekingese, she looked like any Parisian housewife on her daily shopping rounds. She was in her mid-forties, I'd say, with a small pear-shaped body and a fine, proud face, with dark eyes and skin so olive that it revealed an obvious Middle Eastern heritage. Her English, which she spoke with a kind of breathless alacrity, was perfect, without any trace of accent, and she moved with the same kind of breeziness despite the cast.

"Here's the plan," she disclosed, leading us around the corner into the Poncelet Market district, a warren of shops and outdoor stalls along the Rue Bayen. "We'll see what looks good, then decide what to cook, after which we'll head back to my flat and get started."

We went along the bleak, crowded street, intermingling with the everyday shoppers. This was one of the local marketplaces where Parisians bought their essential groceries. Women with straw baskets slung over each arm picked through the stalls in as routine and impersonal a manner as they might select socks. For them, this was no more unusual than a tour through the aisles at Stop & Shop, but to me it was pure romance. There were fruits and vegetables of a quality I had seldom seen—tomatoes that actually smelled like tomatoes, pears bursting with perfect ripeness, eggplants whose skins shone like the finish of a new Saab. Bouquets of

clumsily tied herbs spilled from baskets, and the variety of beans and berries was extraordinary. Daringly, when no one was looking, I palmed a few
of the tiny *fraises des bois* and gobbled them with silly pleasure. The taste
shocked my mouth with a kind of tart, anesthetizing sweetness, which
lasted an unreasonably long time, until I blunted it with some bread.

In the stores behind the stalls, vendors tended counters of fish and
chickens and smoked meats and cheese and bread right out of the oven.
Each gave off a smell as identifiable as my own skin, but it was invigorating to walk down the street and inhale the lush combination of scents in
the morning city air. The smells were fruitier and more pungent than what
I was accustomed to, from the lack of packaging or refrigeration, especially in the summer months when freshness was insanely volatile. Even
so, the straw baskets filled up fast. Women who'd arrived empty-handed
left the market loaded down like pack mules. I gazed with envy at their
bulging baskets, imagining the simple meals they would yield.

As soon as we hit the market, I scampered up and down the stalls,
gaping at the embarrassment of riches, while my classmates took pictures of mussels and tender lettuces and cradled vegetables as if they'd
been handed Fabergé eggs. "Oh, just *look at these*," Penny cooed, fingering a crate of black figs. Her husband tickled her neck with fennel fronds.
Everyone ogled the langoustines.

I felt a flash of mortification. We behaved like goddamned . . . *rubes
. . . tourists . . . Americans.* For a moment or two, I became self-conscious
and drifted a few steps behind, pretending to be on my own, lest anyone
mistake me for a comrade. When Samira explained how to differentiate
between male and female eggplants, I wandered away on the pretext of
inspecting radishes. But almost at once I realized my mistake. There was
nothing shameful about exuberance. We had come to Paris with the spirit
of discovery and fun.

"This looks promising," said Samira, holding up a plump piece of fish
with a blue-gray skin as snazzy as a Missoni weave. "Anyone have an idea
what it is?"

I had a sneaky feeling it was cod. In fact, it was *dos de cabillaud*, the
thick, sweetest fillet of cod from the part not touching the stomach. But I

hesitated a few seconds before blurting out an answer, lest anyone think I was a know-it-all. I kept it to myself, looking sideways at the keen, joyful faces of my classmates, who stared with fascination at the meaty, milk-white surface of the fish.

"What about the salmon family?" I asked Samira. "Is salmon caught around this area?"

"Not even close!" She sounded pleased. "Salmon is usually smaller and has a more colorful, reflective flesh. This has a big, white flake and is less oily. Most of you should be able to recognize this because, at one time not too long ago, it probably fed more Americans than beef or chicken."

She was wrong in that respect, but I wasn't going to queer her credibility. "Then it must be cod," I said aloud, as innocently as I knew how.

She patted me tenderly on the head, teacher's pet, and marched off to have our aquatic treasure skinned and cleaned.

The menu took shape as we made the rounds: a citrusy salmon appetizer; cream of artichoke and Armagnac soup, followed by *fruits de mer à l'armoricaine*—a Brittany-style fish stew starring two kilos of that gorgeous cod—fingerling potatoes perfumed with olive oil and *herbes de Provence*; saffron basmati rice; arugula salad with raspberry vinaigrette; and, for dessert, a deadly chocolate Grand Marnier tart. It was an ambitious program, loaded with challenge. An hour later, steering Samira's swollen shopping cart through the streets of the seventeenth arrondissement, we tromped into her flat, ready to cook.

The place was tastefully posh, somewhere on the fringe of the sixteenth, near the Bois de Boulogne, in a building that had been commissioned by Napoleon III. A young Russian maid dressed in jeans and an obscenely skin-tight T-shirt unpacked our groceries while we waited in a room that had been recently enlarged by combining an adjoining apartment. A postcard view of Paris glistened in the picture window, whose curtains had been drawn to make an impression. Samira's food must be pretty sumptuous, I thought. She sure played to the crowd.

The three-hour class, held in a commodious, fully equipped galley kitchen, was more like a cooking party than formal instruction. In situations like these, where everyone was new, there was always a feeling-out process, like a blind date, when the personal baggage gets unpacked and you begin to realize who and what you are up against. There were a few awkward moments. But a camaraderie developed from the get-go as we gathered around a granite-topped island, sipping sauvignon blanc, trading kitchen-disaster stories, and gaping at the food. In the meantime, Samira cleaned and arranged an array of equipment in preparation for our lesson. I eyed a razor-sharp mandoline with extreme prejudice.

"The main thing I want all of you to do is to relax," she said, wielding a gizmo suitable for a pelvic exam that turned out to be an olive pitter. "I'm going to make things easy for you. We're going to have fun, so that you'll enjoy cooking. This isn't LeNôtre, where you have to measure every ingredient to a fraction of a gram. And my food isn't *haute cuisine* intended for royalty. But it tastes and looks great, and you can make it in your own home."

For the most part, Samira lived up to her promises. Within half an hour, she had each of us chopping, slicing, dicing, and grinding faster than a Veg-O-Matic. We learned the proper way to fillet a salmon, removing the minuscule pinbones with a needle-nose pliers, and to skin and seed tomatoes. Piping out whipped cream from a plastic bag—a task I'd always equated with quantum physics—was conveyed with calculable ease. Eventually, individual assignments were handed out to speed the process, while Samira hovered, critiquing and offering tips. Squeamish Penny, who refused to touch the fish, was assigned to clarify the butter; Howie, who refused to touch alcohol, reduced the stock; Stephanie, who refused my advances, prepared basmati rice; and I rolled out a sweet pastry for the tart.

"I always do the desserts first," Samira said, "so that if it's a disaster, there is still plenty of time to come up with something suitable in its place."

Her crust skipped a few steps that were part of every classic pastry preparation, but she insisted they weren't necessary. Later, when it was time to peel and seed six plum tomatoes, she stopped me from making little slits in their skins before plunging them into boiling water.

"I don't bother with that," she said, taking them out of my hands. "I just put them into a bowl, cover them with boiling water, count to eighteen, and then run them under cold water." Incredibly, her method worked. The skins peeled neatly away from the fruit, which remained firm to the touch.

"What about an ice-water bath afterward?" I wondered.

"Nope. Feel this." She cut one of the tomatoes in half and held it out for my inspection. "The inside is still cold. All that stuff about making slits and ice-water baths—forget it!"

Samira Hradsky, as it turned out, was the Rachael Ray of the French cooking-school circuit. But it was hard to fault her shorthand methods. Somehow they worked, worked without fuss. Besides, she knew exactly how to keep things on track, with the right mix of instruction and giddy encouragement. When the situation threatened to overwhelm us—at one time we juggled six dishes in various stages of preparation—she summoned her young housekeeper to help with things like debearding mussels and washing the lettuces.

Through it all, I couldn't help noticing the dining room across the foyer from the kitchen, where a long antique table had been set with a gorgeous hand-embroidered tablecloth, bone china, and heirloom silverware. Napkins were folded like swans above each place setting. Sterling knife rests were placed to the right of the plates, long tapers were positioned in silver holders, with enough glassware to stock a bar. A cross section of fine wines stood at attention on the sideboard. This was going to end well, with a lovely meal, and I picked up my pace a notch in anticipation.

We worked all morning and through much of the early afternoon without coming up for air. As the lesson progressed, Stephanie and I seemed to take more interest in the work and broke down the recipes, often on our own, while Penny seemed a little bewildered. This type of cuisine was way beyond her ken. Certainly she never cooked this way at home, and I doubted she ate in restaurants where gastronomic food was featured. From what she told us, she had no palate to speak of. She was determined not to put any unusual food in her mouth, especially the mussels or anything with fins or animals that might have been raised in a dark pen. But our excitement was contagious, and after much grimacing and eye-popping, she found everything "just fabulous . . . oh, just out of this world."

Samira knew exactly how to deal with a student like Penny, taking great pains to make sure that a lack of sophistication, if that's what it was, didn't spoil the experience for her. "Look," she told me in a private moment, "you've got to hand it to Penny. It took a lot of courage for her to enroll in this class, considering she knows practically nothing about food. She did this to expand her horizons, and to have fun. If anyone wants to apply some snobby standard to her, that's their business. But I know women like her. They go home, they head for the kitchen, and they begin to experiment, even if it just means eating more daringly."

She was right, of course, which contributed to another aspect of my education. I was so quick to judge people, typecasting them by what they ate and how they behaved around food, that I feared becoming what I dreaded most: a self-righteous food snob. And something of a show-off, to go with it. Earlier, in the throes of prep, I had suggested to Howie that he chop some onions and peppers into a *mirepoix*, suspecting that he wouldn't know the term (just as I hadn't when the journey began). It confirmed every suspicion when he returned a helpless blank stare, and I might have made something more of it, thrown him a snooty biscuit or two, until I looked up, over his shoulder, at my reflection in the kitchen mirror, and thought, "Only an asshole would do something like that."

The truth was that Howie, Penny, and I were on the same track. Unlike me, however, they had never regarded food as an obsession, most likely not even a passion. But this experience—for all of us—was transforming, in one respect or another. Here we were in Paris, preparing *fruits de mer à l'armoricaine* on a day when the rest of the world was on a meat-loaf trajectory. (At least we imagined it that way.) If you consider that Penny and Howie had never tasted fennel or monkfish, never prepared a mayonnaise from scratch, their presence here was quite remarkable. Their sense of a travel detour—taking a cooking course in the home of a serious international chef instead of a *Bateau-Mouche* down the Seine—was pretty adventurous. I had to hand it to them, they surprised me.

Their openness was refreshing, a wonderful thing. It was unconnected from the effluvia of urban pretensions, trained noses, and jaded palates. They had no expectations, other than a kitchen safari into the unknown.

"This is a good group," I muttered, looking at my hands and mincing

some garlic that was already chopped too finely. "Isn't it funny how everything tastes better with a good group? A good group, for cooking—or
afternoons in Paris."

"All right, everyone, let's concentrate—let's finish the tart," said
Samira.

She stood across from us at the counter, with a pale-yellow pastry
wrapped around a porcelain rolling pin. She unfolded it over the tart pan
and pressed it snugly into place. She gave me a murderous stare when I
offered to prick the pastry shell with my fingernails, as I had seen Kate
Hill do during a similar demonstration.

"Not in my kitchen, buster," she said. "It's not elegant. I don't want
your dirty fingernails in my pastry, no matter how scrubbed they look. It's
disrespectful toward the food. We're going to do this with a fork."

For the tart, Stephanie had made a thick, fudgy filling of melted semi-
sweet and dark chocolate beaten with sugar, eggs, cream, and more than
a snootful of Grand Marnier, all of which she scooped into the shell and
smoothed with a spatula. Howie piped fancy rosettes of whipped cream
around the edges before his wife punctuated each white swirl with a raspberry. As an afterthought, I shaved curlicues of Belgian chocolate over the
top, using a vegetable peeler. Then we popped it into the refrigerator to
set for a few hours.

Samira fussed with each twist and turn we made, pulling us steadily,
assuredly, toward the grand performance, when our haphazard preparations coalesced into a spectacle of gorgeous dishes waiting to be served.
The dessert and salad were already spoken for, as were the herbed potatoes, roasting slowly in the oven. The artichoke soup, which needed to be
finished with *crème fraîche,* gave off a wonderful nutty aroma, but it was
the fish stew simmering on the stove that tantalized us most of all.

One of the best things about it was the simplicity of its preparation. As
with most stews, it called for a quick sauté of vegetables with the right mix
of herbs, followed by a reduction in some combination of wine and stock.
This could be simmered and thickened as much as necessary, as long as
the liquids did not cook out. If meat happened to be the primary ingredient, it would have to be browned in advance, but with fish, all you had to

do was add it a few minutes before serving, simmering until the flesh was cooked through. Conveniently, it could be made in one pan, which is satisfying in a pinch, and we threw it together in no time at all.

FRUITS *de* MER À L'ARMORICAINE
(BRITTANY-STYLE SEAFOOD STEW)

4 Tbl. clarified butter (or half
   butter, half olive oil)
8 shallots, chopped finely
5 garlic cloves, minced
3 Tbl. fresh tarragon,
   chopped
1/4 tsp. cayenne pepper
4 Tbl. Cognac
1 cup dry white wine
1 cup fish stock (or clam
   broth)

1 lb. plum tomatoes, seeded
   and chopped
1 Tbl. tomato paste
1/2 cup heavy cream or half-
   and-half
salt and pepper to taste
4 large fillets cod, halibut, sea
   bass, or fleshy white fish
   (about 2 lb.)
chopped parsley for garnish

Melt the butter (or butter and oil) in a large sauté pan over medium-high heat. Add the shallots and sauté 3 to 4 minutes, stirring constantly until softened. Stir in the garlic and cook 1 minute; stir in the tarragon and cayenne and cook a few seconds more.

Carefully add the Cognac off the heat, then boil until it is evaporated. (You can also flame the Cognac, which heightens and enriches the flavor.) Add the wine and let boil until it is reduced to about 4 tablespoons. Blend in the stock (or broth), tomatoes, and tomato paste and bring everything to a ferocious boil. Reduce heat to low, cover, and simmer gently 30 minutes.

Add the cream and simmer, uncovered, 5 minutes, tasting to correct the salt and pepper. Increase the heat to medium-high, add the seafood to the sauce, bring it to a boil, and simmer until the fish is opaque, about 5 minutes. Cover, reduce the heat, and cook 10 minutes more.

Transfer to a large, deep serving dish and garnish with chopped parsley.
Serve with rice on the side.

Serves 6

We improvised a bit with the stew, adding a handful of mussels, shrimp, and scallops to the pan a few minutes before it was due to come off the heat, slapping on the lid just long enough for the mussels to open. Stephanie had noticed them on a shelf in the refrigerator, and Samira, as giddy as a schoolgirl, urged us to experiment—experiment!—indulging our creative imaginations at will. The shellfish added something richer and slightly fatty to the dish, giving it a hearty southern twist; you might see a stew like this served in Marseille or Nice. I've made it both ways many times since then, and I prefer the pared-down version for more elegant affairs, adding the shellfish when friends crowd around the table and the mussel shells start to fly.

By the time we brought it to the table, the place looked like one of those feature spreads in *Bon Appétit* in which an impossibly handsome couple entertains impossibly beautiful friends at their impossibly picturesque chalet in Aspen. Suddenly everything seemed possible. We were no longer peons with our faces pressed to the pane. The four of us—strangers only a few hours earlier—knew that we had pulled off the perfect dinner party. We knew that no attack of pretense, no fear of insecurity could exclude us from this elegant scene.

The ride back to the hotel was a long, oppressive, forty minutes on the *Métro* through a succession of dreary stops. The car was practically empty, and its emptiness made me even lonelier than I'd felt on the platform. The day's cooking class had been a huge success. But being alone here in Paris, as I have indicated, felt strange. It wasn't a good place to visit with a broken heart. Everywhere I turned, there was romance of some sort, from the way the sun hit the red-tile rooftops at sundown to the handsome couples crowding cafés on the Boulevard St.-Germain. It was impossible to walk ten feet without feeling the unyielding grip of love. An odd mix of resentment and sorrow filled me as I realized that the only role here for me was that of envious observer.

It was difficult keeping my eyes open on the train back to Nation. I felt listless and a little wasted, no surprise considering all the wine that had been consumed. The shuffle of songs on my iPod kept me alert and amused. No deejay in his right mind would follow Jimi Hendrix with Peggy Lee, then Bryan Ferry, as compatible as guests at a Balkan mixer, but somehow it worked in this context. There was something deliciously absurd about the mix, even more so in this era of focus groups and play-lists. I shrugged, thinking that maybe machines *were* smarter—better suited to entertain. Perhaps there was a machine that could sort out my dinner parties.

It was just after eight when I arrived at the top of Rue du Faubourg *St.-Antoine.* The streetlights had just come on, and the processional to and from dinner destinations had shifted into gear. I'd decided to pass on an evening meal. I thought of going to Pierre Gagniere, as a treat, or back to La Régalade for the umpteenth time, but getting anywhere from here was such a schlep, and anyway the food at Samira's was enough to hold me for the night. We'd done a hell of a job in that tiny kitchen of hers. The class was first-rate, jam-packed with useful tips and instruction, and the dishes we prepared were excellent, as good as any restaurant food I'd eaten since arriving in France. The fish stew was a cross between *bouil-labaisse* and *bourriade,* loaded with chunks of moist, succulent cod, and a thick, rich sauce that everyone lapped up with spoons. It surprised us how we'd brought it together so fast, without much fuss.

The same with the potatoes, which we'd roasted with copious herbs. At the last minute, Samira gave them an extra-large splash of olive oil and a handful of bay leaves—there must have been a dozen, at least —which released an extravagant, tropical perfume into the room. Nothing to it, but the result was wonderful, incorporating a greater intensity of flavor saturated with spice. "A nod to my Middle Eastern heritage," she said, claiming "half Lebanese, half Saudi, and a quarter Kurdish" ancestry (to say nothing of being mathematically challenged). There was a wonderful bluntness about Samira; she was gregarious and warm and exhausting, perhaps in response to a rigid upbringing that confined her to Mama's kitchen, especially during summers, when all her friends went off to camp. That, according to Samira, was where she learned how to cook—a prelude to marriage—which her mother enforced by browbeating her with a doctrine meant to prepare her for the future: *Burn it in my house, instead of your husband's house.*

In any case, there was no burning that afternoon, not even any singeing by her impetuous students. The cooking had been intensive, a thorough five-hour marathon covering all bases, and the meal a celebration of our collective effort. I only really began to appreciate how productive we'd been when we were finally seated and took an overview of the table. The amount of food was stunning, a feast—nine or ten dishes spread around like artwork on display. Everything looked and smelled sumptuous, handled with a skillful touch. Even the rice, generally a throw-in, had been adorned for the occasion, unmolded from a rounded pan and dressed with fresh herbs and pimiento slices.

The touches were subtle and real. You can't learn how to cook in such a short-term class; that is, you won't leave Samira's having mastered a full repertoire of recipes. But it went a long way toward demystifying the process, along with staging an enjoyable cooking experience, and for all of that I was grateful.

The lobby of my hotel was as deserted as those onrushing *Métro* platforms. The desk clerk, an elderly Sikh with a dark purple bruise on his cheekbone, gave me the once-over when I asked for the room key. After he pushed it very solemnly across the counter, I told him I would appreciate it if he would send up a half-bottle of Champagne, some cheese, and a slice of the apple tart that I had spied in the coffee shop earlier in the morning. He said nothing but wrote it down, with the tip of a stubby pencil scratching across the paper like a scurrilous cat.

It took me a long time to crawl out of the shower. I didn't want to leave the cleansing warmth but was pleasantly surprised, if somewhat suspicious, to find the refreshments on a tray by the bed. Even more incredibly, the Champagne was very special, one of the best of its kind. As I tore off the foil, the phone began ringing. It was a representative from Delta calling to say they'd found a seat for me on a flight from Paris to New York. Home . . .

I hesitated, glancing out the window onto a nearby flat. I became hypnotized, bewitched by the rhythms in the surrounding courtyard, conjuring up a replay of the day. My mercurial, offbeat mind kept returning to Samira's kitchen, to the reward of solid instruction and vibrant social exchange.

"Thanks," I said into the phone, "but I've changed my mind."

After hanging up, I popped the cork and muttered an appropriate toast, wondering, in fact, whether the glass was half empty or half full.

I had no business being in the kitchen of the Meurice. A friend had persuaded its executive chef to take me under his wing for a day, but I could tell from the moment I entered what a mistake had been made. The place hummed with precision; it was a citadel of culinary perfection, with standards of discipline right out of the Koran. It reminded me of a bottling plant, if you've ever been to one, except that it was two rooms instead of one. Besides, it was *Le Meurice*, the chilliest joint in Paris—all Brioni suits, Chopard jewelry, and a lobby with the coziness quotient of Versailles. On the way in, I'd already passed Warren Christopher, Sting, the entire ministry of an emerging African nation, and that ladies'-apparel big-shot from Long Island, you know, the one who stays at all the five-star hotels and regards them as if they were discos. There was a stiff unerring orthodoxy to the Meurice that I could appreciate from afar, but as far as cooking there went, it intimidated the hell out of me.

The real reason, though, for putting myself through such an ordeal was that the chef, Yannick Alléno, had the reputation for being the most talented cook in Paris. You couldn't walk into a serious restaurant that season without hearing his name. When he took over the kitchen in the summer of 2003, *Le Figaro* proclaimed it "the gastronomic event of the year." I happened to have dinner there the night of his début, and it was the kind of mouthwatering experience that surpassed the hype. The food was just brilliant. The most jaded pickle-faced epicureans twitched like marionettes in their seats as one dish after another appeared like the highlights at Sotheby's spring auction. I overheard someone at a nearby table say Alléno's menu charted the crossroads of French gastronomy, but if so, it was the kind of crossroads Robert Johnson sang about. Waiters served wild duck in a crust of Indian spices nesting on a plump roasted peach half. Mounds of puffed potatoes studded with *girolles* had been sweetened with dried apricot. Alléno presented a sea-bass fillet with aromatic herbs, sweet-pepper fondue, and sardine cream. If you were lucky, there was room for one of his signature desserts. I did hand-to-hand combat with *crème brûlée* ice cream swaddled in an orange-flavored biscuit and decorated with tiny wild strawberries that someone had shipped from Andalusia.

Alléno bagged his first star faster than a hooker on Hollywood Boulevard. By the time I walked through the door again, he'd received a precious second, with rumors of the third being withheld simply to stabilize his ascent. (He has since hit the trifecta.) Some said the Michelin judges were influenced by reports of fiery tantrums, which were legendary. In any case, the starriest object in the Meurice was Alléno himself, a ridiculously handsome character, so suave and utterly French, with an ever-ready smile that was more like a fixture than a warm embrace.

He charmed me from the get-go, which was his manner, and I was duly taken in. It took a certain style to run such a fabulous establishment, and he had it in spades. He knew how to set a room in motion just by walking into it. There was something commanding about him. It had nothing to do with the way he cooked or his exquisite suit or the fine bones of his face. It was the aura, the star power he radiated that made people react so spiritedly.

He gave me the first-class tour, including a peek at the process he used for "a new creation" that involved alternating slices of grilled eggplant, *cèpe, boudin noir,* and Granny Smith apple in an apple-basil vinaigrette.

I was beginning, though, to feel like a politician on a fact-finding tour. I'd met the mastermind, seen the kitchen, and glimpsed the *creative process.* Now, if I guessed correctly, we'd probably go play golf.

Next best thing: Alléno turned up his smile, patted me on the head, and stashed me at an out-of-the-way station to clean a tubful of *cèpes*. This was his lame device for letting an outsider feel like part of the kitchen crew. It almost felt as if he were making fun of my pursuit. Well, I'd be damned if I would give him the pleasure of seeing my abject disappointment. Not a flinch or a hesitation showed on my face. Smile frozen in place, I slipped into an apron, cursing my luck, and wishing I had gone somewhere more sensitive, more willing to play. I was serving a purpose, and even a worthwhile one, but I resented it.

It is amazing how many shapes and idiosyncrasies you can attribute to a *cèpe*. After an hour brushing those babies, I'd identified half the animal kingdom; in the third hour, I discovered one in the image of the Virgin Mary. If I called the tabloids, it occurred to me, vengeance would be mine.

I wasted the whole day doing KP at the Meurice. Around six, during dinner prep, I spotted my friend Claudia talking to a waiter and waved her over.

"You're getting very special treatment," she said, without a trace of irony. "Few mortals ever spend an entire day with Yannick."

"I can only imagine," I mumbled, wiping the *cèpe* doo off my hands. "Most, if I've guessed correctly, die of boredom. Am I right?"

Somehow I managed to convey my frustration and begged her to intercede with Yannick on my behalf.

"I need to learn something constructive," I pleaded. "Anything—a recipe or a preparation. But, please—no more scut work. I don't iron, clean blinds, vacuum carpets, or *clean fucking cèpes!*"

It worked. A half-hour later, Yannick walked over with that smile fixed on his face.

"So I hear you want to learn how to cook. Okay," he said, steering me toward the stove, "let's see you make an omelet."

I must have stared at him, blank-faced, for an impudent length of time. Finally, I muttered: "You son of a bitch."

It was a trick, and his delighted laugh told me I had caught him red-handed. Making an omelet was a litmus test in practically every good kitchen in France; it determined whether or not a chef got hired. Stories abounded about seasoned cooks who bungled once-in-a-lifetime opportunities, scraping omelets off a cast-iron pan while a stone-faced chef harrumphed in disgust.

"If you have the skills to make an omelet, it means you have decent hands," my friend Sandy once told me. "A cook has to make his hands do what his mind wants them to do, without thinking about it. That's what makes a cook so valuable working the line. When you're under huge pressure like that, you need to have skills that you aren't thinking about. Chefs are always saying to each other, 'I'll send you this guy—he's got good hands.' It means that he is a real craftsman. Everyone is always talking about the *art* of food. Well, if you can't be a craftsman, you'll never be an artist."

An omelet took skill; it was an accomplishment, a work of art. At my best, I turned out a Greek diner special.

As if to prove a point, I whipped out a fluffy three-egg specimen that never failed to satisfy my daughter. Yannick sat behind me in a chair, with one leg crossed over the other. I could feel his smug grin burning into my back.

"What's this?" he asked with mock disdain when I presented my omelet.

I stared at him, refusing to answer.

"I thought you were going to make an omelet. So?"

The weight of the pan felt good in my hand. I could kill him with one well-placed blow.

I clapped a hand to my heart. "I suppose I don't get the job."

"You wouldn't get the job in a brasserie. But you're in luck." He stood up and took off his jacket. "I am going to teach you how to make an omelet."

Big fucking deal, I thought. You get to show off and put me in my place at the same time. At least I had the sense to keep this to myself.

A transformation came over Yannick as he collected a few utensils for the demo. I watched him with bemusement as he combed the fringes of the room, picking up this and that—a whisk, a metal bowl, a fork, a dozen eggs.

He was no longer the debonair two-star impresario but a journeyman cook, eyes hard and focused, all business, with a steady, sure touch. He clutched a scratched-up nonstick pan, not a pretty thing, but well seasoned. With all the instinctive moves, he poured a little straw-colored oil in the bottom and swirled it around. I stepped back to allow him more room.

"Let's start with the base," he said, breaking three eggs into a small metal bowl. He beat them with gusto, dipping a fork deep into the bowl and lifting the egg high in the air. "You have to get underneath it, getting a good amount of air into eggs, beating until the mixture forms a mousse." A fine spray of bubbles frothed along the surface. He sprinkled a pinch of salt into the bowl, followed by a grind of white pepper. When the oil began to sizzle, he turned up the flame.

"It has to be very hot. You wait for a moment until the oil separates in the pan." After a few seconds, he dropped a half-tablespoon of butter into the pan and immediately poured in the eggs. "Now watch carefully. Everything happens very fast."

The process reminded me of a choreographed dance routine. His whole body moved with fluency as he swirled the egg around the pan, hands, shoulders, hips, back, tilting the pan this way and that, bent over the stove like an evangelist. There was a flow and authority in the way he worked. Order reigned. Standing before his steamy pulpit, he conveyed the impression that the stove's heat was his heat, and if the burners ceased to function, he would conduct the body heat he generated to finish the job.

"It's all in the wrist," he said, transferring the pan to his left hand and using his right to run the flat end of the fork back and forth across the bottom, slurrying the egg, as it firmed, toward the center. "Now we change," he said, gripping the handle in his right hand and tilting the pan away from him. The omelet began to slide a bit, just an inch or two toward the edge. He changed hands once more, holding the handle with his left and hitting his wrist three times—"*Boom! Boom! Boom!*" he intoned—causing the omelet to roll gently his way in three neat folds. Grabbing a plate, he took the pan handle in his right hand, tilting the pan at a forty-five degree angle so that the omelet simply rolled over itself onto the plate.

"*Voilà!*" he said, as if it were the most natural outcome.

As far as omelets went, it was a masterpiece. There was nothing to it but egg and expertise. It had a beautiful, unblemished texture, glistening with a faint perspiration of butter on its brow. It was everything an omelet should be—downy, creamy, with a slight spring, almost like pastry in your mouth. After my first delicious bite, Yannick grabbed the plate from me and slid the omelet into the trash.

"Now you make one," he said.

I nodded brightly and took up the metal bowl. I tried to seem confident, a little cocksure perhaps, especially when it came to breaking the eggs, which I did one-handed like a pro. Even the mousse produced an approving nod from Yannick.

"Okay, here you go . . . ," he said, winging a chunk of butter into the pan.

He stood over my left shoulder, gently barking out directions. "Good, good," he said encouragingly, when I scrambled the egg on the bottom of the pan. "Now, begin to roll. No . . . no! Change hands. No—hold the pan differently. Okay, good. Now, hit your wrist—*Boom! Boom! Boom!*"

I didn't know omelets were alive. Mine jumped out of the pan and landed on the counter. He picked it up with a thumb and forefinger, holding it to the light. My cheek flushed under the discipline.

"Okay," he said flatly, "now we do another one."

The second, third, and fourth weren't bad. I was particularly fond of the ninth one, which seemed to scroll at will. From the eleventh omelet on, Yannick took over the *Boom! Boom! Boom!*—pounding me on the wrist with an open fist. After the sixteenth, a red strawberry formed on my forearm where his knuckles made contact. Finally, the eighteenth was perfect. I gazed up at him with pride, handing over the sweetest, purest, smoothest omelet that I had ever seen.

He studied it expressionlessly, his pedagogic spirit spent, and, after a moment, he nodded: "Now let's make an acceptable one."

Once we edged into the twenties, I was like any other torture victim lapsing into delirium. Nothing of consequence mattered anymore. I would even tell him where Jimmy Hoffa was buried.

"Boom! Boom! Boom!"

"Beneath the visitor's goalpost at Giants Stadium . . . the Secaucus toll booth on the New Jersey Turnpike . . . the pilings under the Verrazano Bridge . . ."

"Boom! Boom! Boom!"

Wasn't this covered under the Geneva Convention, I wondered, as omelet number twenty-three hit the pan with a splash.

"Ah . . . ," he sounded impassive. *"Voilà!"*

"What do you mean—*voilà?*"

"You understand French. It is an omelet, as I have taught you."

"You're kidding, right? What about doing another one? What about *Boom! Boom! Boom?*"

My pleas blew coolly on Yannick's face as he took the plate from me and decorated it with chervil and a few slices of fruit. With the flick of a hand, he signaled a cook's assistant.

"Where are you going with that?" I snapped at him, slightly louder than I had intended. Lowering my voice, I said, "That's my omelet," in the way a parent says, *my baby . . . my first born!*

"One omelet," Yannick said scornfully, taking a small slip of paper from his shirt pocket, "Room 609. We are sending it up." He put the paper on the plate and handed it to the assistant.

With Yannick's firm, dismissing nod, the omelet disappeared on a tray down the hall. Jarred by the speed with which it was gone, I wanted to race after it.

Suddenly, Yannick began to chuckle in a soft, sly, satisfied way and draped a brotherly arm over my shoulder. Like Louie and Rick after Elsa's quick departure, we walked off, shoulder to shoulder, in the direction of the freezers.

"Now," he said, "let's see what you do with sweetbreads."

⁂

After cooking at the Meurice, what do you do for an encore? That was easy for me, considering I was so good at courting trouble.

The next morning, just after ten, I wandered out of the garden at the

SDQ1xlldvb

Your order of October 2, 2015 (Order ID 113-2275254-6197868)

Qty.	Item		Item Price	Total
1	The Saucier's Apprentice: One Long Strange Trip through the Great Cooking Schools of Europe Spitz, Bob --- Paperback (** P-1-B180F144 **) 0393335380		$15.64	$15.64

This shipment completes your order.

Have feedback on how we packaged your order? Tell us at www.amazon.com/packaging.

Subtotal	$15.64
Tax Collected	$1.37
Order Total	$17.01
Paid via credit/debit	$17.01
Balance due	$0.00

Return or replace your item
Visit Amazon.com/returns

19/DQ1xlldvb/-1 of 1-//OAK5/second/5893516/1003-04:30/1002-21:15   JM2

Musée Rodin, walked across Rue de Varenne, and knocked on a warped, unmarked door that opened into a busy kitchen. It was Arpège, where they were expecting me: the frying pan into the fire.

If the Meurice was a new shining sentinel in the gastronomic universe, Arpège was a longtime superstar. The best French cooking was often conducted on its queue of stoves. The restaurant had soared into the three-star galaxy under *Überchef* Alain Passard, whose menus famously pared down overwrought traditional dishes to their most essential ingredients. Vegetable consommé replaced cream, herb emulsions stood in for butter. No effort was spared to create brilliant compositions with lightness and clarity. But Passard was known to get weird. In 2001, he announced a culinary fatigue with meat and fish, pledging to cook only vegetarian dishes from then on. Sandy D'Amato had eaten there soon after the reformation and told me, "The place was in the shit." A turf war raged among members of the waitstaff. It angered him to see Passard camped out by the door, chatting and autographing menus for *pensionnaires* while the kitchen was plunging down a slippery slope.

Among the Michelin aristocracy, there were a lot of places like that, grotesquely overpriced and riding on a reputation. They were big, stuffy rooms, with white-glove service at the tables and *maître d*'s whose ghoulish smiles softened you up for a proper roasting. If you were careful with the menu, you could still eat well; there were always one or two dishes that stood up to the glitter. But most people couldn't see past the VIP treatment and paid dearly for it.

Arpège, from what I could gather, never really suffered for its decline. The knowledgeable clients stopped coming, but there were more than enough high rollers willing to take their places. The status of eating there, the name, still gave off enough steam. In the meantime, the kitchen managed to work through a lot of internal strife. A kind of innocent excitement crept back into the food. Word on the street was fairly promising. By the time I hit Paris, I was excited about the opportunity to spend a few days there, hoping Passard would be back to form, newly inspired and creative and generous.

I knew enough not to interrupt the lunch prep and stood motionless in the doorway for several minutes, hoping for an invitation. The kitchen surprised me. It was small, shockingly so, in a way that had been dictated by history; the building must have been here, in the same condition, for hundreds of years. It reminded me of the cafés in the storefronts of Greenwich Village brownstones, those funny knock-kneed little places where every last inch was pressed into service. There were four stations with fourteen people shoehorned in, and a lot of touching, turning, and bumping in the lurch. A surprisingly young staff, in their mid- to late twenties, performed the line dance with panache, and there was an ambitious intensity in the bustle of prep.

I took off my sunglasses and replaced them with regular frames, wondering where Passard fit into the picture. I was curious about him—how he operated at the three-star level with a seemingly inexperienced crew. Restaurants like this usually maintained their culinary excellence with a strong personality at the helm, someone who ran the kitchen with a mix of discipline and fear. But I could see nothing of that here.

A door opened behind me, and I was greeted by Frédéric Le Clair, the restaurant's longtime manager and *maître d'*, who was handsome enough to play Ralph Fiennes's father. He certainly had the polish and personality to command the big screen. I can't remember much about what he told me except that I should enjoy my visit to Arpège and not hesitate to ask him for anything I might need.

"I'll try to stay out of everyone's way," I promised. "But I hope Mr. Passard will allow me to participate in the prep in some small way and possibly walk me through a recipe or two in a spare moment."

Frédéric threw me a most poignant look of condolence. "I'm afraid Mr. Passard doesn't cook much anymore," he said, bowing his head slightly.

I felt my exasperation surge back, anticipating yet another setback to my plans.

"But his son, David, is an excellent chef," he went on. "Perhaps you will find him a little more approachable than his father. In any case, you will have lunch in the dining room at the end of service, and there will be a chance to meet Mr. Passard."

Lunch . . . meet . . . It sounded like a brush-off to me. For the next hour, I did nothing but watch the kitchen at work. It flattened me. I felt forlorn, but I said nothing to Frédéric. Besides, there wasn't much I could do to insert myself into that tiny space. Lunch prep was breakneck, like a military exercise. The room spun in a perpetual blur, everyone performing specialized tasks, and there was no time for anybody to stop and teach an amateur. But I learned a great deal just by watching—how cooks held their knives and chopped, handled food, organized their *mises-en-place* and cooking agendas, and used such basic ingredients as butter, cream, and oil. Even the most basic enthusiast could absorb some of the kitchen confidence that the cooks had and develop a sense of organization, especially when it comes to preparing five or six things at the same time.

Months later, after I returned home, there was an opportunity for me to cook dinner for a few friends, but without enough time, really, to labor over the recipes. It was supposed to be a casual get-together, but, of course, I was determined to put on a show. An hour before they arrived, I felt the nerve-racking surge of adrenaline, the charge that churns in your gut and turns your hands into clumsy, defective machinery. More often than not, this was usually the point at which I'd begin to lose it—storming around the kitchen, rushing steps, getting sloppy, regretting the whole frantic affair.

Instead, I remember putting down my knife and taking a few steps away from the counter. There was a bottle of wine, a pretty good Chinon, that I planned to serve with the meal, and I poured myself a glass. I sipped it with care and closed my eyes, allowing the warmth to wash over me. Relax, I insisted. Picture the kitchen at Arpège.

I felt a sweet smile of recognition spread on my face. The entire cast of characters danced behind my eyes: Frédéric, David Passard, the cooks from Mali, Spain, Japan, and the young guy with the perfect hair from Sweden. Kurt? Klas. Head of the klas. As systematic as a smorgasbord. There was a tempo I was searching for in the dreamy memory, a particular rhythm that syncopated the energy at Arpège. It wasn't high-strung or florid. If anything, the pace of work there was constant, metronomic. Precise. Nothing at all manic to disrupt the easy flow.

Water began boiling in a kettle, and I allowed its whistle to break the

dreamy spell. As a rule, I keyed in on sounds and movements to help settle any anxiety I felt, the vibration of a crowd, the mechanics of a brick-
layer. Something about their regularity had a soothing effect on me. It
also worked when I focused on Arpège. As the hour wore on, I used the
rhythm in that kitchen as a cushion against adrenaline. Chop the vegetables, check the pan, whisk the dressing, lower the flame, mince the herbs,
reduce the sauce—every detail of every recipe handled meticulously and
dispassionately, calibrated to fit in the overall scheme. Turn, check the
sauce. Okay, wash the lettuce. Good. No hurry. Now, blanch the broccoli
rabe. Umm-hmm. Keep your eye on that sauce. Mince some garlic. Easy
does it, watch the fingers. Thinking, always thinking, that a little composure kept everything in check. Don't rush it. Maintain a calm, steady
pace. See what happens? Nothing to it at all.

I definitely benefited from watching them, but I coveted the distinction
of belonging. Of course, I couldn't take my eyes off David Passard, who
worked the quad of burners just off to my right. He seemed impossibly
young to supervise such a kitchen, much less tackle the dogma of French
cooking. (I assumed he was in his early thirties; months later, someone
told me he was only twenty-two.) But there was no doubt about his stat-
ure. He was the master of the kitchen and moved from station to station in an unobtrusive way that seemed more supportive than demanding,
while leaving nothing to chance.

It looked to me as if he'd been raised in the kitchen. His skin had the
pale, chalky pallor of a photographer who never left the darkroom. His
expression was guarded and he never altered it. It was almost spooky the
way he worked with an unspoken peripheral awareness of the other cooks
on the line. Passing to the freezer, at the end of the tiny room, he wove
among them without any kind of exchange. No one acknowledged David.
A balloon-shaped steaming *saucier* caught his eye, and he stopped to dip
a spoon into it.

"The sauce is too thin," he said, without looking up, "and the color is
wrong—it's not bright enough."

The cook, a young Spaniard, nodded imperturbably. Without any to-do, he puréed a bunch of coriander with some olive oil and salt to bring up the color of the sauce.

"Yes—perfect," David agreed as he helped to dress the plate. As he worked, his eyes scanned the kitchen, an attribute of accountability that seemed to alienate him, or at least set him apart, from the camaraderie in the downtime.

This time, his gaze fell on me, then it shifted toward a young American named Alice, from New Jersey, who was in training at Arpège. A few minutes later, she walked over and motioned for me to follow her.

She placed a little bowl filled with *haricots verts* next to her on the counter. "Do you know how to snap off the ends?" she asked.

I stared at her with something less than kindness before answering. "I'm a quick study," I said finally. While I blazed through the task, Alice went to fetch a container that looked like the footlocker my mother used when packing me off to summer camp.

"This is the reward for your good work," she said, flipping open the lid.

The trunk was filled with green beans, thousands of them piled like some smuggler's personal stash. So . . . this was how they intended to keep me busy and out of their hair.

"Can you do this?" David Passard asked me in French, dead serious, as if offering me a Mission Impossible assignment.

I found it hard to keep a straight face, but I threw him a nice, crisp, *"Oui, Chef,"* and set about the work.

The first hour was Zen. I settled into a meditative swoon and felt good about my contribution to the essentials of gastronomy. But no matter how fast I worked, it hardly made a dent. The amount of beans seemed infinite, like autumn leaves. Eventually, sore spots developed under both thumbnails and my index fingers cramped.

I was beginning to feel almost victimized, invited here under false pretenses and pressed into slavery. Ostensibly, Arpège participated in the Relais et Châteaux *École des Chefs* internship, but the program was bogus. There was no cooking school here, as far as I could tell. No facilities, no teacher, no lessons. The *carte du jour,* if you will, allowed an outsider to hang around the kitchen and watch. That's all. And while you're standing there . . . can you snap the ends off 16,000 beans?

Fortunately, I knew how to sulk. I'd learned this as a preschooler and had refined it over the years, developing it into an art form. The trick is the shoulders. You can wear the best hangdog expression and mumble like a malcontent, but if the shoulders don't slump at exactly the right angle, there is no use even showing up for work. I was so good at it, so glaringly pathetic, that David Passard picked up on it right on cue. He felt *guilty*, I could tell—it was all over his face.

"You should see this," he said, beckoning me to his station. I walked away from those beans faster than an illegal immigrant from a cop. In a bowl, he was mixing five pounds of gray sea salt with a little egg white to form a glutinous paste. Instead of packing the paste around a leg of lamb, as Madame had done, David selected a four-and-a-half-pound chicken that had been brushed with oil. That was the extent of it, aside from a rosemary sprig stuck decorously in the top. "It roasts for one hour and twenty minutes in a 325-degree oven, which keeps the chicken perfectly moist. Nothing else. *Voilà!*"

I smiled weakly at him as I described Madame's lamb misadventure. For a second, his lips twisted into a smirk before recovering a professional pose. I knew that he had heard this before; it had somehow justified his noble pursuit in a personal and private way.

"The secret to a perfect recipe is in here," he said, tapping with two fingers above his heart. "And in here." He repeated the gesture on his forehead. "Intuition—but no guesswork, like a doctor who delivers babies. The dish arrives perfectly every time." He stuffed his hands in his pockets and shrugged with comical nonchalance: "Really, there is nothing to it at all."

He gave me a bite from a finished bird. I assured him, rather obsequiously, that I was impressed with the results, that I had never tasted such a moist and succulent chicken. He reached back across the counter and picked up a smaller, salt-encrusted orb.

"I forgot the most important ingredient," he said, palming it like Dontrelle Willis before throwing a splitter, "—imagination. Why, with imagination any cook can perform miracles." He pushed his thumb through the surface of the salt ball, cracking it open like an egg. Inside was the most dreadful-looking lump.

"It is nothing but a beetroot, you see. Something as ordinary as that has no right to taste so heavenly. But, believe it or not, it is the specialty *de la maison.*"

I bit into it carefully, expecting a rather bitter, nose-tickling flavor, completely unprepared for the mouthful of buttery sweetness. Feeling almost deceived, I asked him with fascination, "How do you get it to taste like that? Do you marinate it for a long time in advance?"

"I do nothing of the sort." He sounded offended. "That would be what you Americans call overkill. If anything, in addition to the salt, only one ingredient gets added, and that, as I have tried to explain, is a kilo of imagination. Without it, you have nothing but a scrubby beetroot."

I was about to beg for the source of this imagination when a man walked into the kitchen dressed as a chef. His face was an actor's, luminous and handsome and charismatic, with eyes as powder blue and piercing as Paul Newman's, to whom he bore a close resemblance. A neckerchief was tied expertly under his chin. He moved from station to station, shaking hands with everyone, right down to the dishwashers. Only David Passard avoided his embrace by leaning halfway into the oven. When he came to me, he turned on a hundred-watt smile and said, *"Bonjour, bonjour—je suis Alain."*

Actor, indeed. This was none other than the star of the Arpège extravaganza himself, Alain Passard. He appeared just in time for lunch service. In fact, lunch was already prepared, the restaurant achingly full, when Passard veered into the dining room, arms outstretched like angel wings. Not veered, but bounded, the way Jay Leno bounds on stage each night to exultant fanfare. I half-expected theme-song music, applause, and a follow spot. His aura, such as it was, lit up the otherwise dark, shaded room.

The whole thing happened so fast that I didn't know what to make of it. Curious, I glanced over at David, who wore the blank stare of a defendant awaiting a jury's verdict. He seemed vigorously dispassionate, although a chemistry of unrest churned in his body, and I wondered how he dealt with it day after day. It must have frustrated him no end to inhabit his father's long shadow. All morning, David had run the kitchen with distinct personal style, expressing his jaw-dropping talent in every phase of the cuisine, only to have his father turn up to take the bows. It didn't seem fair. Alain Passard, for all intents and purposes, was retired. He had no right to claim the glory when he hadn't contributed so much as a grind of pepper.

I neglected the pile of green beans in front of me and watched the master work the house. Out on the floor, every silver hair neatly lacquered in place, he held himself poised to oblige the giddy idolaters. Every table demanded his presence: a hand on the shoulder, just a word or two, a small measure of recognition. A comforting warmth infused Passard's greetings as he waltzed through the clutter of tables, switching from language to language according to each client's need. Something in German led to a clinging handshake. House secrets concerning the risotto were passed in . . . Spanish? No, Portuguese. Even the nodding old couple from St. Louis got the full treatment.

"He's in his element," I said, as David plated a lobster braised in a wine broth infused with hazelnut oil.

"Who?"

"Your father."

"Ummm."

I could tell by the way he worked that he was deliberately engrossed. I have behaved this way myself when it was prudent to mask churlish feelings, staying coolly, purposefully steady for as long as I knew how. After a while, perhaps because it is impossible to hold it in any longer, or because you get weak, or because you just don't give a damn, or because something inside finally snaps, you let the feelings leak out, just enough to make your point. That was the place David had reached. He remained preoccupied with the food in a cross, tense way, and then, looking up from the plate as I watched his father perform, injured eyes betrayed him.

"You don't approve, do you?" I asked boldly for a guy in charge of bean-snapping.

He turned away from me and stared at the scene for a long moment, his hands forgetting a pile of shallots on the cutting board. "It is the arrangement."

"And what is your part?" It just slipped out. The instant the words were out of my mouth, I regretted them.

There was a brief bump of silence. David looked down sharply and took a clumsy whack at the shallots. They scattered across the board like frightened ants. As a rhythmic chopping resumed, his pallid face became very distant.

"Could you shell those pistachios?" he said, pointing to a bowl on the counter across the kitchen.

Pistachios. More diabolical than *haricots verts* when it came to crippling pain. What was next, I wondered, bamboo shoots under the fingernails?

I felt chastised, deservedly so, and slinked off to do penance, wondering how much damage I had done and whether I could recover my meager standing. I could have kicked myself for not holding my tongue. More than anything, I wanted to get out of that restaurant and take off across the Left Bank. There was a strong urge to cut and run, to throw in the towel on this foolish charade.

I positioned myself at the counter so that I could keep an eye on the situation. David was working busily at the far end of the room under a cloud of steam, but I could tell by his body language that he was distracted. Every so often he glanced toward the dining room, ostensibly to gauge lunch service, but there were stolen glimpses of his father's performance. A wrinkle of pleasure flashed across his face.

This was most likely a deal they had struck, roles they had rehearsed. It was the final act of a still-vital chef who had grown bored and passed the torch as a way of avoiding inevitable decline, as well as a son's duty to preserve his father's interests and reputation. A rite of passage that took place in every important French kitchen, a tradition as old as cave painting.

It was obvious from David's stare that he knew the score, that he'd made peace with his situation, and not a bad one at that, with abundant respect for his father's legacy. There might have been envy, animosity, regret, but David shied from those ghosts. Besides, there were debts to be paid; he was cooking his father's recipes in a restaurant his father had made famous. The old man had earned his bows. He was Arpège, Arpège was his.

I almost didn't return for the next day's *stage*. Convinced that I had profaned my welcome, I contemplated sleeping through the morning, yielding to the fatigue and languor of the seemingly endless *stage*. I had been on the go for nearly a month without a break. Since leaving Madame's, I had been stumbling through the days in a kind of aimless exhaustion. In another way my willpower, the mechanism that allowed me to keep my head above water, was gently giving way.

Instead of moving on, moving on, moving on, which, so far, had worked as my defense, I flirted with surrender. There was a fragile throbbing between my eyes.

"You are so fucking soft," I told myself, throwing back the covers and climbing forcefully out of bed.

I dressed and shaved and sprinted to the *Métro*. Today was supposed to bring me quality time with the chef, and I was now set on pressing the opportunity. From the train, however, the prospects seemed fairly remote. The list of hurdles was daunting. An overworked kitchen. Allotted time at a premium. Complicated recipes. Any distraction a burden. I was beginning to chalk this up as a lost cause. Another lost cause. On the Rue de Varenne, there was already gridlock outside Arpège. Beetle-shaped cars were heaved up on the curb, while deliverymen convoyed boxes of provisions through the kitchen door. Horns blared in protest. But inside the cooks, oblivious to the uproar, performed their feats of magic with God's bounty, extracting nectars, essences, pulps, and froths from a cornucopia of seasonal vegetables.

Alice was waiting for David with a problem, a truffled salad dressing that had emulsified. He gathered me up on the way to rescue it: all apparently forgiven. He showed her how to avoid the breakdown of oil, combining the ingredients —oil, wine vinegar, shallots, a hint of mustard—with a nice economy, then beating the phlegmy puddle with short, even strokes. *The trick to it is whisking only until it peaks, like so, otherwise it falls apart like a jilted lover.* If he only knew.

There was nothing to the dressing, a delicate, savory vinaigrette with only the lightest notes of acidity. Since most of the restaurant's salad greens came from the sweet, inner leaves of lettuce, the object was to focus on their natural flavor as opposed to masking it with dressing, which was so often the case. This only worked, of course, because the young greens were so exceptional, grown hydroponically and tweaked by the Passards, *père et fils*, to maximize flavor and character. Back home, the stuff from the supermarket, the so-called mesclun sold in ready-paks or bulk, was mass-produced and, for the most part, tasteless. I couldn't remember the last time my lettuce outshone the dressing.

Alice, who took her duties seriously, tasted each of the greens before she dressed them. She did it automatically, but with great deliberation, nibbling the leaves with her front teeth to release the flowery juices and then letting the flavors expand on her tongue. She repeated this ritual after each spoonful of dressing. I watched David go through the same process while making blinis. Before he cut them with a mold, he selected one from each batch, smelled it, broke off a small piece, and smelled it again, before popping it in his mouth. His face never changed, it remained impassive, but occasionally, and only rarely, his eyes narrowed and that batch would be swept into the trash bin.

"You have to taste everything," Klas instructed me later, while I was helping him with the gazpacho. "The tongue: the most indispensable instrument in the kitchen."

We were whipping up huge vats of the soup, a creamy salmony-pink foam that was one of Alain Passard's signature dishes. It was basically an intense, silky-smooth vegetable cocktail processed entirely in the blender. They served it icy cold, in a wide-lipped martini glass, with a spoonful of sherry vinegar to finish, waiting until the last minute to top it with a dollop of mustard-scented ice cream that melted on contact.

"So—taste," Klas said, handing me a tablespoon.

It took a few random samples for me to realize that constant adjustments were necessary. More salt, or, when it was too salty, more tomato; more or less fennel stalk according to the strength of the bulb; striking the right balance with onion, cucumber, and garlic. Tasting, always tasting, after each ingredient was added.

"Now taste this," Klas said, his Nordic face ablaze with mischief. He dipped my spoon into a metal saucepan and practically shoved it into my mouth.

I pulled back in anticipation of a wicked scorching. Of course, a good bowl of soup can blow hot or cold, but I hadn't been prepared for a fruity one. Especially a broth consisting almost entirely of melon. It was made by swirling a little extra-virgin olive oil into a canister of ripe honeydew chunks and "blending the shit out of it," as Klas so eloquently put it. We must have let that blender run for a good ten minutes, banging the sides of it like a pinball machine while adding some salt, the juice of half a lemon, and just a sprinkling of sugar before straining the liquid through a *chinoise*.

When we had finished, David waved me over to watch him assemble a dessert. He was putting the finishing touch on an avocado pistachio soufflé, which released a cloud of steam so sensuous that it seemed more expedient as an aphrodisiac than as food.

"You know how to make a *tarte-Tatin*?" he asked.

Oh, shit. This was another one of those buggy tests, like the omelet at the Meurice. Anyone with a stove made a *tarte Tatin*. For my money, it was the perfect dessert: large chunks of firm, ripe apple caramelized to perfection in a pool of butter and sugar. The whole thing was done in a skillet, with the pastry baked on top, and then inverted onto a serving dish just before bringing it to the table. As I've mentioned, I'd made it often over the years, with varying degrees of success. There was always an even chance of its falling apart or sticking to the pan. Too much syrup proved as deadly as the lava at Krakatoa. But even a *tarte Tatin* disaster was a delicious treat.

Yeah, I knew how to make it, but I'd be damned before I'd dance around like a trained poodle, whipping out twenty-three versions of it for a fussy French chef.

I put down my notebook, let out a sigh, and struck a pose that left no question about my willingness to bark and roll over. David looked curiously at me, thinking perhaps that this was too much instruction for a gringo.

"This is something I don't demonstrate very often," he said, "but I thought you might like to learn one of our most requested dishes."

"Oh, that'd be nice. Yes, I'd like that very much."

We peeled six Gala apples, which were on the small side but juicy, and then carefully cut each one into six even wedges. The size was important so that they would cook evenly. Then we rolled out a *pâte feuilletée* that had been resting under a cloth, fitting it to the diameter of the pan.

I skyed an eyebrow at the renegade puff pastry, thinking perhaps it was left over from a ladies' luncheon or some wingding that served pink souf-flés. Traditionally, with *tarte Tatin* the pastry is a butter dough as sweet and crisp as a sugar cookie after it's baked. Bob Ash made no pretense about it; with the remaining dough from his *tarte Tatin*, he whipped out a dozen biscuits, perfect for dunking in a sweet dessert wine. A puff pastry seemed so delicate, prissy. It's true enough that everyone puts his own spin on the recipe, even though the basics generally remain the same. But I discovered that nothing at Arpège was straight off the rack—and here is David's method of turning a *tarte Tatin* into a three-star extravaganza.

TARTE TATIN ESTRAGON

6 Gala apples, peeled and
   cored
12 Tbl. butter, divided
3 cups sugar, plus extra for
   sprinkling

splash of Calvados
1 1/2 cups fresh tarragon
   sprigs
pâte feuilletée [puff pastry]

Preheat the oven to 325 degrees.

Cut each apple in half lengthwise, then lay each half on its cut side and slice each half into 3 equal wedges.

Put 4 tablespoons of butter and 1 1/2 cups sugar into the bottom of a 12-inch cast-iron pan or skillet and melt the mixture over medium-high heat, stirring until it forms a golden syrup. Carefully add 3 of the apples cut into sixths (18 wedges in all), combine with the syrup until they are well coated, and cook for only 4 to 5 minutes, until the apples begin to soften. Splash the apples with Calvados, allowing them to flame up. When the flame subsides, transfer the apples to a bowl with all of the syrup. Repeat the procedure with the three remaining apples.

Add 1 1/2 cups of tarragon to the apples in the bowl and combine gen-
tly. Allow the apples to stand 15 minutes.

In another cast-iron pan, press all the apples into the bottom, remov-
ing and discarding three-fourths of the tarragon. Add all of the sugar
syrup and dot the top of the apples with the remaining 4 tablespoons of
butter, cut into chunks.

Roll out the pâte feuilletée *very thinly and fit it over the top of the*
apples, tucking it into the sides of the pan and sprinkling the top with
sugar. Bake 1 1/2 hours, placing the pan on a baking sheet so the ooz-
ing caramel won't trickle on the oven floor. After removing the tart,
weight down the top of the pâte feuilletée *with the bottom of another*
cast-iron pan and very carefully pour off any excess juice. Let it rest 5
minutes before inverting the tart onto a large serving dish.

Serves 8

It was almost impossible to view the result without also imagining a
fist-size scoop of vanilla ice cream pinned to a slice like a corsage. There
is something indecent about serving apples straight out of the oven without the inalienable scoop, much like appearing undressed in public or
hearing opera sung in English. Anything but vanilla would probably com-
pound the sin, but when I mentioned this to David, he shuddered: "That
would be"—he nearly cursed, then swiftly recovered—"*inappropriate* when
it comes to this tart." I was skating on very thin ice.

Frédéric must have witnessed the exchange and understood its por-
tent, because in an instant he had me by the elbow and was turning me
toward the dining room. "It's time for Bob's lunch," he announced, with
the kind of unctuousness you learn at *maître d'* school or perhaps in French
politics. As he guided me toward a table, I watched his bearing lift with
esteem. He seemed to unfold, like one of those flat sponges after it has
been dipped in water. The kitchen was David's; now we were on his turf.
"You've got the best seat in the house. I've put you in the corner by the
kitchen, so you can see the entire restaurant."

Filled with people, the room seemed astonishingly small, less austere.

It had once functioned as a stable but had been a restaurant of one type or another since 1760. Across from where I sat, horses once munched hay while their masters had a meal at one of the communal tables. New owners changed its configuration over the years, but there was no way, short of demolition, to increase the square footage. To keep the place profitable, the food had to be sensational and the prices frighteningly high. The Passards, who had cooked here since 1984, managed both tasks with genius. Lunch went for a heart-stopping 320 euros, and everyone left feeling it was more than worth it.

The food, as expected, was incredible, a culinary epiphany. I'd managed to nibble during my *stage,* sampling a little from each dish we'd prepared, but on a plate that had been dressed to kill, everything tasted different. Better. The gazpacho had a voluptuousness that was missing when right out of the blender; the beetroot, served atop a paper-thin sheath of its own skin and drizzled with a balsamic vinegar older than my daughter, made me laugh out loud going down. Its presentation was a showstopper, a daring bit of theater that came off with resounding triumph.

When the waiter returned, he was carrying a trio of small tartlet shells filled with cilantro mousse that Klas had been making when I left the day before. I'd watched him collect a bagful of leftover salad greens and blanch them in a bath of hot water and gelatin, before blending them with oil. He scooped the whole grassy mess into a CO_2 canister and shot a salvo of curlicues into the shells. Just before serving, Alice intercepted them and decorated each tart with a few grains of *fleur de sel* and a microscopic coriander flower that looked too pretty to be real.

It was delicious. I patted my stomach and smiled meekly to indicate the mounting impression, but my waiter only grinned before disappearing into the kitchen. The appetizers were filling, little meals unto themselves, but as I feared, my colleagues were only warming up.

There were more appetizers followed by more appreciative grunts: a *carpaccio* of langoustine covered with thin slices of raw *cèpe* and drizzled with basil oil and sea salt; a caramelized onion gratinée dusted with Parmesan; a red-pepper *velouté* surrounded by an infusion of crème chantilly and *Speck* (a German ham) that, because I'd made such a fuss over it, was twice the size of a regular serving; and spinach cooked with a carrot mousse in a langoustine caramel sauce and sesame seeds.

There were two or maybe three more dishes; I'd lost count. I felt practically assaulted and sat there staring in a daze at the fresh setup they were arranging on the table.

"David thought you'd like to try the scampi pan-fried with a Thai curry of lemongrass and ginger. He also suggests a cappuccino of potato mousse, and afterward *foie gras grillé* with *citron Japonais.*"

"He's trying to kill me, isn't he?" I asked with complete sincerity.

"Not at all." The waiter recoiled as if I'd offended him. "Really, everything I'm serving is part of his standard repertoire. It is the restaurant's *carte dégustation*, the tasting menu. You'll have to wait until dessert." He leaned close to me and whispered into my ear: "Then he's going to kill you."

The *sommelier* refilled my glass with a viognier from South Africa and I swirled the wine absentmindedly while fighting off encroaching blues. Dining was an exciting social pastime for me. At best, I could seem, for prolonged stretches, to exist within the contours of a warm cocoon, a small untroubled child curled up as if to nap. On those occasions, I felt something close to love. But Arpège made me lonely; it was too full of romance and intimacy. My focus slipped from the food being served and skimmed across the faces seated around me, the traits and mannerisms of total strangers, and then to a familiar figure, Alain Passard, who was sitting with three women at a table against the wall. One of them, leaning toward Alain in midsentence, dipped her creamy décolletage flirtatiously under his nose. He obediently put a cigarette into her mouth, lit it. What an operator this guy was! Meanwhile, without a place setting, he ate from everyone's plate.

In a few minutes, he got up and began circulating around the room, doing the dance: shaking, kissing, signing. Schmoozing. I smiled at his finesse and rocked back in my fabric-covered chair, taking pleasure in the reaction of his acolytes, and an accommodating waitstaff forced to dodge the outstretched arms. There was a good feeling in the restaurant. The drone of conversation hummed under the back-and-forth.

A waiter strode over, balancing a piece of David's *tarte Tatin* on a plate, his other hand folded correctly behind his back. "You should recognize this," he said, placing it before me, and at once I inhaled the musky plume of apples laced with anise that rose off the crust. I ran a finger through the puddle of light-brown juice and licked it with delight. "But first . . . compliments of the chef . . ." And, with that, he brought out his other hand, which cradled a small decorative bowl, and crowned the tart with a scoop of vanilla ice cream.

Amazing: a formidable French chef with a sense of humor. I was beginning to feel almost hopeful for the world. Perhaps there was even a rubber bodysuit hanging in David's closet. God knows, Arpège wasn't the place to thumb your nose at propriety. *Tarte Tatin à la mode*—one small step for identity, one giant leap for mankind.

A forkful of the *tarte* made me forget everything but the combination of flavors afizz in my mouth. The marriage of apple and tarragon was brilliant, a natural.

I positively glowed with pleasure. The waiter laughed but cautioned me about finishing the entire portion. The *tarte,* he said, was only a teaser— "to open your palate."

Let me admit right here: My self-control was horrible. I gobbled down the *tarte* and licked the juice off a spoon, worried that I'd never be able to duplicate such a treat. I'd never eaten anything so sweet and savory. If this was to be my last experience with it, I was going for broke, ice cream and all, wondering only how I might wangle seconds.

Again, a wave of sadness swept over me. An experience . . . a meal such as this was meant to be shared, remembered. The empty seat opposite me tugged at my heartstrings.

A bottle of Cognac and a wooden humidor made the rounds. Across the room, Alain Passard paused by a table of four dignitaries and shared a joke whose punch line rippled from man to man to man. The one sitting with his back to me laid a meaty hand on Passard's wrist, and in reflex the chef signaled for the humidor. The box was presented, a selection made, the end guillotined as only the French know how. Way to kill a great meal, I thought. Part of me wanted to rush over and snatch that stink bomb before it poisoned the air. The man bent sideways to take a light from

Passard, and in profile I recognized the florid forehead, bulbous hound's nose, hair sprouting from the ears: Maxim.

Only . . . the disheveled, uncombed, pouchy-faced, slightly grubby man I'd met the other night had morphed into an ad for *Vogue Homme*. He was dressed impeccably in an Italian pin-striped suit that gave his well-upholstered torso a fine, tapered alignment. An extraordinary sage-green silk tie was knotted the way a sailmaker might fasten it, and—he was *groomed*. Someone had given Maxim the full-press makeover. His face was smoothly shaven and free of that dusky cadaverous patina. And his hands . . . was that a *manicure*?

His hooded amphibian eyes rotated from the cigar to my table, locking in place until I came into focus. Not a spark of recognition registered anywhere on his face. I winked at him and lifted my glass, conveying my delight in seeing him again.

Nothing doing. He regarded me as one might a saltshaker. With determined emphasis, Maxim puffed on the cigar, sucking on it the way I first encountered him at the café, two nights earlier. His eyes blinked involuntarily but did not change. We stayed like that, wordless, staring keenly and imperviously at each other.

From behind me, a waiter poured some Cognac into a large glass and handed it to me. I took it without looking and swirled it around. A dozen thoughts went through my mind. Perhaps he didn't recognize me. Or maybe he was stunned. What were the chances of our both turning up here like this? I hadn't mentioned Arpège to him. Did he think I was stalking him?

I picked up my glass and walked over to his table.

"Maxim," I said, taking in the grand spread, "I'm proud of you. It seems you've overcome your *petit bourgeois* leanings."

Maxim looked up at me, coolly, the surprise on his face tightening with something less than politeness. Several looks crossed at the table. He wiped his mouth and smiled impersonally: *"Désolé, M'sieu'. Je ne parle pas anglais."*

Some kind of strange game was being played. I made up my mind not to let it rattle me.

"That's odd," I replied in French this time. "You spoke it better than me a couple days ago. What happened? Run over by a *cabinette* with American plates on it?"

He continued to hold his stare, ostensibly bewildered. I stood my ground. We were beginning to attract attention. Alain Passard started toward us, but Maxim briskly motioned him away. If I pushed it, there was going to be a scene. Instead, I chuckled humorlessly, contemptuously, like a politician, before turning away.

As I walked back to my table, I heard him make some lame excuse for the interruption, and he used a vulgar French word to describe me that was impossible to translate. I had heard it before, of course. But it hurt like hell to hear it used about me by someone who had shown me such unsolicited kindness.

Sitting down, I refused to look away from the table where Maxim was sitting. No one in the party cast a peek in my direction. Several minutes passed. Cigarette and cigar smoke clouded the room, but that was the norm in France. Maxim gestured animatedly while he talked, and perversely, touchingly, I recognized all of his idiosyncrasies.

I kept thinking it might be a good idea for me to hit the kitchen until he left, to cool off with the waitstaff. But all at once everyone at his table rose and waddled off uniformly like penguins, congregating in the little reception area at the front of the room. Passard himself shook their hands, one by one, ushering out each man with a soft, persuasive shove. Maxim took extra time with the chef, chatting with surprising familiarity, before hurrying through the door. Weird.

I was left staring at the newly empty space when the waiter returned. He leaned like Isadora Duncan across my table and filled a flute from a magnum of excellent Champagne. We looked meaningfully at each other as the foam edged up the slender glass. I wasn't sure if he'd seen what had happened, but he seemed to be genial and accommodating, following the action with a mischievous smile.

"As promised," he said, placing a set of forks at my elbow, "prepare to be killed in the sweetest possible way."

I thanked him and declined politely. If the truth be told, I'd already been killed enough for one day.

Chapter Six

FRATERNITÉ

After a week in my next stop, Théoule, I would be more than ready to head to Italy. There had been a dim, bad juju at the cooking school, Le Mas des Oliviers, where I had gone to chill out after leaving Paris. This feeling was easy to dismiss, at the outset. First impressions are powerful, and it was impossible not to be blinded by the beauty. In all my travels, I couldn't recall ever laying eyes on a more spectacular setting.

The road led up from the sea in a series of steep hairpin switchbacks that seemed lifted from the outtakes of *To Catch a Thief*. Five miles farther along, surrounded by the ledgy Tanneron woods, was the village of

Mandelieu, a tiny coastal nook, and a few miles more, straight up, Théoule. Almost at the top, a hidden drive opened onto a cliffside retreat overlooking, in dizzying perspective, an enamel-blue swath of Mediterranean Sea, with huge views of the Riviera all the way to Cannes. The jagged hillside below was blanketed with oleander, bent away from the kite winds. A cluster of sailboats bobbed and drifted in the harbor below, and along the distant shore the lights of Nice winked in the shadow of the Swiss Alps.

Le Mas itself was a peaceful little oasis, a two-story dusty-pink villa with cornflower-blue shutters whose reflection shimmered in the surface of a quaint pool. It had been built as a private bungalow in the early 1970s. By 1990, however, it was a roofless crumbling ruin, when it was renovated by a couple whose modest resources rescued it from certain ostentation. Now it was a lovely glinting jewelbox, by no means as opulent as the neighboring pastel mansions. The couple added six tasteful suites and a whirlpool, too, which gave off a regular hearty burp that defied the persistent wind. Around it wended a terra-cotta terrace, suspended in the air above the sea by a rise of stone walls.

At first I rejoiced in the house and the riot of scenery. Beyond the sanctuary, the weather was surpassingly tonic: salt air, tropical bleached light, a fine scent of mimosa and pine. It was exactly the kind of place to collapse in idle ease. In Paris, there was so much to absorb every time I turned another corner; the excitement and glamour of the city kept me so jacked up, leaving little downtime between the cooking shifts. There had been plenty of fireworks to go around. But in Théoule, the warm air and expanse of sea felt liberating in other ways, and I began to seek convalescence in its leisured embrace.

On top of everything else, the resident chef, Frédéric Rivière, turned out to be a sweetheart of a guy. He was a fair, brown-haired man in his early forties, going gray around the edges, yet his trim physique showed no trace of the rich food he cooked. I liked him instantly. There was an unruffled easygoingness about him. I got the impression, however, that he was holding something back, although that may have been due to the constant turnover at Le Mas. Otherwise, he had a good laugh, unself-con-

scious, low and musical. His every gesture seemed informed by gracious-
ness and honesty.

Whatever grounded Fred came in handy at Le Mas des Oliviers
because the character of the place demanded it of him. Le Mas was a
cooking school in name, but that was about it. First and foremost, it was a
getaway, a resort. You went there to cook a little; to eat like a pasha; to sit
by the pool lacquered with sunscreen or gape at the view; to take one of
the excursions offered by the young, attractive staff; to play golf or shop;
to socialize with the other guests; to enjoy the facilities; and maybe, just
maybe, to perfect a recipe or two you might duplicate back home when
showcasing the slides from your "cooking school" vacation. That didn't
mean the guests weren't interested in cooking. They were *interested*, the
way they were interested in gardening and the national debt. "I'm going
to a cooking school in the south of France": it had wonderful cachet. But
Le Mas wasn't selling the cooking so much as the package.

So it was up to Fred to keep everyone happy—the elderly sisters who
traveled together once a year with their niece, the languid husband who
couldn't boil water, a single woman who bemoaned the lack of available
men, the class clown whose wisecracks annotated each lesson, the couple
from Tulsa whose midnight fights rattled the stucco walls, the earnest car-
diologist who shrank from gutting fish, the rogues' gallery of significant
others, and, of course, me, the mutt in this pedigreed group.

Of course, none of them had bargained on a classmate like me—by now
so obsessed with my cooking mission that I found it impossible to relax.
From the moment I hit the property, I was in overdrive. I was impatient,
fidgety, like someone with too much caffeine. (Richard Dreyfuss in *Jaws*
comes to mind.) My eyes kept darting toward the kitchen. Fingers twitched.
To the others filtering in, I must have resembled one of R. Crumb's speed-
freaks. I was a nightmare for anyone looking for easygoing fun.

Fred, I'm sure, had me marked for trouble, though, to be fair, the first
morning he hitched his geniality to our apron strings. There were fourteen
of us, all ostensibly committed to an intensive cooking experience, but, as
is often the case, not everyone was really . . . that is, they wouldn't know

a *bain-marie* from Donny and Marie, despite the fact they talked a good game. That, I suppose, was to be expected. In some ways, a little bluster offered a bit of self-protection, an attempt to establish individuality in a group experience. It must have been obvious, as well, to Fred, who had seen it all over the years, but as we arrived at Le Mas in the hours before lunch, his sunny grin took on a cautious overcast.

"You ask so many questions," he said to me, while cutting up two chickens for a late lunch. Everyone else was unpacking, or collapsed, so we had gone off to the kitchen, a modest three-room suite with a large stainless island that would serve as our classroom. Fred invited me to assist, which seemed like a great opportunity to learn something new, and while he trimmed the pieces, I sliced onions and cut a bunch of carrots to size, grilling him about every technique he used. "I'm impressed by how much you want to know," he said.

"Isn't that the whole point of this place? We've only got five days to learn as much as we can."

He looked up from the work wearing a funny little smile. "Oh, I wouldn't expect too much from the other guests. You'll find they're not that interested in specifics."

That seemed like an odd thing to say, coming from the chef at a French cooking school. In as nice a way as possible, I asked him what these people were doing here, if not to hit the stovetop running.

"Everyone is here for a different reason—and most, let me assure you, aren't serious cooks. This is their holiday, it's very social. We have to respect everyone's needs."

Obviously, he had heard through the grapevine that I was a little nutty about cooking. Someone must have tipped him off, which was fine as long as he respected my needs as well. But there was something in his tone that sparked some reflection.

When I thought about it, I realized I had been rather spoiled so far, the beneficiary of mostly one-on-one instruction. For one reason or another, I'd received the kind of individual attention that is unavailable to most amateur cooking enthusiasts. Classes had either been ridiculously small or constructed especially for me, which was unheard-of on the cooking-school circuit. Usually, it was all groups: fifteen, twenty-five, even more, squished together as if on a Carnival Cruise. Somehow, up to now, I'd managed to avoid the factories. I had been thankful, naturally, but not particularly gracious. Now, the prospect of group lessons offended me. The thought of sharing a chef's attention with others seemed like a punishment, like having my pocket picked. I'd gotten a look at the guests as they'd drifted in. It seemed doubtful any of them would know how to make a soufflé, I thought huffily. Or a proper omelet, forgetting for the moment my sorry output in the bin at Le Meurice. I think it was Spinoza who said that ambition was nothing but a species of madness. But who was Spinoza? I asked myself. Nothing but a skinny little philosopher on a low-fat diet. I wanted to cook, and the others had better strap on their stick blenders.

The fact of the matter was, I was already ahead of the curve. The lunch Fred and I whipped out, a curried chicken fricassee, was among the best recipes I learned while traveling abroad. It was simple to prepare and anything but bland. The curry gave the ordinary chicken an exalted magic. This was a perfect meal for either summer or winter, lunch or dinner, and heartwarming, full of aromatic herbs, and served at the table with noodles or rice. We threw it together in no time at all, and I have made it, along with a baguette and a big salad, whenever I needed instant comfort at the end of a difficult day.

CURRIED CHICKEN FRICASSEE

8 chicken thighs with skin,
   bone in
2 Tbl. olive oil
salt
1 Tbl. curry powder (or more,
   to taste)
10 Szechuan peppercorns,
   crushed
1 1/2 Tbl. fresh thyme,
   chopped

1 1/2 Tbl. fresh rosemary,
   chopped
3 med. onions, chopped
5 cloves garlic, crushed
1 cup white wine
3 cups (or more) chicken
   stock

Wipe chicken thighs dry so they will be sure to brown, then sauté, skin side down, in a deep stockpot or casserole with 1 to 2 tablespoons of the olive oil (the chicken will give off a lot of its own fat) and salt well. Cook over medium-high heat about 10 minutes, until the skin develops a golden-brown color. Add the curry powder, crushed peppercorns, and herbs, sprinkling them evenly over the chicken.

Turn the chicken with tongs and continue cooking. After 5 minutes, add the onions and continue cooking. Add the garlic and wine and deglaze the pan, scraping up the brown bits. Boil only 2 minutes, giving the wine just enough time to lose its acidity. Add enough stock to cover the chicken. Bring to a boil, then cover the pot and reduce the heat to simmer.

Cook slowly, 1 1/2 hours. Remove the chicken and keep warm. Reduce the sauce slightly until thick and serve.

Serves 4–6

Cooked long and slowly like that, the chicken practically fell off the bone and the sauce developed a thick, syrupy consistency. Of course, it helps if you throw in a wodge of butter at the end, as I have been known to do without apology. The stock is also a last-minute improvisation. Fred just used water, which was fine if you had a good farm-raised chicken. His was from Bresse, the Beverly Hills of chickendom. But those pitiful yellow birds we get in the supermarket are about as tasty as latex, bringing nothing whatsoever to the sauce. So the stock helps to give it a flavorful boost.

We also marinated a slew of *niçoise* olives by rinsing them thoroughly and adding a fresh, fruity olive oil; a splash of balsamic vinegar; two crushed garlic cloves; a dash of cumin powder; a few sprigs each of sage, rosemary, and parsley; a pinch of *herbes de Provence*; and Fred's special twist, a touch of soy sauce. I didn't see the olives for another two days, but when he served them with drinks before one of our communal dinners, they were the runaway hit of the cocktail hour.

Lunch on the patio was a pleasant enough affair, a feeling-out process to determine who we were getting into bed with, so to speak. Everyone seemed to get along, or at least made an effort to talk to each other. In fact, there was so much chitchat it bordered on the excruciating. Life stories were exchanged in shameless detail. Pictures of every child, grandchild, and family pet were passed from hand to hand. One man pressed a snapshot to his heart and sighed, "My baby," but when it finally reached me, I saw it was a single-engine plane. Other hobbies were recalled with slightly less affecting endearment. It came as no surprise that every woman was in a book club and reading one of those soft-core literary fiction paperbacks about earnest servant-girls or matriarchs. The men all seemed to be working on the latest Harry Potter. When I proposed dissecting the works of M. F. K. Fisher, they wondered who he played for.

Mostly, there was good, friendly engagement among the guests, as opposed to obvious long-term friendships to be made here. It was fortunate we were getting along well, I thought, because the cooking instruction wasn't going to sustain the week. Fred, as it turned out, was a wonderful man, but, despite the chicken dish, a disappointing cook at best. The first class was a harbinger of the week ahead. We made three different recipes in the morning: starter, main course, and dessert, but there was so much crisscrossing among the three that we were never sure what was in play at any given moment. The recipes and ingredients were listed in a spiral-bound course book placed at each station, but Fred improvised at will without advance notice. I found myself playing sheriff, always catching him in the act.

"Excuse me, Fred," I interrupted, during a demonstration for mango sorbet, "there doesn't appear to be any lime zest in our recipe."

"Yes, yes, I know," he said, barreling on, "but I am putting some in because it brings out such a nice flavor."

"Should we add it to our recipe?"

"Yes, you can. I am going to put in an egg white, as well." That wasn't on the ingredients list, either. "It gives the sorbet smoothness, but Americans are uneasy about uncooked egg whites, so I don't list it."

The scampi *mille-feuilles* and Mediterranean/Asian pork recipes were both haphazard dishes. The recipes were sloppily written, and Fred veered from the printed instructions without warning or a notation so that we could adjust it in our books. I couldn't always follow his sudden detours and became frustrated.

"What is going on here?" I whispered to the woman next to me, whose face was knitted into mystification.

"He's improvising," she said, "although I'm not sure which recipe he is improvising right now."

I glanced around at the others. They seemed happy, sipping wine or Coke, making jokes, enjoying the way Fred poured his mixtures from a flask above his head—as if they were at home watching Emeril on the Food Network. He was entertaining as hell, they were in a beautiful place—life was grand. They were getting their money's worth, and soon they would be having lunch on that lovely sun-drenched patio. But I felt like I needed to pounce, to pounce now, or this would elude me forever.

"How long did you blanch that spinach?" I asked, as he lifted a soggy green clump out of boiling water.

"Oh, just a little while," Fred said, smiling.

"Umm, yes. But how *long* of a little while?" I persisted. "A minute? Two?"

"Yes," he said, blotting it with a towel. "Now we are going to put paprika on the wontons. . . ."

I searched madly through the ingredients, looking for paprika. *Nada.*

". . . and we'll put them in the oven until they turn a lovely golden color."

How long might that be? I wondered.

"Now, we'll put on a few spoons of scampi stock."

"Uh, how do we make that stock?" I asked.

"It's in the back of your recipe book," Fred said, "but I made some earlier. Oh, and I scented it with a squeeze or two of lemon, which you won't find there."

I realized that the *mille-feuille* recipe was completely different from what was in our book, so I scrambled to rewrite it as he plated the dish.

"Oh, good, I see you are writing this down," said a woman named Pat, who was busy snapping pictures of her niece. "Will you make sure we all get it later?"

Sure, lady, I thought, right after I finish cleaning up the dishes.

While Fred struggled to explain the assembly of the dish, one of the couples expounded on their cooking ordeals during a recent camping trip to the Tetons and another guest shared his recipe for grilling salmon poached in orange juice. Fred finally sent us out on the patio for a snack, while he and two assistants finished off each of our recipes.

A lesson the next day went from bad to worse. The class had requested a fish-soup recipe, which seemed like a natural, considering where we were. Every restaurant had one on the menu, and each soup defined the character of its inimitable chef. (Alain Llorca's was fiery hot; Fred's, it turned out, was watery, bland. The model couldn't have been more precise.) There was a lot to prepare: cleaning the fish, chopping and sautéing vegetables and herbs, and making the stock, a delicate court bouillon. Because it wasn't in our recipe books, there was plenty of head-scratching. Perhaps too ambitiously, Fred paired it with a recipe for curry beef *paupiettes*, which required an elaborate veal-stock preparation, as well as spaetzle, and a nougat glacé with candied olives for dessert that called for an Italian meringue.

An hour into the class, things had spun into a nosedive.

At one point, Fred had twelve different pots working at one time, and we weren't sure which went with what recipe. The nougat glacé, especially, required a PhD in chemical engineering. It took real skill to pull off the meringue, a skill none of us had, and the egg whites in the cream kept collapsing. As if the situation weren't disorganized enough, the recipe was confusing; someone suggested it had been written by Kafka. Fred kept adding ingredients, pulling out the stops, trying to correct a looming disaster. Finally, during an onslaught of our questions, he looked up, grinned, and said, "I am never making this recipe again."

It was the perfect retort to defuse the comedy of errors, perfectly Fred—but things grew progressively worse. At the height of the chaos, Bucky, the class clown, broke into a medley of songs from *South Park*, entertaining us with half a dozen foulmouthed routines. As Bucky tuned up for an encore, Fred's nougat glacé was pronounced DOA. Nothing was going to save that gloppy mess. To his credit, Fred never lost his composure, but it was clear he was as frustrated as we were.

"Next time," he said, "I think I will teach everyone how to make *croque-monsieur.*"

That evening, the mood on the patio was subdued. The light and vibrancy off the water had been so constant and strong that even nightfall couldn't darken the horizon. The view to Nice was enchanted, grand in the dying day. Everyone kept commenting about it, hoping that it wouldn't disappear all of a sudden. A galaxy of candles struggled against the warm, itinerant breezes. But when the chatter started, with everyone comparing class notes, a pall fell over the atmosphere that was stronger than cloud cover. No one wanted to hurt Fred's feelings. Everyone appreciated his joyous spirit, adored the ambience at Le Mas. But when someone mentioned they had better food on the flight to France, the nodding of heads was ominous.

Earlier, while they were dressing for dinner, I had crept back into the kitchen and found Fred, whistling to himself as he touched up each of our beef *paupiettes*. On his face, concentrated downward, played the ghost of a smile. He fussed over the plates like an undertaker preparing an accident victim for a viewing.

"Can you save them, Doc?" I asked, dipping an index finger in some veal stock that was puddled around a fillet.

"We'll see," he said. "At the very least, I can make them look . . . respectable."

The subject of taste was underscored by its very omission. The scattered debris on the table, zucchini stems and eggshells and crumpled paper towels, seemed to epitomize the character of the recipes.

Still, there was a demure, precise detailing to his knife work that no one else had the chance to see. He worked instinctively, by feel, adding a chiffonade of basil to the curry paste, even though it was store-bought. A splash of wine gave it a nice home-cooked lift. Someone might have concluded that perhaps Fred was underqualified for this job. But he had been at it since he was nine years old, serving cheap, hearty lunches to men in overalls and working banquets at his grandmother's restaurant, L'Hôtel du Cheval Blanc, in Brittany. At fourteen, he left home for cooking school and three years later began the journey that marked a serious, albeit agonizingly lonely, gastronomic apprenticeship: a few years' *stage* on the deserted Atlantic coast, graduating to a bistro in Cannes-sur-Mer, followed by a two-star restaurant in Avignon, and finally the grand prize, apprenticing under the late, great Fernand Point at La Pyramide in Vienne. He had had enough training to launch a culinary institute.

"I get the feeling you'd be more fulfilled cooking at a restaurant," I said.

"Oh, I'm not complaining," he responded. "Everybody thinks the best job I can have is to be a chef. But restaurants, as you know, are often nightmarish. They make you—how do you say?—nuts. Here, at Le Mas, there is beauty, serenity."

There was also, I concluded, an extravagance of dilettantes. I couldn't think of a place, other than perhaps an anorexia clinic, where people had less appreciation for food.

"I'm not so sure about that," he said. "There is a good spirit here. No matter what goes on, I can always sense it—the desire to learn more, to experiment, to expand tastes. People just need a little incentive. The problem with Americans is that they have very little culture of food. In a French home, food is always prepared with a lot of care, and the same goes for presentation. But it is nothing we work at. It comes naturally, because it has always been so much a part of our lives. The vegetables are not just peeled, but shaped; we finish them with olive oil to make them glisten. Most Americans get their food already prepared, so they don't think about it in the same regard.

"You know, five years ago, Americans came to cooking schools here without any basic knowledge. It was frustrating. We couldn't just demonstrate recipes without first teaching them how to dice and chop. Everyone here today already knows that. I mean, look at all the questions they fired at me! No, I think the Americans are taking the next important step. And when Americans want to learn something, they go do it—" pushing both hands out from his chest like a rocket launch "—*immediately! Now!* Unlike the French, who have to think about everything before they take the first step."

"It might help if they listened to you, instead of chatting like magpies."

"It might. Their attention span is not what I'd call enduring. They are often like children, *very much* like children. They don't seem to have the slightest degree of self-discipline."

"It's not in our genetic makeup," I said.

"That may be so, but if they ever give an award for *fraternité*, it would go to this group, and others like them. I'm impressed by how well everyone gets along."

I had to hand it to Fred, he was a diplomat extraordinaire. He could find a diamond in an acre of sand. His tone implied a real affection for camaraderie mixed with the understanding that in any connatural group, he was the odd man out. Studying his face, composed around the intention of a smile, I felt as if I were looking at someone living in a detached utopian realm who craved carefree friendship. It seemed that, somewhere in those years of training, he missed out on that part of life. His need to please was palpable. Concerned that it showed on my face, I hastily asked, "What are all those chicken wings for? Are you moonlighting for TGI Friday's?"

"It's for a little snack," he said, using his corruption for hors d'oeurves. "You can help. Here—I'm going to show you what to do."

I have to admit, I never cared much for chicken wings. Eating one required too much time and effort in exchange for the hard-won scrap of meat on those scrawny bones. But Fred's recipe made it worth the struggle. We laid a half-dozen wings on a baking sheet, sprinkled on some *épices riz parfumes*—a zesty potion of onion powder, ground coriander, cardamom, cumin, and salt—hit them with successive splashes of balsamic vinegar and soy sauce, and baked them slowly, at 350 degrees, turning them once during the scant half-hour cooking process, until the skins caramelized, reaching a nice nutty-brown color.

They disappeared almost as soon as they hit the patio, all eight servings, along with a fig-and-chicken-liver canapé in a tangy shallot reduction that he and I threw together, almost as an afterthought, at the last minute.

Dinner was a cozy, candlelit affair, despite the unexciting food we'd made during class, which figured prominently on the menu. It seemed that a level of comfort had been reached as we'd gotten to know one another these past few days, such that guards gradually came down, intimacies were exchanged freely. I think it was safe to say that, had we been anywhere else, many of us would hardly have made social overtures to those with whom we were now locked in conversation. It said a lot about us that we strove to find common ground. We looked past the stratified places from which we came, with their artificial distinctions, and tried to forge here a more considerate community.

We should have known better. We'd all read *Lord of the Flies*.

Merry group that we were, we decided we would stay up together later and watch the Bush–Kerry debate, which would air live in France sometime after two that morning. Almost on cue, opinions started to misfire on all cylinders. Bud lit the fuse when he announced that he stood "somewhere to the right of Genghis Khan."

"So I guess that means you are holding Bush's dick," Bucky said.

"At least he has one," Bud replied.

And it went downhill from there. Somehow, I managed to hold my tongue until a few drinks later, when everyone was lobbing their best political grenades. I overheard the oxymoron "compassionate conservative" and was about to pull the pin on my own device when a member of the house staff, Chloe, tapped me gently on the shoulder.

"There's a phone call for you," she said.

I was expecting to hear from a friend in Nice, but the voice on the other end of the line caught me entirely by surprise.

"It sounds like you're having a high old time," Carolyn said, the note in her voice ringing with innuendo. "Was that a special friend of yours who answered?"

I ignored the gibe. "It's great to hear your voice. Where are you?"

She was at home, of course, and still hadn't the slightest intention of joining me. Nor did she embrace my suggestion that I see her when I returned to New York. "If you do," she said, "I won't be here. I mean it."

Then why was she calling? I felt exasperated. Still, I was torn.

The silence on the other end of the line crackled with impatience.

"I just wanted to hear your voice," she said, "but apparently it was a mistake." Her own voice was empty of warmth, mechanical. I half-expected her to hang up and waited for the line to go dead. Something like a sigh broke into the vacuum, but it could just as well have been an electrical hiccup. I waited, obediently silent.

In the background, I heard whoops and shouts coming from the patio. Something was going on down there. I could hear Bucky's voice rising over everyone else's. It got louder and louder—and more and more heated. I couldn't make out exactly what they were saying. Intrigued by the commotion, I tried to make some kind of conversation with Carolyn, telling her about my cooking to avoid the demeaning crisis in our hearts. Eventually, we said goodnight and hung up.

I sat by the phone for a while. Why was I still bothering, I asked myself? We were like the guests at Le Mas, essentially incompatible. Yet we seemed to have moved into that sorry, unavoidable purgatory occupied by couples who realize their bond is broken but can't stop making a desultory effort to repair it.

In the distance, a muffled shout was followed by wicked, barking laughter. Through levels of dissolving discomfort, its overtones enticed me. I considered rejoining the guests, who had started gathering in an upstairs drawing room for the debate. In the end, however, I declined. I felt let down, another letdown. Instead, I returned to my room determined to take an unbreakable oath: to keep concentrating on cooking and forget about Carolyn; beginning tomorrow, I would put her out of my heart.

In the morning, as the sun crept across the patio and I sat there struggling with my notes, I felt a little queasy. It was almost like indigestion, but I'd barely touched my food the night before.

I found Megály, the housekeeper, straightening up in the kitchen. "You missed all the excitement last night," she said, gingerly picking pieces of broken glass out of the sink.

Apparently, the shouts were part of a melée that erupted in the swimming pool, thanks to the incendiary highball of politics and wine. Bucky and

Elliott, along with one or two of the women, goaded Bud about his politics until Bud, the outspoken conservative, had just had enough. He was drinking pretty heavily, but he was no match for Bucky, who was loud and a bit of a bully and never backed off. Finally, inevitably, blows were exchanged.

By all accounts, Bud bore the brunt of the battle. "First he got all flustered," said one of the Midwestern aunts, a little too eagerly, "then he got *spanked*."

"Yeah," her sister chimed in, showing a good one-two combination with her delicate hands. "And if that wasn't bad enough, his wife lit into him. She stuck her head out the window and shouted, 'You never spend a minute in the bedroom with me. Some vacation this turned out to be!' Actually, this is turning out to be more exciting that I'd ever expected."

While everyone went on a shopping excursion to Antibes, I stayed behind, writing and lounging in the whirlpool. Later, I wandered into the uncharacteristically quiet kitchen, where Fred was prepping a recipe for "Mediterranean Bass Cooked in the *Herald Tribune*." He had fifteen black-and-silver beauties lined up on the counter and was gutting them with a well-practiced flick of the wrist.

"Will you teach us how to do that?" I asked, running my hand over the skin of a slender fish. It was spiky firm, with bright red gills, and it actually gave off a sweet saline scent.

"No, I do it for everybody." Sun glinted off his chef's blade in bright prismatic quills. "Most people . . . they get uncomfortable."

Again, I reminded him of my reason for coming to Le Mas des Oliviers, until he eventually relented. It occurred to me as we plotted our exercise that Fred secretly enjoyed my incessant probing, had done enough hand-holding and nose-wiping to consider me a serious student, a budding cook among the resort's go-go party crowd. This appreciation sent an eagerness through my hands as I took a knife and traced a line on the fish's soft underside, from the tip of its head to the tail, before making an incision, using a scissors, to define the cavity.

"You have to make the incision at the gill," Fred instructed, "which opens up the fish's insides. Now, just reach an index finger in, beginning at the head, and rip out everything in one easy motion."

Alas, I was reminded again why medical school wouldn't have suited me. The thought of groping blindly around Moby Dick's belly wall was about as appetizing as a colonoscopy. I wanted to say: Jews don't do this. But without missing a beat, I stuck a crooked finger in the cavity and pulled out its slimy guts. The swollen little GI system fell neatly onto the counter.

"Nice," Fred said, which seemed like a howler of a compliment.

"Who's going to tell the next of kin?" I asked.

Fred shook his poised half-cocked head. "You did so well," he said, "you can do all the rest."

Emboldened, I envisioned the sterile calm of an operating theater and set about the work like an assembly-line surgeon. Unlike my fish-gutting experience with Bob Ash, this time I got it down. It took about half an hour to clean all the bass. Then we stuffed each fish with a bouquet of fresh thyme and rosemary stems, a laurel leaf, and a good pinch of fennel and coriander seeds. Just before we wrapped them, Fred inserted lemon slices into each cavity, along with a few chunks of garlic.

Later, when everyone returned, they brushed sheets of the *Trib* with water and wrapped the fish five or six times in a single page, continuing to brush water on the paper with each successive fold. The packages were placed on cookie sheets and baked at 350 degrees for about twenty-five minutes. When the newspaper was entirely dry, the fish was done.

The sea bass was part of a lovely composition involving a daisy-petal of crisped potato slices, a colorful trio of sautéed peppers, ruffled arugula leaves, and a shot of warm cilantro coulis—all in all, a pleasing interaction of tastes and textures.

The appetizer, a Lyonnais cauliflower soup, was less of a success, due to the difficulty of creating the garnish—poached quail egg and sliced duck. Several impetuous students broke their yolks but insisted on continuing the delicate process. Despite Fred's warnings that it wouldn't work, they pushed on and sullied the water for the rest of us. Hard feelings crackled through the kitchen like electricity. You could feel the backfire of disenchantment.

Bucky's girlfriend, Marylu, was one of the earliest offenders, and when her yolk streaked the water, Bud clicked his tongue and glared.

"You want to make something of it?" Bucky growled. His chin came up fast.

Marylu put a firm, slim hand on his wrist: "Button it, chief."

"You're in my crosshairs, fella," Bucky said, stabbing a finger at Bud.

The others looked about uneasily, holding their collective breath. Bud said nothing. I found his lack of a comeback discomforting, as though he were giving up any pretense of brokering peace.

"Is Bucky always such a handful?" asked an older woman named Jeanie.

Marylu glanced nervously in Bucky's direction before answering, and, when she was sure he was distracted, nodded slightly: "Always. My mother refers to him as a man-child."

Well, I thought, she's batting .500 on that one.

Fred managed to defuse the situation by popping the cork on a bottle of Entre-Deux-Mers. "I think what we need right now is a cool glass of wine," he said.

The others drifted outside, whipped up by the prospect of some more poolside fireworks. I kept my eye on Bucky, who was still muttering and seething.

"Do you think we ought to stand between those two?" I asked Fred, who was whistling jauntily, cleaning up the mess we'd made.

He flashed me the most innocent smile and said, "Us? No . . . no. This is tradition at Le Mas. There are always two guests who cannot get along. Usually it is the women, too many queens of the kitchen. But you'll see, it always sorts itself out. We haven't lost anyone yet."

Perhaps this time his luck had run out. I stood watching the scenario through the kitchen doors. Bud and Bucky were standing on opposite sides of the patio dining table, talking to their respective allies. You could see everyone rehashing the quarrel and offering advice. Periodically, the two men glanced at each other with evident hostility.

People mellowed out a bit after the food arrived. Even Bud managed a few dear smiles and wiped up all of the sauce on his plate with a crust of baguette. He drained his glass and said to his wife, "Sweetie, can I interest you in a . . . nap?"

At the other end of the table, I saw Marylu give Bucky a convincing elbow to the ribs. He was on a short leash as far as that mouth of his was concerned.

As the couple made their exit to plenty of eyeball-rolling, Fred and his staff arrived carrying a bowl of chocolate mousse infused with a buttery jasmine cream. We ate a little, to be polite, but it was too heavy for a summer afternoon. A tea-scented sorbet would have finished the meal nicely. At times like this you wanted to get up from the table without feeling grotesquely full, but these sessions were structured to cover the bases.

Somehow, miraculously, we did it again later that night. We prepared our farewell meal, a menu featuring a variation on the fish soup, vegetable timbales, and mango chicken *papillote*, pulling out all the stops so that by dinnertime, in the midst of the fourth course, nobody even felt like talking. For dessert, there were individual apple tarts framed in a cloud of Vietnamese cinnamon, and just as everyone was drowning under its perfume, a tiramisu hit the plates, followed by wedges of zucchini cake topped with pumpkin *coulis*. The quantity of food was obscene.

I found it almost difficult to breathe, but, of course, that might have been due to a confluence of factors. At any rate, I knew it would be futile to stick around for coffee. There was a tension at the table that strained toward self-punishment. It would be better to avoid another sticky scene.

"See you tomorrow," I said, hoping to sleep late, or at least until everyone had departed. I barely made it up to my room before I was sick.

The next morning, I determined to head to Italy. There was nothing left for me to glean from France. That isn't to say I had mastered its cooking. If anything, I had learned that my knowledge of *la cuisine* was superficial, at best; my instincts were largely uncultivated, my skills raw and only emerging. I was worn down, but I had scored a sheaf of fabulous recipes. More important, all the French experiences, even the strange ones, had fed my passion. Throughout my journey, I realized I'd been happiest when I was most fully engaged in the cooking.

France, for me, had always been the epitome of passion, but I had been in too many French kitchens without a breather. There were other cooking schools in the area that might have sharpened my focus or at

least given me the confidence to experiment with impunity, but I didn't
have the willpower to face another fish *en papillote* right now.

Instead, I packed my bags and hugged Fred Rivière before slipping
quietly into a van bound for the train station in Nice. It took a long time
to wind down the mountain. Each mile I put between myself and that
little haven on the cliff made me feel more human again, inching toward
civilization. Our isolated little world had been splendid . . . up to a point.
Whenever twelve or fourteen adults cohabit in close quarters for any
length of time, there is bound to be friction, and God knows we had generated our share. Of course, proximity breeds its own special crises, like
Jerusalem or the New York Yankees. The presidential politics didn't help,
but there were plenty of petty quirks that fed the fire. By the end of the
week, with egos still smoldering, there was a fragile peace, at best.

I thought about all the tension in that kitchen and all the disappointing food that had resulted. It was no secret why my cooking at home was
marked by confusion and anxiety. I enjoyed the process, the creativity
involved in preparing a delicious meal, but the undue stress was a clear
expression of my discontent. All that misdirected fury took me farther
from the goal. Pressure, I knew, had no place in cooking. It should be
almost Zen, contemplative, a meditation of sorts. All those pots on the
stove, in the oven: under control. No wonder line cooks rely on instinct—
guys with good hands, no thinking involved.

The best cooks I had seen were smooth operators, unruffled by the
press of action. They took particular pride in the way their kitchens
hummed along, everything in its proper place: the cupboards organized
like research labs, the fridges neat as pins, even leftovers wrapped like
gifts and labeled in smart, exact hands. Cooking, for the great chefs of
France, was a form of discipline—the proper *mises-en-place*, the proper
techniques, the proper preparations. Order and restraint in the kitchen
were indicative of being centered in other phases of their lives.

I thought about my own kitchen, with its organic clutter. The room was
practically an obstacle course, and I lunged and lurched through it like
a taxi driver in rush-hour traffic. Becoming aggressive with a whisk—as
a cabbie with his horn—seemed a reasonable upshot of working in that

environment. And of course it explained why my recipes were a series of unstable experiments. I wasn't an incompetent cook but rather a man whose life resembled a soap opera. Le Mas had lapsed into another wild episode. It stood to reason that the more distance I put between me and those circumstances, the better my cooking would fare.

It hit me that my relationship with Carolyn had been like one of those cooking fiascos: tension-filled, joyless work. Too much effort, too much thinking involved. People are always saying that you have to work at a relationship, but it shouldn't have to be so hard. Shouldn't it be more like the seamless harmony in the kitchen at Arpège, and with the same results?

If I had kept trying to spackle things together with Carolyn, like the salt-encrusted lamb at Madame's, it might have led to the same sad, dried-out outcome, suitable for chucking in the bin. Or we'd wind up like the group on that night at Le Mas, all broken glassware and mayhem in the pool.

The *gare* in Nice was teeming with travelers. Saturdays were impossible, when most people on holiday were in transit, and the crowd swept along the platforms at fast-forward speed. Some of them, I imagined, were running for their lives. Before boarding, I stood outside on the sidewalk for almost half an hour, shading my eyes, trying to pinpoint Le Mas in the far-off hills.

In a car at the back of the train I leaned my head against the cushion, sipping from a water bottle and watching sunbathers dragging their blankets across the Riviera sand. By the time we crossed into Italy at San Remo I felt somewhat reborn, though still pursued by familiar pangs. There was a *pâté en croûte* or two I still lusted after, and technique for a strawberry charlotte . . . pork *rillettes* . . . *truite au bleu* . . . profiteroles. . . . But I was about to trade in butter, cream, and shallots for tomatoes, garlic, and olive oil. A change of saucery was exactly what I needed.

Chapter Seven

THE TOWER OF THE GUELPHS

From the window of the train as it headed out of Florence, the Italian countryside was a succession of ruddy stone villages, wobbly roads, and tightly braided vineyards, all washed by swashes of Crayola color, oranges and mustards and the entire spectrum of green. Mark Twain had gotten it exactly right—that the Creator made Italy from designs by Michelangelo. Fortunately, redevelopers hadn't left their prints on this part of the world. It would be a pity to travel through Tuscany, the most charming of Italian regions, in a landscape designed by Calatrava.

I will always remember the mysterious enchanted feeling of walking with my bags through the piazza in Figline Valdarno. It was a gorgeous Sunday evening, an hour or so before dusk, and the villagers had gathered there, I suppose, to let off a final burst of weekend steam. The square, which dated from the twelfth century, seemed like a stylized movie set. Shafts of ghostly warm light sliced across the yard, striking surfaces at uneven intervals. There were the requisite cobblestones, of course, a repeated fan-shaped mosaic, surrounded by palazzos and ancestral halls whose irregular cracked walls and archways resembled a medieval fortress. A quintet of gangly boys knocked around a soccer ball in front of the Church of San Francesco, over the objections of a woman selling flowers by its door. Pigeons waddled cautiously along the fringes. Outside an unnamed bar, two tables of old, pinch-faced men sat drinking something strong enough to fortify the debate that had engaged them for half a century, while their women leaned over windowsills watching them, occasionally barking out ultimatums.

I came at the square from around the austere Teatro Bonaparte, cutting through the *passeggiata* of strollers making their way along the darkened storefronts. The crowd seemed weighted with good-looking young couples. The men wore tapered linen shirts, with sweaters draped over their shoulders and knotted loosely at the neck. The women, artfully made up, wore fantailed sunglasses large enough to create wind drag. In my rumpled sport coat and jeans, I stood out like a sore thumb.

The train had been hot and stuffy, not one of the Eurostar coaches that serviced the main routes, and the walk from the station seemed endless. I was down a quart of water, most of which sluiced along my neck like a tributary of the Arno. I walked straight ahead, past the Palazzo Pretorio, an edifice that reminded me of the duke's house in *Rigoletto*. There was a restaurant hidden somewhere in the shadows that I needed to find. The information in my itinerary was sketchy: "Look for Torre Guelfa toward one end of the piazza."

The name was from a page right out of local history: Tower of the Guelphs. In the mid-fourteenth century, the town was part of the Florentine Republic, which was muddled in the siege of two warring political factions—the Guelphs who were loyal to the papacy and the

Ghibellines who supported the emperor. It was Florence versus Rome, vying for access to the sea, with bystanders like Figline Valdarno caught in the crossfire. Figline, known as "Florence's barn" for its vast agricultural bounty, thus sided with Guelph towns in a blood feud that lasted for generations.

It seemed like a joke to honor the Guelphs, kind of like naming a New York spaghetti joint Fortress of the Gottis. Maybe it was to ward against partisans with long memories. In any case, the Torre Guelfa restaurant was tucked into the piazza much like a steakhouse at a strip mall. It looked modest enough from the square, nothing more than an innocuous brown entrance shaded by the overhang of an arch, but once inside the doorway, there was no question of authenticity. There was the indisputable presence of the holy trinity: garlic, onions, and olive oil. The walls were stained with the odors; it was in the woodwork and the curtains. It had been weeks, maybe months, since I'd savored that aroma. I closed my eyes and inhaled like a junkie.

It was a catalyst to be sure, firing up a memory bank of Italian food debauchery that ran the gamut from the spaghetti and bocce-size meatballs served at my hometown diner to the mom-and-pop joints on New York's Mulberry Street to the transcendent menus of Lidia Bastianich and Mario Batali. How many *saltimbocca* conquests were notched on my bedpost? I'd lost count years ago. Or my enduring addiction to risotto? Does anyone ever get over that? The notion of a long-simmering *Bolognese* sauce made me drool. A nicely charred crust of pizza. . . . *Good God!* Was there no mercy? After so many weeks in the grip of French food, the soft swing to Italian was irresistible.

Tuscan food, especially, would be a gift to my palate. As my friend, Fred Plotkin, noted in his landmark *Italy for the Gourmet Traveler,* "Tuscan food corresponds to our notion of eating well" . . . *crostini,* minestrone, *ragùs, tortelloni, pici, pappardelle,* wild boar—*cinghiale!*—*bistecca alla fiorentina,* white beans, and fragrant olive oils. Five or six courses at each meal—sign me up, baby. I could hardly contain myself.

It took a while for me to locate the chef, a wiry, dapper man with the unfailing smile of a game-show host. Claudio Piantini's English seemed lifted from an American newsreel, an endearing vowel-heavy singsong that tickled my ear, except that my name came out sounding like *Boob*. His sister Sabrina introduced us in a train wreck of two languages before erupting in a clitterclatter of Italian that went on and on for several minutes, without any pause or punctuation as far as I could tell. Claudio nodded every so often and smiled patiently, but I could see he had tuned out somewhere around the two-minute mark, blurting out a *si* every so often in order to placate her. When it was over, she folded her hands across her chest and jerked her head toward me to indicate that Claudio should translate.

"Yes, well, my sister wants to remind that there is other two American groups cooking here at present. Tomorrow you come with small class and we learn some good recipes. I teach you myself. Tonight you eat here in dining room with big class, twenty-five women." His eyes sparkled impishly. "You be—how you say?—lucky dog."

Obviously he wasn't familiar with my track record. The women were mostly hearty country gals, amateur artists, from what I could gather, on some kind of a landscape-drawing retreat, whose interest in me ranged from frosty to hostile.

"We are a close-knit group," one of them informed me, scowling, as I settled in at the end of a long refectory table. And those were the last six words anyone exchanged with me that night.

I was the Invisible Man throughout dinner, an uninvited guest, a gate-crasher. At first I was annoyed at being treated so rudely, but once the food started coming out of the kitchen, hurt feelings were the least of my concerns. The variety of dishes placed before us was extraordinary—an *antipasto* platter sagging under the weight of fresh, air-cured salami; fat succulent gnocchi slathered in sage brown butter; hand-rolled *pici* served *al funghi porcini*; free-range beef marinated in garlic, rosemary, and juniper berries; roasted potatoes strewn with parsley and drizzled with a local fragrant olive oil that was regarded as one of Tuscany's very best.

Claudio was as talented as they come, a real artist, but in that honest, homespun way that was devoid of culinary flash. It was two-fisted food, the kind that extolled grilled meats, soups that required a knife and fork, ancient family recipes, and house wines harvested in the proprietor's back-yard. One dish, a concoction he called *francizina*, looked like the Tuscan version of Sloppy Joes.

"What do you think this is?" a woman from Alaska asked her friend, holding up a small bowl of white crescent-shaped cheese segments.

"It's pecorino with grapes and honey," I said, although evidently my form of English was a dialect she didn't understand. When no response was forthcoming, I added: "A fresh sheep's-milk cheese. It's really delicious."

Alas, nothing I said was going to melt that glacial armor. It seemed pointless to stick around for a nightcap with this crowd, so I skipped dessert and grappa in favor of turning in early.

Accommodations for the cooking school were a short drive from the restaurant, a bourgeois B&B on property owned by Claudio Piantini's mother. When I arrived, it was already nightfall and sealed in eerie pitch darkness, but when I awoke before dawn, thanks to an overzealous rooster, the sense I had of my whereabouts was that it resonated with spiritual warmth.

I popped the blinds and looked out on a gilded Tuscan landscape. Somehow I'd landed in the heart of the Chianti hills. The cottage was ringed by level expanses of vineyards, with their vanishing horizon back-lit, on days as clear as this one, by a band of silver-tipped olive trees. Overhead a jet left its imprint on the painted sky. Aside from the obvious fact that Claudio farmed the land to provide for his restaurant, it was useful to note how it influenced his food. I stepped out into the garden. There were patches of wild fennel and sage to saturate his dishes with sharp earthy flavor, black cabbage for the *ribollita*, the kind of spicy arugula that made your eyes squint, and the ugliest tomatoes I'd ever seen—squat and wrinkled with folds that looked like lips injected with Botox—called *florentino*. Later that morning, when Claudio joined me, I asked him how they differed from other varieties of Italian tomatoes. He responded, "San Marzano and Roma are long and for the can, but *florentino* are for fresh sauce." He broke one in half with his thumbs and put it under my nose. "See . . . ," he said, laughing at my reaction. I pulled back, eyes skeptical, looking for the trick. The flesh gave off strong notes

of herbs, especially oregano and basil, which made it smell more like seasoned sauce than tomato.

Tangent to the vegetable garden was a grove of fig trees, and behind it
another dense copse of olive trees, with branches sagging from the strain
of ripe fruit. "This is very good year," Claudio said, delighted by his crop.
"I will get eight hundred liters of oil."

If you ask me, he'll definitely need it. The kitchen of Torre Guelfa,
I deduced later, must have a trade agreement with OPEC. The cooks
burned more oil there than a fleet of thirsty Hummers.

At the edge of the garden, where a narrow strip of gravel separated the
pasture from the main house, sat a motorcycle, engine revving as if it were
preparing to peel out and turn a wheelie. A tiny, shriveled woman worked
the handlebars with an impatient touch.

"My mother," Claudio said, punctuating the absurdity with a shrug.

She gave me her mummified hand, ice-cold like a slab of stone.
"Piacere," she said, before barking out a passage of Italian, *prestissimo,*
forcing a smile onto Claudio's lips.

"Si, Mama, *si,"* he repeated futilely throughout the barrage. When his
last *si* earned a sharp nod, the woman dropped her head down, released
the gears, and left us standing in a cloud of exhaust, eating her dust.

"I imagine she cooks like she rides that bike," I said, while brushing off
my sweater. "Did she teach you everything you know?"

Claudio shook his head vehemently. "No, no—she *very* good cook, but
she make the kind of food Italians eat in their homes. I wanted to do
something more special, so I go to school in Florence, and afterward I
work for fifteen years in five different restaurants. My food, it simple, too,
but simple *à la mode.*"

A little before noon, when we got to Torre Guelfa and after Claudio
had a chance to leaf through the reservation book, there was time for
an informal cooking demonstration. The class squeezed into the back
of the tiny kitchen through a snugly constructed galley. On a stainless-
steel counter, purple onions were stacked like a display of new baseballs.
The set of couples joining me was from Kansas City. I got the impression
they were longtime friends, but as it turned out, only the husbands were

acquainted, both traveling pharmaceutical salesmen who had won the trip to Italy as part of a corporate incentive program. Neither Todd nor Scott had spent a minute cooking before departing for Italy, unless those big honkin' steaks on the barbecue counted as *cuisine généreuse*, and they were determined to have a blast. Claudio liked their enthusiasm but kept them away from the stove.

"We do preparation here," he said, slapping some potatoes on the counter, "then I cook what you make and serve it for your lunch."

The women groaned in earnest.

"I spent half a day scraping the last thing Scott made off five or six burnt pans," said his wife, a pretty blonde with a constellation of freckles over the bridge of her nose.

"You told me you enjoyed it," he protested, playing his part.

"I tell you I enjoy a lot of things, Sweetie Pie, just to give you encouragement."

Todd lifted a pinch of flour from a cup and flicked it at his friend. "*Ooooo*, that felt so good, Sweetie Pie," he moaned, teasing.

Claudio followed the horseplay with a perplexed smile. "Okay, now we make some gnocchi and then *braciole alla Livornese*."

Gnocchi, as I was to discover, was the omelet standard in Italian cooking schools. No one got past a *trattoria* door without first learning how to master it. Its presence on Tuscan tables was ubiquitous, eaten *primi*, as a starter, in place of pasta or risotto, or alongside the main course instead of potatoes, though many meals included both. The traditional recipe, implanted at birth, was nothing but a sloppy mixture of mashed potato, flour, egg yolk, and occasionally Parmesan cheese. American chefs tended to blend in ricotta, which was viewed here with about as much enthusiasm as baseball. Otherwise, the formula was set in stone—three parts mashed potato, one part flour, one part egg yolk, the dough formed into pieces the size of Tootsie Roll segments and served in either a creamy sage butter or fresh tomato sauce.

From what I knew about gnocchi, most of it practical, there were two basic varieties that prevailed throughout Italy: the supple, densely rich dumplings that just about melt on your tongue, and those that are on the

ATF's list of restricted weapons, right under the entry for dumdum bullets. There was no in-between. The secret, Claudio said, was choosing white-fleshed potatoes instead of yellow ones, which become too starchy and invariably turn to mush. Properly prepared, that is to say, without improving on the recipe, gnocchi is hard to ruin and just as easy to perfect.

GNOCCHI

1 1/2 lb. white potatoes, skins on	1 egg yolk
salt for the boiling water	Parmesan cheese, grated
1/2 lb. semolina flour	extra-virgin olive oil

Boil the potatoes in plenty of salted water. When they are soft but not mushy, remove them and, as soon as they are cool enough to handle, peel them. Mash.

In a bowl, measure out enough of the mashed potatoes to serve as a foundation for the formula (roughly half the potatoes in this recipe will accommodate four people), then add one-third the quantity of flour and the egg yolk. Combine well, using discretion to add enough Parmesan (about 1/4 cup or more) and some salt to flavor the mixture without overpowering it.

Meanwhile, bring to a rolling boil a large pot of very salty water.

Make a dough of the potato-flour mixture. The dough should be smooth, soft, and slightly sticky. On a floured surface, using your hands, roll out "snakes" of gnocchi about 1 inch thick. Dust with some flour to keep them from sticking. Cut into 1-inch segments and roll each segment over the tines of a fork, pressing them lightly in the center with your thumb so the grooves can hold the sauce.

Cook the gnocchi in the boiling salted water. They are finished when they float to the top, about 2 or 3 minutes. Remove with a slotted spoon, transfer to a bowl, and glaze with a little olive oil to keep them

from sticking, until they are ready to be sauced. Reserve 1/4 cup of the
water if you intend to sauce gnocchi.

Serves 4

Because every Tuscan kitchen seems to have fresh tomato sauce simmering on the stove, the urge was to splash a little over a bowl of gnocchi. A little pesto spooned on top wouldn't hurt matters, either. Given the choice, however, I prefer the sage butter sauce, which is creamier and a bit more delicate, and almost as easy to prepare.

SAGE BUTTER SAUCE

2 Tbl. unsalted butter	*1/4 cup of the hot gnocchi water*
3 or 4 sprigs of sage, chopped	*salt and white pepper to taste*

Melt the butter in a very hot frying pan, then add the sage. Add enough water to keep the butter from burning. Swirl until creamy, seasoning with salt and pepper.

Place the gnocchi in the frying pan. Swirl to coat them well with the sauce, and only long enough to reheat. Serve.

Scott and Todd breezed through the preparation, while their wives stood to the side, drinking wine and taking notes. The looks on the men's faces told the whole promising story.

"Check out my gnocchi," Todd beamed, putting a spoon into my mouth and puffing up with delight at my reaction.

Scott was equally carried away: "Honey, the kids are gonna love this, won't they?"

"I don't know," his wife demurred. "You know we've got four of 'em. Odds are they won't all go for it."

The three of us had a blast cranking out those potato dumplings in assembly-line mode. Making gnocchi in an Italian kitchen was instant gratification for an American wading into authentic regional cuisine. There was practically nothing to it, nothing tricky; nor did gnocchi require a prissy preparation, unlike so many of the French recipes I'd observed. You rolled up your sleeves, got your hands dirty, put your own decorative touch on each piece. Once the potatoes boiled, the whole process took about ten minutes, start to finish, about the time it takes to make a box of Kraft mac-and-cheese. I'd tried gnocchi at home a few times, winding up with either rubber or mush. But Claudio's formula was foolproof, a sign that the relative ease of Italian cooking might do wonders for my kitchen confidence.

The two drug salesmen were smitten by the experience of having made something unfamiliar and better tasting than they'd ever eaten in a restaurant. In retrospect, that sounds patronizing, but for many Americans, especially many American men with limited time at the stove, making an elaborate recipe, that is to say, a recipe necessitating more than salting a slab of beef, was a revelation. The encouragement of cooking for themselves was considerable. Todd was having so much fun, he shaped the last snake of gnocchi into a giant penis and had a picture taken as he slid it into his wife's open mouth. When he realized that Claudio was watching, he yanked it out, leaving a gruesome set of teeth marks on the head, though the chef's laughter defused any embarrassment.

We worked through *braciole*, the traditional Italian preparation of either top round or flank steak sliced thinly and pounded before receiving a quick sauté and optional sauce. I'd eaten many versions of this recipe over the years, each one a testament to the gospel of rustic cooking, and I knew the best ones were down-and-dirty: no fuss, no frills, nothing to embellish the unembellishable. As for rusticity, Claudio didn't disappoint. Everything about the recipe, including the ingredients, was bare-bones basic. No one, I can assure you, had altered it since the Guelphs threw a Ghibelline Val di Chiana steer into a pan. The incredulity on my face must have been apparent, because Claudio fixed me with a slit-eyed stare.

"What have you been doing since you arrived in Europe?" he asked, with a tone that suggested I might have been kidnapping children.

Perhaps too smugly, I ticked off the places in France where I had been cooking.

"Ah, France . . . ," he said. "The difference between our food and . . .

theirs . . . is that in France the sauces and the presentation are so important. But Italian kitchens are like poor kitchens. We use all the principal
ingredients of home cooking—no cream, no butter, just tomato, garlic,
onions, and olive oil."

There was a flip side to his argument, of course, which was that it
depended on whose home you were cooking in, to say nothing about those
succulent pastas and sausages. Nevertheless, I understood Claudio's point.
The essence of Tuscan cuisine is its simplicity. There is nothing precious
about it, no fidgety exploration of texture and flavor. Much of it, in fact, is
instinctive. The recipes are merely blueprints to guide a cook through the
process, allowing plenty of leeway for whim and imagination.

Simplicity was the norm in the kitchen at Torre Guelfa, although
Claudio's touch and feel were instincts of the ages. Most of his recipes
were handed down from relatives—his mother, naturally, but she was the
last in a line that reached back to the Renaissance. "This is the kind of
food Italians eat in the home," he said, "but with twist, *my* twist."

That wasn't to imply he was a local star. Most Tuscans, he told me,
hardly ever ate out in a *trattoria* or restaurant. In fact, in Figline Valdarno,
there were only five restaurants for its 22,000 residents. They existed basically for business and special events. "In Figline, everyone cooks and eats
at home."

To that extent, Claudio made his *braciole* for Italians who expected
nothing more complicated than what they cooked for themselves. "It is
what I make when I hungry," he said, cracking the lid on a new vat of olive
oil. Without apology, he poured into a frying pan an amount that would
keep my Saab humming for a week. Todd whistled appreciatively, wearing
a twisted grin, and wondered aloud if the company he worked for had a
drug to combat its effects.

"I don't suppose you could use canola oil?" his wife asked.

There was nearly an inch of oil in the pan, at least a cup's worth, which
took a few minutes to bring to a temperature just under the smoking
point. While that heated, Claudio peeled two potatoes and sliced them
lengthwise, about a quarter-inch thick, frying them in the oil with four
cloves of sliced garlic. It took about ten or fifteen minutes until they'd

begun to turn golden. When the potatoes developed a nice crust, he produced five steaks cut to the same thickness, nicking their sides with a knife, he said, so they wouldn't curl in the oil. He plopped them right in the same pan, allowing them just to lose their raw color before adding two cups of canned and hand-crushed plum tomatoes, a sprinkling of salt, a few grinds of pepper, and a tablespoon or two of very potent chopped garlic.

"Boil together for three minutes, and serve," he said.

"*Voilà!*" I exclaimed, as he took it off the stove.

Without warning, Claudio wheeled on me, nearly splashing my sweater with hot sauce. He shook his head with exaggerated vehemence. "Not *voilà*, not in Torre Guelfa," he said, pinning me with a stare.

A little touchy about those French neighbors, I thought, deciding not to compliment him on those freedom fries in the *braciole*.

This dish, because of the tomatoes, required a good deal of salt, but the seasonings combined with a kind of aggressive exuberance. It also received an unexpected boost from the nutty starch released by the potatoes and the flavor of good fried meat, which I later enhanced at home by using fattier rib-eyes.

"This is one of those one-dish meals that Martha Stewart advocates," said Scott's wife, as she double-checked the ingredients for her husband's recipe card.

Our lunch was served in the restaurant's main dining room, a spacious L-shaped affair whose walls had been washed in that toasty orange color you see everywhere in Tuscany. Large round tables had been laid with linens, the place settings spaced so evenly they appeared to have been measured to within a quarter inch. In an alcove at the back, partially hidden by a frayed, plum-colored curtain, half a dozen waiters shared a staff lunch that had the look and heft of a banquet, passing around platters mounded with pasta, grilled meats, and sautéed vegetables, accompanied by flasks of red wine. We took our seats at a table along the wall nearest to the reception desk. It was still an hour before lunch service, and our high-spirited chatter echoed through the empty restaurant. The two drug salesmen, especially, were pumped.

"I eat on the go," Scott explained. "As it is, I've never given much thought to what I put in my mouth." Career, family: those were the priorities. Food was fuel; fill 'er up. "If you told me I'd ever cook a lunch like this, I'd have called you a rude name."

I decided to keep my adventure with the strawberry soufflé to myself.

Both Scott and Todd were more at home in diners and family-style restaurants, where the nightly specials had an easy familiarity. They had few opportunities to experiment with ethnic food. Their sales routes wound through Kansas and the south, into the Texas panhandle, and they put thousands of miles on their cars every month.

"We're basically on the road all day," Todd explained, "always by ourselves. It's a godsend just to have the radio. I don't really listen to it, but it's nice just having those other voices with me on the long drives. When it comes time to eat, I survive mostly on steaks. This gnocchi business is way out of my league."

I knew exactly what he meant. My upbringing in Pennsylvania wasn't much different. There was little contact with food aside from the most basic of basics. An artichoke or even eggplant would have thrown me a curve, much less a tongue-twister like gnocchi, which never crossed the plate. There was a Cantonese joint that served our idea of exotic dishes, like chop suey and sticky-sweet spareribs. A special-occasion restaurant, Nick's Chat-A-While, dished up steaks, chops, and an adventurous veal Parmesan. (Nick's Greek salad, with iceberg lettuce and a sweet, vinegar-laced dressing, was legendary.)

It's not easy for anyone from Middle America—that is, anywhere outside the key cultural centers—to decipher the mysteries of cuisine. What is it that arouses our curiosity, forces us to push the margins of taste into territory unknown? For me it was easy: Moving to New York thrust me into the epicenter of gastronomy. Friends I made there talked about food the way I talked about music and sports. They were consumed by it and lived from meal to meal. The entire city was caught up in food; it was a way of life. I accepted gratefully the importance of a liberated palate. Today, there are more interesting places to eat throughout the country, but for Todd and Scott, the choices were bleak.

"There is so much to learn," Scott said, a note of futility rising in his voice. He glanced at his wife, who was languidly devouring a crust of rosemary-scented *focaccia* that had been dipped in a puddle of olive oil, so that her lips glistened, evoking something primal.

"By all means, educate yourself to your heart's content," she said. "Nothing would make me happier. The kitchen is all yours."

Todd's wife laughed, displaying large perfect teeth: "The same goes for me, Sweetie Pie. I'm happy to retire from this point on."

I wondered whether they had noticed the heat in their husbands' eyes, the eagerness in their voices. A door had opened. They had discovered something about themselves, something they never knew was there. All these years they had gone without. From here on in, there was no turning back.

After lunch, Claudio took us through a few more recipes, including pasta *carbonara* and the preparation for duck *ragù*. The levels of experience in the kitchen frustrated the chef. Clearly, Todd and Scott demanded more of his attention, so I excused myself and took a walk around the village. When I returned a short time later, the men from Kansas City could barely contain their excitement. They'd turned out some home-made pasta, zucchini cream soup, roast stuffed pork, and a bowl full of marinated *cipolline* onions.

It was like encountering two junkies. They had the same steamy energy about them, working off a food high, and I stood off to one side, envious of their discovery.

"You need to go to France," I told them. "You'll never think of food in the same way again."

Scott smiled skeptically: "I'm already in heaven, pod'ner."

"No, you don't understand—you're merely outside its gates. There's a TGV to the Promised Land and its streets are paved with *béchamel*."

"That sounds too extravagant for my taste," Scott said.

For the time being, he and Todd were satisfied with sticking to roasts and economical sauces —the backbone of Italian cooking—which are the essence of simplicity. For the time being. But I was convinced that their curiosity would get the better of them. It is not hard to acclimate one's palate to pasta and even *braciole*; spaghetti and thinly sliced steak are, in many ways, integral to American cuisine. Preparing a mousse or an aspic, a soufflé or a *crème anglaise,* even a chicken *blanquette* requires a fair amount of work that, on the surface, intimidates the beginner cook. Words such as *deglaze*, *blanch*, and *caramelize* hit a novice the same way that *bisect, decimalize,* and *extrapolate* cause my eyes to cross. But a tantalizing bowl of gnocchi almost always leads to the discovery of other cuisines. I'd spot Scott six months before he fricasseed something or reduced a sauce to a thick glaze.

An hour after lunch, during some downtime that had been set aside for a swim, I ducked back into Torre Guelfa to use the house phone. Everyone was already back at the B&B, presumably splashing around in the pool. The restaurant was deserted, aside from the dishwasher, working her way through a tower of grimy pots. I'm not sure why I wandered through the dining rooms, but for the next few minutes I perused the cupboard of local wines, the stack of linen, the silverware drawer, and the reservation book. There was a curtain separating a back room, where earlier I had seen the staff having lunch. I had decided to explore further when a faint sound stopped me from barging inside. Gently, I pulled back the curtain a couple of inches and saw Todd. He was sitting by a window, his feet up on the sill, with a cookbook open in his lap. For a moment, I thought he was asleep. Sun streaked across his face and his body was still. But eventually he smiled at something, picked up a pencil, and made a few notes.

I left without interrupting him, but one thing I knew for sure: Sooner or later, he'd be taking that trip to France.

Another day, Claudio gave a cooking clinic at his B&B test kitchen, a spacious underground setup in a bungalow at the foot of his vineyards. Despite a dire lack of ventilation, there were two hulking restaurant ranges going full blast and enough counter space to land an F-16 fighter jet. Little parcels of utensils were laid out every few feet so that students could work in a structured space. Even so, the basement seemed unnecessarily cramped. I did a quick head count of the parcels and got only as far as fourteen when the doors banged open and the students filed in.

They were a familiar bunch—the art class I'd eaten with a couple nights before—and I could tell from the looks on their faces that they were as happy to see me as I was to see them. As I'd learned at the restaurant, they weren't prone to mince words.

"Who invited you?" asked a woman wearing an indecently stretchy tank top that said JUICY across an ample fold.

I averted my eyes. "I'm with the band," I replied, clinging for cover to the chef's side.

"It might be better if you just observe," Claudio suggested, rescuing me with a knowing look. "Tonight, you come to Torre Guelfa . . . we cook there together."

I stuck around for a few minutes, hoping to pick up a few pointers, but the class was too big and unwieldy. There was a lot of horseplay. To his credit, Claudio behaved like a *padrone,* steady and imperturbable, in spite of the conditions. It may have been that his tenuous grasp of English shielded him from the monkey business. Perhaps he just tuned them right out. It was difficult to say. From my brief appearance, I could tell that the menu he prepared was top-notch. Those students who paid attention and took good notes would come away with six great recipes for a beautiful slow-paced dinner. But most displayed absolutely no interest in the cooking. They will have Italian food back home: all-you-can-eat scampi for $11.99 at the Olive Garden.

Instead, I went back to my room and, after a period of restless deliberation, I began writing a long email to my daughter, describing the extraordinary places I'd visited, the fantastic cast of characters along the way, and, of course, the food, the incredible food. "People cook with such passion," I wrote. "Their devotion to tradition humbles me; the respect for ingredients astounds. Each meal is an adventure, an education, an act of love."

I spent a few paragraphs recounting a day trip to Florence and the unexpected payoff, thanks to my compulsive curiosity. As always after some sightseeing I was slow to leave town. Instead, I wandered around the maze of streets behind the magnificent *Duomo,* with Brunelleschi's dome and Giotto's bell tower, where the hustle dissolved into residential serenity. The day had been blisteringly hot, leaving me flushed, parched. A tiny *alimentari* seemed like the perfect place to grab a bottle of water. Inside, beyond the open beaded entrance, it smelled of *soffritto* and pesto and lollipops. It reminded me of my grandmother's house—the visceral connection, the odor of cabbage and cucumber, the feeling of separation from all things modern. I felt, timid hot American tourist, like a stranger in a town where my fractured Italian could cause an international incident. On the shelves, cans of exotic-looking staples appeared to have been glued together, everything in its place. The skeletal stooped-shouldered woman behind the counter motioned me presumptuously to one of the three small tables pushed, as an afterthought, I gathered, against the far wall. Instead of shaking my head, refusing, I sat down, suddenly consumed with hunger. Was this even a dining room? What was I expecting—a display of Tuscan fireworks? No menu was evident or offered, and when the woman disappeared without a word or gesture, a feeling came over me that perhaps I'd made a huge mistake.

I glanced around the store feebly, feeling increasingly foolish. What was I thinking, I wondered, waiting here like a hungry puppy and with a train to catch back to Figline and Claudio and his recipes? I grabbed at the bottle of water from the cooler and drained it, gazing at the prints of Pompeii, several Fellini posters, and a map of ancient Florence that hung above the cash register. Some creaky sounds emanated from a confusion of old pipes. I could hear a radio clattering in the back.

Eventually, the woman returned, carrying a bowl of steamy soup balanced on a tray. "*Prego*," she said, banging it on the table.

Ribollita! A paean to Italian ingenuity. You could cook for days and not produce a masterpiece like this. It requires alchemy, a clever touch, otherwise you wind up with gruel. Those who call it soup are idiots. An authentic *ribollita* lies somewhere between stew and compost, a dense, full-bodied concoction made from leftovers simmered in their juices, with garlic, leeks, and black cabbage added to deliver a pooty tang. Even then it needs to sit, allowing the flavors to combine. Hours and hours, even days. To finish it, old bread is submerged to absorb excess liquid. Claudio made a version that was intense and heavily salted, so thick, in fact, that he discussed its mass in terms of being tender. For good measure, he removed the bread before serving and fried it in olive oil, because, he noted, *ribollita* meant "cooked two times."

This porridge was silkier, luxuriant, drizzled at the table with the kind of just-bottled citrusy olive oil the gods intended when they created the fruit. Every spoonful from the bowl seemed as satisfying as a sigh.

The woman watched me from her post behind the counter, eyeing me with a guarded, congested expression that I chose to read as pleased. As soon as I rested my spoon, she swooped in, snatched the dishes, and rushed from the room.

The next two hours reminded me of the Macy's Thanksgiving Day parade—a culinary spectacle with wave after wave of dishes, like floats, each one as grand and glorious as the next. No marching bands in between, of course, but there was an angelic harmony to the flow. *Tagliolini* in a rich meat-and-chicken-liver sauce. Eggplant Parmesan shriveled like birds' nests. *Porcini* caps seared in oil with garlic and hot pepper and speckled with an herb Italians call *nipitella*, which a friend later identified as cat-mint. A slow-cooked pork loin with garlic and lemon zest roasted on wood and sliced with surgical precision into thin rosy slabs. Spinach sautéed in oil flavored with garlic and hot peppers. A few leaves of lettuce tossed with lemon and oil. And, just to prevent me from going away hungry, she cut a wedge from a tart of jammy figs encrusted with burnt sugar, and stared until I finished the last crumb.

After the meat course, I began worrying that I wouldn't be able to get up from the table, but when the espresso finally came, I was down-right panicked. How much food had I put away in the interim? (I didn't want to know.) I'd been victimized in the past by a cabal of Jewish grand-mothers—the refrain "Eat, darling, eat," still gives me indigestion—but Tuscan women, hands down, put them to shame. When it comes to food, Italians never know when to quit. What's more, they plan a menu from which there is no shortcut or deviation. You could always push away from my grandmother's table without touching a fork to that fourth helping of brisket. *Hey, stop it, Grandma, you're killing me* always brought a comic exchange of faux grimaces and hand-wringing. But in Florence, where the procession of courses is predetermined, inviolate, there is no joking around. Refusing a dish is considered an insult; you offend the food, the cook, the family recipe, even the honor of the infant daughter who *one day will cook this same dish exactly as her ancestors did.* Everything served is to be eaten, down to the last bite. You should suffer a heart attack before leaving a wretched meatball on the plate.

Somewhere in the evolutionary process, Italians developed a stomach quite different from the American model. Theirs, it seems, is a limitless receptacle into which food is packed like a compactor. There are not even slowdowns during dessert, whereas my friends suffer openly during the throes of eating; they are always one bite over the limit or one bite away from it. Here, the gesture of anyone gasping at his plate is completely alien. Italians get up from the table after a four-course lunch with a bounce to their step; most Americans can barely make it to the TV after Thanksgiving dinner.

During a hospital stay (perhaps that hernia operation, or when they removed my tonsils), my stomach must have acquired a few spare Italian parts. Somehow, the coffee and its zing had fortified me, and I gazed plaintively at the unexplored kitchen in the back of the store.

"*Mostrare* . . . ?" Show me? I muttered and pointed, flashing my best ingratiating look.

A darkness crept over the old woman's face, as if I'd crossed a line. She worked her jaw back and forth. All the while, she never took her eyes from me, perhaps deciding whether it made sense to invite a total stranger into her kitchen. We held our positions for what seemed like an embarrassing amount of time. Finally, a stubby finger appeared from under her apron.

"*Prego* . . . ," she said, jabbing it toward the kitchen.

I practically tiptoed into the back, careful not to seem threatening—or insane. Sunlight blazing through a window rendered obscure a room that looked ready to administer a medical examination. It was neat as a pin; a few pots and pans hung on a rack bolted above an ancient stove; a stack of spotless dishes, alongside a *mezzaluna*, rested in the drainer next to the sink. Aside from a stockpot simmering on a lonesome burner, it was impossible to imagine that a feast had just been cooked here. The look on my face must have revealed disbelief, because a flicker of a smile played on the woman's pursed mouth.

You old rascal! I thought. This was a role she'd played before, and often.

While I stood scratching my head, she walked over to the stove and removed the lid from the pot. Sharply scented steam rose from the rim, engulfing her. She dipped a wooden spoon in and blew on it.

"*Prego*. . . ."

It was some kind of tomato sauce, but with a deep, earthy aftertaste redolent of smoke and meat.

"*Fabuloso*," I exclaimed to her utter stupefaction. Pointing to my chest, I begged: "*Insegnare?*" Teach me?

That elicited the laugh I'd been searching for all afternoon. Up to this moment, the woman had seemed humorless, cautious, and put out, displaying a vocabulary that was, by my count, limited to a single ambiguous word. Now she lifted her mask a bit, giving me an opportunity to make my case. I tried to explain to her in my broken Italian what I was doing in Europe, where I had been, and what I had learned so far. You might have thought, from her reaction, that I was the world's funniest stand-up comic. The Italian she rattled off mystified me, but it probably translated as: "That's a good one!" She stood, grinning at me, expectantly. All I could do was nod and say, "*Vraiment*," which, of course, was French and utterly useless. I searched my memory for the right word. "*Veramente*," I said, at last. "*Veramente . . . veramente.*"

"*Veramente.*" The spin she put on the word made it sound shifty: *indeed*.

It wasn't until I pulled out a photo of my daughter that the old woman changed her tune. In Italy, flashing a picture of your kid opens any door. That waiter who treats you like a hat box? A picture loosens him right up. Want to cut the endless line into the Uffizi? Fan those photos, brother. What little I could convey made an impact: how I'd left my daughter behind in the States—a motion over my shoulder was the best I could do—and called her every chance I could. (Thank God for that cheesy phone signal, with the thumb and little finger to the ear.) But . . . oh, how we missed each other, called every chance we got. I laid it on thick. A few more minutes, I'd squeeze out a tear or two.

That sauce recipe was as good as mine. *Veramente,* baby.

The woman shook her head in a way that acknowledged my pathetic little performance. "*Ecco . . .* You cook Tuscan style, you must know Tuscan meat sauce. No like *salsa di pomodoro,* no red. It turn brown, color of *terra. Prego. . . .*"

Unbegrudgingly, she brought out a hamper containing the essential ingredients and taught me the following recipe with firmness and precision.

TUSCAN MEAT SAUCE

3 or 4 stalks celery with their tops	8 bay leaves
3 red onions, cut in quarters	3 1/2 lb. ground beef and pork
5 carrots	salt
1 1/2 cups extra-virgin olive oil	2 cups fruity red wine
	2 1/2 Tbl. tomato paste

Cut the celery, onions, and carrots into chunks and grind them together in a food processor, pulsing just until coarsely chopped. Sauté the vegetable mixture (what Italians call the soffritto) *in the olive oil over medium heat, adding the bay leaves after it softens a bit. Cook the soffritto a long time—almost a half hour—and vigorously, stirring regularly until the vegetables brown. Add the ground beef and pork and salt well. As soon as the meat loses its pink color, add the wine all at once. Cook at a boil until the wine evaporates. Lower the heat considerably. Add the tomato paste and enough water to keep the sauce moist. Bring to a simmer and cook 2 to 3 hours uncovered, adding more water as necessary. Taste, and correct the seasoning. Remove and discard bay leaves. When the sauce is finished, it should be brown, not red.*

Serves a crowd

My *soffritto* didn't brown enough, so she made another one, and then another, so that I could spot the right color. It was essential that the vegetables be dark brown but not burned, smoky but not toasty, sweetly slick but not greasy. Nor was translucence acceptable; there is no such thing as *soffritto* lite. Achieving the right texture comes with practice; once you finally hit the formula on the nose, it comes easy every time out, much like what happens to Albert Pujols every April, once he finds his swing. It took me only one more try before I made a respectable *soffritto* the color of shoe leather, then we began adding the other ingredients to the cast-iron pot.

The old woman gave me a steady, inquisitive look. I thought maybe I had done something out of turn or, worse, corrupted her recipe. Double-checking my notes, however, I decided everything seemed in order, and when I glanced up again into the same curious stare, I raised my eyebrows, hoping it would generate a response.

"You no little *Italiano?*" she asked finally, holding her thumb and index finger a half inch apart.

"Not even a kilogram's worth," I said.

She nodded in one of those gestures that conveyed defeat. "*Ecco,*" she said, "but you have *Italiano* . . ." She tapped a spot over her heart two or three times with her tiny fist. ". . . here."

I couldn't argue with that. It was impossible to cook in a Tuscan kitchen without feeling instant affinity. Here, in an ordinary *alimentari*, the kitchen reminded me of my grandmother's, nothing fancy, but functional, a place that inspired good, simple food. The same went for most *trattorias* or *ristorantes*, usually family affairs featuring cluttered, no-frills kitchens run like those in the home. The idiosyncrasies are heartfelt and real. First of all, women—old women—preside over most Italian kitchens. Even in a beloved *ristorante* named after its virile chef (Da Alfredo in Lucca comes to mind), you can bet his mother is lurking in the shadows, tweaking the recipes. In Livorno, I watched an old woman order around an executive chef with a household name—her son, of course—as if he were the bus boy. "It's always been harder for Italian chefs," Sandy D'Amato once reminded me, "because while they were growing up, the cooking was done by the women in the family. That's why in Italy, especially, a man's food is more splashy, while the woman's is more nourishing, and that carries over into most kitchen operations." There is also, for familiarity, the science of simmering. Pots bubble with sauces for *days on end*. A fussy braise, as practiced in France, would be disdained here, as would the *sur la plaque* method I observed at Arpège, whereby a cook turns a single chicken over low heat in a pan until it has been cooked to perfection. The pots on a Tuscan stove mimic the witches' cauldrons in *Macbeth*. They are, for the most part, crusty, battered relics. There is the *ribollita* simmering on one burner, *salsa di pomodoro* on another, *fagioli*—beans of one sort or another—steaming in the back, and water for pasta churning at a slow boil. Claudio had his sludgy *francizina*—its name surely a swipe at French affectation—stewing on a burner for days.

There was a comfort factor built into the cooking of Italian food. The practice was less rigid than in France, less uncompromising, more forgiving. What the old woman took to be *Italiano* was, in fact, my passion, a quality she recognized instinctively. Imagine that: A stranger—an American, no less—walks into her place and swoons over the food! This delighted and amused her. There were a few dishes stored in her fridge, and I asked her to deconstruct them for me. It took a little coaxing, but she shared her recipes for *pasta e fagioli*, the traditional bean soup flavored with pork ribs and grated cheese, as well as risotto, and a simple pan roast of veal with garlic, rosemary, and white wine.

"You cannot imagine the degree of generosity I've encountered," I wrote to Lily that afternoon, "or the pleasure of people teaching me something they love. Most of all, I've been watching their faces—the way they light up at meals, the way they express themselves. I'm learning so much about how to live my life. And at this age! What a gift."

There was so much more to tell her, but with every attempt to put it into words, I was overcome by excitement. I found it impossible to finish sentences without sounding rhapsodic, a bit mad. Perhaps it was because most days, out of necessity, I tended to take these experiences for granted. Then, in my room or during some downtime, they snuck up and clobbered me. My head spun, trying to process everything I'd learned.

The email went on, of course, getting loopier and more breathless. I realized that if I had been sending it to Carolyn, I would have highlighted the text and hit the delete key. She already thought I was on some weird private crusade. But Lily would understand. You'd know what I mean if you saw that kid tear through a platter of *calamari*. She is a girl after my own heart—maybe a little *Italiano* herself. Writing to her made me miss her more than ever. I placed a call for the latest gossip back home.

✤

Dinner service was in full swing when I arrived at Torre Guelfa. The restaurant was already more than half full, and a checkerboard of orders was arranged like *mah-jongg* tiles on the counter. Claudio looked at them, blinking reflexively, without a glimmer of concern.

"How many people are you expecting tonight?" I asked him.

He shrugged, distracted. "Oh, maybe forty or forty-five. Whoever shows up, we feed them."

It took some restraint to keep from laughing. Alain Llorca once had twenty-five reservations for lunch, with a lineup of fifteen or twenty cooks fussing over his food. I looked with fascination around Claudio's shabby little kitchen. There was barely enough room for his ad hoc staff—Enrico Antonio, an eternally jolly man with an enormous Roman nose who shared the major cooking responsibilities, and a stocky young woman standing back-to-back against Enrico, slicing a quart of cherry tomatoes, which she was still doing an hour later.

Despite apparent sweatshop conditions, there wasn't a whit of tension. Everything moved at a dozy, systematic pace, as if the staff had dipped into the Valium reserves. What's more, each dish was cooked to order, which was doubly impressive. I watched as Enrico prepared a serving of *calamari* and cherry tomatoes as if it were the only dish on the menu that night. He made the whole affair seem ridiculously simple. First, he crushed a clove of garlic and sautéed it gently in equal amounts of olive oil and butter, while batting pieces of milky-white squid in a bowl of flour. The squid hit the pan for a few minutes, just to give it color, after which he flambéed it with a splash of generic bar brandy. When the flame subsided, he added ten cherry-tomato halves and a few torn basil leaves. "Some salt," he said, raining a fistful over the pan, ". . . and love. That's all there is to it."

I assumed that Claudio, in the meantime, was shouldering the bulk of outstanding orders, but when I looked up from my notes, he was sitting on the windowsill in the back, smoking peacefully and enjoying Enrico's *calamari* demo.

"Now I show you what we do with some pasta," he said, snatching a few orders from the expanding checkerboard.

He walked me through an *amatriciana* sauce earmarked for a bowl of homemade pasta, followed by *carrettiera*, a spicy and densely oiled sauce with chunks of tomato and garlic that took all of three minutes to prepare.

As soon as he was finished, Enrico abducted me, pinning me against the noisy grill, where he was fixing *tagliata di pollo bianco del valdarno*, which paired a chicken breast, sage, and *porcini* mushrooms in olive oil with enough garlic to clear a dance hall. The dish was a model of simplicity, cooked with a rough approximation of ingredients in a single pan, and finished, as Enrico pointed out, "with a sprinkle of salt, fresh chopped parsley . . . and love."

It went on like that all night. They worked like a tag team, Claudio and Enrico, pulling me one way, then the other, competing to dazzle me with recipes. We made a bean-and-barley soup, *osso buco*, several variations on the *calamari* theme, *crêpes* with something called flour cream, and a gamy wild-boar sauce that oozed red wine.

"I like the wild boar because it is so aromatic," Claudio said. "Deer is not possible to cook without wine because it is too—how you say. . . ?" He pinched his nostrils with two fingers. ". . . too strong. But the boar, very versatile. I have friend here in Tuscany who . . ." He made a pretend gun with his hand and sighted down his arm. ". . . Bam! . . . bam! So I make nice dish with polenta or fried artichoke. Something less aromatic to balance the flavor."

We made the *braciole* again, so that I'd get the hang of it, and two beautifully composed portions were sent out to the dining room—to Todd and Scott, specifically, who were parked at a table with their wives and another American couple. Authentic Tuscan cooking, I thought, as I plated their dinners. Just before the dishes disappeared through the swinging doors, I dressed them with a few leaves of parsley ". . . and love," I said, throwing Enrico a conspiratorial grin.

Claudio was so pleased by my progress that after another few orders were completed, he said, "How would you like to see me make *real* Tuscan specialty?"

As opposed to these . . . imposters? I wondered. But Claudio had something more authentic in mind. There was Tuscan food and *Tuscan* food, and what differentiated the two was class. The *real* food he referred to meant peasant food, and not the chic derivative attached to, say, the funky clothing at Anthropologie. This *peasant* was literal—food that people made out of necessity, when neither money nor ingredients were available.

"This we call *castagnaccio*," he said, taking down a grimy container from a top shelf above the counter, where it had probably stood untouched for months. He pried it open and held the rim to my nose for a whiff. A faint nutty scent rose sulphurously from the taupe-colored powder hugging the sides. "Chestnut flour. *Castagnaccio* was the cake made by poor people in the Apennine mountains, where the chestnut trees grow. They used whatever came from the soil there, nothing fancy—you'll see."

In no time, Claudio whipped up a batter that smelled like damp mountain soil. To bind it, he added only a little tap water. Then he gazed at a few inches of white wine remaining in the shot glass from which he'd been sipping, and threw that in, as well. "The way poor people do," he said. He poured the sticky dough into a small baking square. The only flourishes were a few raisins, some rosemary leaves, and a scattering of *pignoli*, with a tablespoon or two of olive oil drizzled across the top.

Claudio, Enrico, and I ate the *castagnaccio* while standing at the stove, as the orders continued to pile up on the counter. The cake was like poetry in our mouths. Every so often, one of the men would shrug and throw together a lovely little dinner for the punters out front; otherwise, we chatted and laughed, washing down the cake with cold Vernaccia. I felt like a member of the family, warm from the wine, in sync with the laid-back pace.

We followed that routine for several blissful days, my notebook now bulging with Claudio's recipes. Each lunch service brought half a dozen or so new preparations that could easily be reproduced. In the afternoons, I attended his cooking classes, just to observe, but for the most part my education came from monitoring the restaurant service. The nights were long and wearying. The heat in that little kitchen built to an infernal pitch. With eight burners going at full tilt, it felt tropical, like a sauna; at times, it took an extra apron to absorb the sheets of perspiration on my face.

One night, at ten-thirty, with a few stragglers still lingering over grappa, I'd finally had it. The kitchen heat became so fierce, the odor in the air so oily foul from constant frying, that I was dispatched by Enrico before they had to carry me out.

I hauled myself into the deserted piazza, finding a seat outside the Caffè i Pertici. These evenings on the verge of autumn were seasonably cool, prompting a general drift indoors as the last glimmer of sunlight receded behind the hills. Despite the late hour, I was able to wrangle a glass of Chianti, along with a liter of water. I drank like a man released from captivity and dabbed some on my neck and forearms with a paper napkin. The pretty young waitress watched me with foreboding and said, "Mister, you okay?"

Suspended above me, she shimmered like a constellation of stars. I had only enough energy to nod.

My head spun from the surge of recipes that were now as indistinguishable as a list of phone numbers. I'd been overwhelmed, of course, but I realized the treasure I was going to carry off from here when I left at the end of the week. Claudio had done a number on me, locking right into my curiosity. When he summoned me to inspect some new dish, his eyes sparkled in an artless way. It became his mission to teach me as much as he could in the short time we were together, and he rose to the occasion with obvious delight.

It seemed almost spooky when, sometime after eleven, I saw Claudio streak across the piazza looking miraculously refreshed. He'd shaved and combed his hair, which was slicked back with gel—or maybe olive oil. His apron was gone, and in its place was a sport coat and crisply pressed slacks, wingtips polished to a high bronze gloss. Later, I learned that after each long day's work, he drove the pitch-black roads into Florence, where his girlfriend lived. Wouldn't it be great, I thought, to be that tired from cooking and have someone waiting for me who was worth all that effort? A man can dream.

One morning, after visiting the local market, we stopped in the nearby village of Matassino, at Il Forno, a bakery that supplied the bread for Torre Guelfa. Behind the pastry counter, two women in white hats leaned with long, dull sabers over a large sheet cake, slicing the dough into diamond-shaped wedges. Claudio's pouchy eyes opened wide when he saw it, as though he'd stumbled upon the Ark of the Covenant.

"You *must* try," he insisted, transferring two sloppy slices onto paper plates, licking his fingers. "This is . . ." he searched for the word and sighed, ". . . art."

In fact, the cake was an ancient art made like the *castagnaccio*, from necessity by peasants. It was called *panello con l'uva*, which, according to Claudio, was the traditional *dolce* of poor vineyard people, made entirely from pizza dough, sugar, and wine grapes. My mouth filled with overripe fruit and a kind of sugar syrup that melted off the glaze. The flavor was so intense and gaggingly sweet that I laughed as a means of surrender.

"You must meet Fabrizzio," Claudio said, pulling me by a sleeve as he pushed through doors leading to an adjacent garage.

Inside, a wiry little man, graceful even in a shapeless apron, was muscling his way through a medicine ball of dough, while a trio of helpers behind him shuttled loaves of bread in and out of two industrial ovens. He looked comical, slapping the pasty mass against the little piece of marble whose surface sprayed flour in every direction. His sneakers tracked white footprints on the floor, like an Arthur Murray tango diagram. When he saw Claudio, he waved us into his chalky space.

A flurry of Italian ricocheted like a Teletype. Fabrizzio's head bobbed in time to the staccato exchange. Every few sentences, he'd glance over at me and grin to show that whatever Claudio was saying amused him no end. Their chatter sounded hysterically shrill.

"So, I have been telling Fabrizzio how you like his *panello*," Claudio said. "Is no often an American taste this." Fabrizzio bobbed his head agreeably and grinned wider, even though he didn't understand a word of the English. "And, if you like, he agree to teach you his recipe."

Fabrizzio nodded furiously now, making dough-rolling gestures with his hands.

There was a catch, of course. Fabrizzio only made *panello* before the bakery officially opened—that is, at the crack of dawn, while the ovens were warming up. "And as you see," Claudio said, "he speak no English."

"No, no, I speaka 'gleesh," Fabrizzio protested. He turned to face me, paused dramatically, and bellowed: "A-ruuudy-jooool-iii-yanni."

"*Buono*, Fabrizzio," I said, bowing slightly. "*Inglese . . . perfetto.*"

The next morning, a little before five, a taxi took me back to Il Forno, where Fabrizzio was waiting with an extra apron and a blend of coffee that did the same thing as Liquid Plumber. He seemed awfully cheerful, I thought, for a man whose roosters were still snoring in their pens. A table was set up in front of an oven hissing its rude objections to the cold, and balanced on it were a sack of flour, the ubiquitous olive oil, plenty of sugar, and a bowl of beautiful pearl-shaped grapes with deep, royal-blue skins. It looked like the kind of setup I remember from science lab, as if someone dared us to make something from so little.

For about an hour we wrestled with the formula for a sticky, pliable dough, trying to communicate through a flurry of gestures, head shakes, and grunts. It sounds ridiculous when I think of it now, but for more time than was necessary I struggled with the word *levitato*, scratching my head while Fabrizzio played charades for my benefit. Finally, he became exasperated and stuck a wad of light-brown gunk under my nose.

"*Levitato . . . levitato . . .*" he cried.

Once I figured out it was yeast, he practically jumped on my back and rode me around the bakery.

The *panello* was more rustic than I'd anticipated—nothing but flour and water, yeast, a scattering of fennel seeds, those gorgeous grapes of course, a shocking amount of sugar, and then more sugar, just in case. Fabrizzio demonstrated how to make two of them, until he was sure I'd gotten the hang of it, then we turned out a few variations together, with figs and berries instead of the grapes. In between, he kept plying me with samples of pastry—a lovely, astonishingly plain cake with orange essence that Tuscans eat for breakfast and a hard, unleavened flatbread that gets instantly stale and is used for crackers during aperitifs.

When I made it back to the little *cucina* an hour or two before lunch,

Claudio was wrapping up another cooking class with the angry artists. They were making pizza in a wood-burning oven—or, rather, Claudio was making pizza, while his students all seemed to be talking at once.

"You will not learn anything here today," he whispered between procedures, looking up at me with the saddest beagle eyes.

I started to protest but saw his point. By the *forno*, I could hear Claudio's mother, who was stoking the fire, muttering under her breath in a demonic monotone.

Fortunately, this experience seemed to invigorate the chef for my final *stage* at Torre Guelfa. The minute I entered the kitchen that evening, we were off and running in what became a marathon of new, ever-more-straightforward but inspired recipes. Before I even tied on an apron, Enrico handed me a bowl of thick, well-seasoned cannellini soup made with a rich pork-cheek stock and a slice of what he called *calanco*, a fresh pecorino with great body and texture, lacking the metallic sharpness I associated with other sheep-milk cheese.

When I had finished, he began work on an order of *tagliata di tonno agu aromi Mediterranei*, or sliced tuna with Mediterranean aromas. In retrospect, the dish seemed too simple to be that delicious, but the proof each time I tried it was plainly on the plate. He took a piece of fresh tuna large enough to feed three or four people and coated it with a thick crust of herbs: dried oregano, coarsely cracked pepper, fennel seeds, and perhaps thyme, although I wasn't sure. When I requested the exact ingredients, he said, "Whatever you like, so long as they are in the same proportions." He seared the fish in a very hot dry pan, just two or three minutes on each side, before removing it to a cutting board, where nice, thick slices flaunted a rosy core. Using individual bowls, Enrico laid the tuna over a mound of cherry-tomato halves, some *pignoli,* and capers, seasoning the top with a generous drizzle of olive oil, and salt.

The dish fired my palate on so many levels that I didn't know quite where to begin, but it took no effort whatsoever to finish. When Enrico's back was turned, I lifted the bowl to my face and ran my tongue around the inside. It was that good.

Before I had a chance to breathe, Claudio handed me a plate with another fat slice of the pecorino on which he'd placed three grape halves, face down, with a drizzle of fragrant olive oil. "We use this as *aperitivo*," he said, "or dessert, whatever is preferred. And now I show you how we deep-fry it."

More slices materialized, which he dusted with flour and some egg. Afterward, he brought out a container filled with fine bread crumbs. He rolled each cheese wedge in the crumbs, knocking off the dense eggy clumps, then put the lid back on the container and hoisted it up on the shelf. How many things had been dipped in there in the last few months? I wondered. For that matter, what precautions had been taken to sanitize Claudio's cutting board? During my tenure at Torre Guelfa, I had never seen it be washed—or wiped. He cut freshly killed rabbit on it, wild boar, various cheeses; he filleted fish, chopped vegetables, rolled out pastry. They all succeeded one another on the same wooden plank. Nor, as far as I could tell, was there a washing of hands in this kitchen. Noses got rubbed, cigarettes smoked, garbage tossed, hands coughed into, fingers licked—it all happened in the normal course of events.

Even the *francizina*, his Tuscan barbecue stew, drew a reproachful stare. It had been sitting on the stove since the day I'd arrived—three days, maybe four—without any refrigeration. Yesterday, it sat in a stockpot on the windowsill while flies buzzed overhead. Tonight, it was back on the stove. "Last day," Claudio assured me, when I inquired about its shape. "Afterward . . ." He gave one of those hand signs you see on *Deal or No Deal*. ". . . finished."

To distract me, Claudio uncorked a cold bottle of Greco di Tufo dei Feudi di San Gregorio, a crisp, fruity Tuscan white that we began sipping and eventually killed. Halfway through the evening, another bottle appeared, then another, and my body took on a thickness that slowed me down to 33 1/3 rpm.

"Come watch," he said, throwing me a sly, knowing look. "I make a nice recipe with *calamari*. You learn."

While he gathered the ingredients, Enrico laid a few slimy squid on the same counter where a chicken had just been cut up. I was fascinated by his method of cleaning these strange creatures. He handled them the way

I'd seen electricians strip wire. He peeled a thin, nearly invisible layer of skin, a flimsy coating almost like cellophane, back across the slick white flesh, and I thought for a moment he would break it. Instead, he caught the end of the coating with two fingers and yanked, unwrapping the squid like a cheap cigar.

"Remember," he told me, pulling at sections that came away in his hands like orange segments, "take away the eyes and teeth and the soft spine. They are no good. The rest—good."

I smiled weakly when he passed me several squid to prepare. Cleaning them seemed to require a skill unavailable to the butterfingered novice, although once I got the hang of it, there was nothing to it at all.

In the meantime, Claudio assembled quite a collection of vegetables whose skins glistened from a quick rinse in the communal sink.

"I call this *composa di calamari su crosta di patate*," he said proudly, which sounded infinitely more musical than squid on potato crust.

The recipe was a little more involved than I was used to at that point, but well worth the extra effort. In fact, it was the best of all the recipes I learned from Claudio and not at all complicated once I figured out how to coordinate steps in advance, before assembling it, like a Christmas toy, at the last minute.

COMPOSA *di* CALAMARI *su* CROSTA *di* PATATE

4 russet potatoes, unpeeled (about 1 lb.)	2/3 cup extra-virgin olive oil, separated
water	8 small pieces calamari, cleaned (bodies and tentacles)
salt and freshly ground pepper	
1/2 lb. (2 sticks) butter	2 cloves just-crushed garlic
4 young Italian artichokes	4 sprigs flat-leaf parsley, chopped, for garnish
flour for dredging	

Place the potatoes in a stockpot and add enough cold water to cover them by a few inches. Salt the water and boil the potatoes in their skins until you can pierce them with a knife, about 15 minutes. Drain, peel the skins with a paring knife, and either mash them or put them through a ricer. Season lightly with salt and pepper.

Melt the butter in a large, nonstick frying pan. As the butter begins to melt, add the mashed potatoes and press down with a spatula to form a cake of sorts, salting it very well and letting it cook over medium heat until a little golden crust forms on the bottom. This takes a while, perhaps as much as 20 minutes, and it must be turned occasionally by inverting the "cake" onto a plate and sliding it back into the pan so that the potato browns on both sides. Cook until all the butter is absorbed and the potato cake is soft but doesn't adhere to the pan. Set aside, covered, in a warm oven.

Remove the outer leaves of the artichokes (not those big fat California babies, but the slender Italian models), cut each in half, and scoop out the fuzzy choke with a melon baler, being careful not to remove any excess heart. Slice artichokes thinly with a mandoline or very sharp knife. Place the slices in a bowl and dredge lightly with a handful of flour. Shake off excess flour and fry in 1/3 cup of olive oil until crisp. Remove to a warm plate and pat with a paper towel to remove excess oil.

Meanwhile, lay each piece of calamari flat. Cut bodies open, flatten, and score the inside, about halfway through in a crosshatched pattern. Cut body pieces into 2-inch squares. (They will curl around themselves in a decorative flower shape when cooked). In another frying pan, heat 1/3 cup of olive oil, along with the crushed garlic. When it is hot but not smoking, season the calamari with salt and pepper and add to pan. They are done when they curl up like a flower, 2 to 4 minutes or less, depending on thickness of calamari.

To assemble the dish, cut 4 circles from the potato cake using a 2-inch mold or cookie cutter. On each plate, place a disc of potato. Drape with 3 pieces of calamari and a scattering of the fried artichoke slices. Sprinkle parsley on top and around the plate. Drizzle with olive oil and serve.

Serves 4

There was something so wonderful about the easy combination of textures—the soft potato and chewy *calamari,* with an uncompromising crunch of artichoke lightly between the teeth. It tasted like a snug winter's night in front of a Tuscan hearth, like a gift, an answered prayer. I made such a fuss over it that Claudio brought me a second helping made from the leftover potato cake. Embarrassed, I waved him away, protesting, but only halfheartedly.

"It is extra," he said with an impish grin. "No one will eat it."

He was a prince, I thought, and as I finished the *calamari* and drank more wine, I positively glowed with affection. His kindness washed over me. I felt the slow exchange of information as a path toward intimacy. Here, in an Italian kitchen, I'd encountered real encouragement. The world was more benevolent than I had expected.

Claudio returned, rearranged plates. I opened a plastic container and lopped off a hefty slice of the chestnut cake. Then another. Nibbling at it, I began to think about all the things I'd eaten during these travels. Whenever I turned sentimental or felt lonely, I had rooted through cupboards, each one a dark dry abyss stocked with anonymous boxes, and fed something to the void within. Food had become my trusty fallback, a satisfying distraction. For too long now, I'd been putting off thinking about the obvious: One of these days I'd have to head home to my own kitchen full of cupboards, where there were so many unknowns awaiting me. So far, I'd managed to avoid confronting any of them. There had to be a better answer, something other than the munchies, to settle unresolved issues in my life. Enrico would know what to do. He'd have the recipe, the list of ingredients. *Whatever you like,* he would say, *as long as they are in the same proportions.*

"*Andiamo.*" Claudio's voice sliced through my gauzy reverie. "We make one more recipe, then you finish. Too hot tonight. You have color of pecorino."

Before I could protest, he slapped a three-inch-thick rib steak on the grill and pummeled it with salt. A pop and a sizzle came from the jowl of fat around the eye. While the steak seared, he peeled five artichokes and cut them into large, uneven chunks, rolling them first in flour and then in some lightly beaten egg. Without having to be told, I picked up the chokes, ready to redip them in the flour, but a quick hand restrained my forearm.

Claudio wagged a forbidding finger across the bowl. One dip only— keep it simple. "Tuscan way," he said, repeating the process with zucchini blossoms. Both of the prepared vegetables went into a wire basket that was lowered into a pot of smoking olive oil. He reached under the counter and brought up a bowl of fresh *porcini* mushrooms. "Different for *funghi*. Just flour and cold water. The difference in temperature makes them fry crispier."

I explained that in France they added a little beer to the batter.

"Ah, beer—yes," Claudio sighed. "But the French make it like tempura. That is not Italian."

I cast a wary eye at the steak, which was engulfed in a corona of flame. Claudio, noticing my concern, plunged a long fork into the meat and touched it to his lower lip. "If the fork is warm, the meat is done; cold—not done," he said. A slight hesitation before the verdict. "It will be medium-rare." Tuscan science.

While the steak rested on the counter, he retrieved the vegetables, which had taken on a nice woodsy tan. Flecks of crisply fried flour clung to the sides like a day's growth of whiskers.

"We leave all this here," he said, stripping off his apron. Obediently, I followed him outside, into the piazza, where a table had been set near the restaurant door. A gentle breeze blew, pulling at the slim threads of candlelight, which flickered unsteadily in the glassware. Around us, teenagers huddled in the darkened archways, their cell phones glowing like fireflies. Claudio slid into a seat and motioned me to join him.

"We've been nibbling all night," I said, patting my well-upholstered stomach.

"Yes," Claudio nodded, "and now we eat." He snapped a crisp white napkin, which sent a signal to unseen eyes. As the napkin dropped to his lap, Torre Guelfa's doors burst open and Enrico cha-cha-ed out, balancing a platter above his left shoulder. I could smell the *carrettiera* before it hit the table.

"*Primi*," said Enrico, ladling pasta on our plates. "You taste one of our specialties made by cheap American help. If you not pleased, you let me know. We fire him."

The situation reminded me of the spaghetti scene from *Lady and the Tramp*. If Claudio expected me to chew down a strand of pasta with him, he had another think coming. Instead, I beamed at him with approval. A flush of paternal pride tided into his cheeks. There was no easy way for me to pay tribute.

He'd singled me out from several dozen would-be students who purportedly came here to cook. Whatever it was that had caught his eye—my eager palate, a feel for the "Tuscan way," an appreciation for the mix of artistry and elusive magic that a chef needs to pull off a great meal—he recognized an uneducated instinct worthy of pedagogic largesse. It goes without saying that I'd learned a ton from him. Some amazing recipes, of course, but a lot more than that, something more important. The incredible spirit in this piazza was certainly part of it.

"You cook my food in your house in America," he said, swirling a few inches of purple Sangiovese in his glass.

I smiled and nodded in a way that I was sure he understood.

"So, you remember what I taught you about Tuscan cooking. How our kitchens are poor, how we use only principal ingredients found in home. Just tomato, garlic, onions, and olive oil."

I'd been listening more carefully than he knew: ". . . and love," I said.

Chapter Eight

THE PERFECT LIFE

After a few months on the road and such a transcendent cooking-school experience, I suppose I was due for a spanking.

My next scheduled *stage*, near Chiusi, came highly touted. The chef, I was told, had been teaching Tuscan cooking for years and would welcome a lightly seasoned student like me, someone with a little macaroni under his belt. It sounded like a great refresher after Torre Guelfa, sort of like Pasta 201. The idea of consistency appealed to me; it would give me something to build on and, possibly, to perfect.

The week kicked off with a welcome dinner at "an authentic Tuscan restaurant" in Montepulciano, where others who signed up for the class had gathered. My heart sank as I pulled into the parking lot. The tour buses were a dead giveaway. They were parked bumper to bumper along the curb, like the elephants under Barnum & Bailey's big top. A tourist trap. *Shit!* Inside, the place was a three-ring circus. One side of the restaurant was packed with Germans wedged into tables so close together that the food had to be passed overhead, like recovered luggage. On the other side were my fellow students, thirty-five couples from a small town in Connecticut, chaperoned by a local celebrity who did some cooking on a cable news show. They were already fairly toasted on supermarket Chianti and kept hoisting wine glasses, shouting out "*Ay-y-y-y*," as they imagined an Italian might do, even though it sounded more like the Fonz.

The meal was awful, no better than cafeteria food, and it was literally thrown at us by two scornful waiters, their faces as blank and lifeless as the grilled mackerel being served. The others wolfed down everything in sight.

"Oh, I simply *love* these sugared raviolis," a woman across from me exclaimed, piling enough on her plate for what could only be a relief mission.

"That's actually nutmeg, not sugar," I told her.

"Nutmeg? Can we get that in America?"

I had been on my best behavior up until now. Even during the hors d'oeurves, when one of the tipsy husbands ran down his Sonny Corleone impression, I'd held my tongue. But my self-control, as we know, is about as durable as a strand of pasta. The woman's question struck the wrong chord and I couldn't help myself.

"You're from Connecticut, right? Do you think the fact that it's the Nutmeg State might be a clue?"

After I was moved to another table, the sing-along started. *When the moon hits your eye like a big pizza pie, that's amorrrrrayyyyy.* . . . I excused myself and went out for some air. Through the open windows, I could hear another delirious refrain. *Volare, whoa-ho, contare, whoa-oh-oh-oh.* . . .

This was a new experience for me, of course, thanks to careful planning and good karma; but my luck, it appeared, had about run its course. I had heard all the nightmarish tales about how Americans travel in Europe, the way they insist that everyone, even the pets, speak English. These were the extremes, of course, but this gang . . . they took the cake. They were like the Joad family, only funny. I had interpreted the clowning as something deliberate, reassuring, a familiar chord they struck with each other to give them an identity overseas. That, at least, was the excuse I'd made for them. Now and then I overheard someone express his fear of traveling abroad for the first time, and I felt a little ashamed of my easy comfort level, but any sympathy soon evaporated with a burst of goofy chatter.

The cooking class itself was held in Palazzo Bandino, an eighteenth-century villa surrounded by vineyards that had once been a private residence but had since been renovated for package tours. Aside from me, only women attended the classes; their husbands either played golf or were shuttled around the knotted skein of commercial tasting sites, buying caseloads of wine to ship home. There were so many of us crammed into the class that we were broken up into flights of thirty or so students, each presided over by the TV chaperone, a real go-getter named Hilda, who herded us into corners of the room where we sat by open windows, drinking wine and watching yellow jackets feasting on the fat clusters of Malvasia and Sangiovese grapes clinging to the vines below the sill.

I was becoming convinced that I'd made a mistake coming here. Even though it was in the heart of Tuscany, with a tradition that stretched back to the Etruscans, there was something too slick, too contrived, about the whole glossy setup. It was a take on what Americans thought Tuscany should be, which, of course, was more compatible with the Venetian or the Bellagio in Las Vegas. Nothing about the place felt as authentic as Figline Valdarno, least of all the chef, who came to us by way of Central Casting.

Luciano Benocci was a strange, cold man with hooded eyes and an operatic girth, like Stromboli, whose apparent lack of English allowed him to plow through a lesson without so much as a shiver of interaction. I don't think he even looked up at us once. If he did, it was to shoot someone the kind of bloodthirsty stare that silenced unnecessary chatter. Hilda, standing sentry at his side, provided a running commentary. Actually, it was less a translation than her own unique take on the recipes that cried out for serious editing. Ingredients were misidentified, procedures ignored.

During a demonstration of sausage making, Luciano trucked out a huge metal device that butchers in Italy used for commercial preparation.

"Where in the world am I going to find one of those in New Haven?" a woman asked.

It was probably rhetorical, but I suggested she could do the same thing at home with a pastry bag and some casings.

"No! Impossible!" Hilda said, throwing me a look she no doubt learned from the chef. "Of course, if *you* would rather teach the class. . . ."

This was an ominous development *(another* ominous development). I recognized in her admonishment a certain pattern. Like all cooking-school veterans, I had developed a familiarity in the kitchen and with it a tendency to, shall we say, open my big mouth.

I didn't say anything more—either to Hilda or to Luciano, who had been following our little set-to with apparent relish. His movements took on a certain jaunty bounce, and after each demo he'd glance up over his knife, first at me, then at Hilda, skying an eyebrow as if it might jump-start a spirited reprise.

I had been in some remarkable kitchens and my tolerance for bullshit was next to zero. In any case, the grace period for chefs was dwindling with each day of experience. I was impatient to learn something new, eager to build on the gift I'd been given. A free-for-all like this seemed like a waste of precious time. The truth was, I didn't belong in a class like this. In a perfect world, there would have been categories of cooking schools to satisfy every level of student, but since I'd waded into what was obviously an explosive new phenomenon, there was no way to distinguish among the good, the bad, and the cheesy.

The class at Palazzo Bandino seesawed among all three extremes. There was a *pici*-making demonstration given with a kind of fox-trot monotony, along with four sauces to accompany the dish. The first one—nothing but a sorry paste of bread crumbs, garlic, and olive oil—was ridiculously uninspired and thrown together. (Where was the love that finished Claudio's and Enrico's recipes?) I checked out mentally and stopped taking notes. Eventually, Hilda came around to inspect our results, but she made a detour around me that was comical. Most likely I radiated something scary. In any case, she knew enough not to tangle with me.

The chef also must have sensed my frustration. After the class disbanded, he motioned me into the kitchen like a man with a secret. In what I took to be pretty good English, he said, "I going to teach you zump-zing extra."

He produced a few beefsteak tomatoes, filling several bowls with bread crumbs, parsley, oregano, and chopped garlic. My heart sank again as recognition set in. The bonus was nothing more than a baked-stuffed-tomato lesson, the simplest, most basic of *antipasti* taught in the Italian equivalent of Home Ec. He'd underestimated me, misread my eager smile. Unable to hide my dismay, I watched with indifference as Luciano mashed everything in a bowl, bound it with olive oil, and popped it into the oven, all in less than a minute flat. Afterward, he let me watch him make pizza, with the emphasis on *watch*, and not exactly make it, either. The dough had already been prepared, so he rolled out a large round, spooned on some tomato sauce *from a can*, followed by a sprinkling of grated mozzarella, and slid it into the oven next to the tomatoes. With apologies to Claudio, I clapped twice and said, *"Voilà!"*

Luciano patted me on the head like an obedient dog: "Tomorrow, you come back. We make gnocchi together."

I didn't tell him he'd have to shoot me first.

In the lobby, the Germans and the Yankees were drinking and singing again, this time noisy choruses of their respective national anthems, in a scene that seemed lifted right out of *Casablanca*. Where was Claude Rains when you really needed him? In his place, however, strolled a character named Patrick, a fifty-something pseudo-stud in a white silk shirt unbuttoned to his navel, tight jeans, retro ponytail, and requisite earring. I'd seen him hanging around the fringes, no doubt to provide some mock-hip Italian–LA appeal. From what I could tell, he seemed to be very popular with the Connecticut wives, who flirted shamelessly with him. In any case, he was a facilitator, an aide-de-camp to keep the paying customers happy. The first words out of his mouth to anyone were: "Can I get anything for you?" He was clearly disappointed each time I responded with an emphatic "No."

This time, he popped the question and turned away before I answered, certain that he had me pegged as an American unwilling to play.

Instead, I said, "How about a taxi?"

Fifteen minutes later, I was on a train heading north.

I bought a one-way ticket to Florence on the three-forty train. From the outset, I had been hearing about a cooking school outside Lucca that was worth a separate trip, so I decided to head there right away, as opposed to a few weeks later, when I had planned to go.

My bags had never really been unpacked in Chiusi. I swung by the hotel and, while the taxi idled, threw together the rest of my gear, paid the bill, apologized to the young couple who owned the place, and beat it out of there, as fast as I could, before anyone else could say "gnocchi." There were a few souvenirs from Palazzo Bandino—an apron, some mimeographed recipes, and a gift box containing wine—that I left on the nightstand beside the bed. As callous as it may sound, I didn't want any reminder of the place. The adventure, so far, had been a remarkable, if unorthodox affair, and I wanted nothing to put a drag on the momentum.

Aside from that maniac in Beaune, this was as close as I had come to making a getaway. I was a fugitive from a generic Tuscan kitchen where the sauces were indistinguishable from the paint being slapped on the barn across the road. It was high time I learned this all-important life lesson: There is no point in staying with people who are wrong for me.

The place in Lucca, I was confident, would offer a radically different approach. It was supposed to be a luxurious, highly civilized school that attracted a more worldly, if not serious, crowd of cooking enthusiasts. The chef, Valter Roman, was renowned for teaching an energetic hands-on class, although I heard stories, depending on who told them, that he had either stomped out or been fired from Le Mas des Oliviers in the days before Frédéric Rivière arrived. In fact, this new setup was literally around the corner from Villa Lucia, a sister property of Le Mas that catered to the same clientele. Rumor had it that if you looked up every now and then, you could see the sparks flying between the competing kitchens. How utterly Italian, I thought. In case the school turned out to be another bust, the situation promised the equivalent of good opera.

The Tuscan Chef, as the course billed itself, was located in Vorno, a tony suburb of villas and bungalows that was established in the fourteenth century as a summer residence for Lucca's noble families. All winter, they lived within the walled city, where enormous fireplaces provided heat. But in the summer, when the weather turned sweltering, they packed their belongings into elegant horse-drawn carriages and moved, with friends, guests, and servants, to the higher altitude in the shadow of Mount Pisano, where they remained until just after the October harvest.

Villa al Boschiglia was quite the swanky pad, a seventeenth-century gated mansion on the apron of a magnificent lawn, surrounded by a grove of plane trees and feathery thin larches lining the gravel driveway. A giant urn planted with geraniums stood in a nest of fallen pine needles. The place reminded me of Tara before the war, with its sweep and splendor. A faint sweet fragrance filled the air, lemon mixed with lavender, a scent so delicate, so perfect, that I imagined it was piped in from the Guerlain plant.

An attractive young couple greeted me at the door, and thereupon I was escorted into a formal dining room intended for a banquet. Sunlight flooded through the floor-to-ceiling windows, warming the room with golden heat. Valter Roman took my bags, his wife, Julia, replacing them with a slim flute of *prosecco*. "You look like you could use something delicious to eat," she said, *veddy* British.

What a difference a day made. The room was lovely, elegant, well suited to a segment of *Masterpiece Theatre*. There were several good antiques, muted pastel-colored silks on the chairs and draperies. The table was laid with sculptural arrangements of flowers and tapered candles to match the silks. I can't remember if there was art on the walls, but archways carved out along one side of the room opened onto a handsome kitchen, where unseen elves and gremlins labored over God's work.

It seemed as if only seconds passed before a feast appeared on the table. We ate some fresh homemade pasta and creamy sharp sheep cheese sizzling in a casserole; grilled zucchini and roasted peppers; and plump, well-charred boar sausages oozing garlic and wild fennel. The mixed green salad with Parmesan shavings was worth the journey by itself.

Valter Roman was boyishly handsome, fine-boned and slim, with a voice that had traces of a flinty German accent. There was something standoffish in his nature, something impersonal, but perhaps that was Germanic too, although I suspect it had more to do with the circumstances at the villa. Valter was a chef's chef, the real McCoy, you could see it in his eyes and the way he carried himself in the kitchen, with confidence and imperiousness, but the cooking school demanded more of a stretch, so that he doubled as a sort of jack-of-all-trades. He planned the menus, of course, and taught the daily lessons, but there were various marginal responsibilities, like welcoming the guests, assigning rooms, conducting tours to markets and vineyards, handling complaints, all the frothy details that impinged on his craft. He was running a camp instead of a kitchen, which must have frustrated him no end.

Still, he made the best of it, as far as I could tell, without apparent condescension, and when the guests began filtering in a few hours later, he and Julia launched into action.

It was an odd unusual group, not at all what I'd expected. There were several couples in their sixties drawn from all corners of the States; two longtime friends from Massachusetts—she a working mom, he gay; a few gals from the Deep South; and that familiar compulsive cooking-freak writer nursing a broken heart. As always, there was an awkward cocktail hour during which we stood around shyly, giving each other the once-over. And, as always, I jumped to a few rash conclusions. It was easy, considering the revolving doors I'd spun through, all the characters who'd left unexpected impressions. It was a form of self-protection, I guess, seldom accurate but a resourceful gamble nevertheless. Valter predicted an intriguing week, but judging from appearances it was anyone's guess.

We cooked together that first afternoon, and later that evening we sat down at the long table and ate platters full of stuffed, deep-fried zucchini blossoms, several types of crostini, paper-thin *tagliatelle* with rich wild boar *ragú*, toasted almond biscotti, and tiramisu made from ladyfingers soaked in rum with a coffee-and-cocoa-flavored mascarpone.

The recipes were good, very good, and the working conditions, for the most part, were sprawling and well equipped. It was the best-appointed kitchen I'd been in so far: thoughtfully designed, acres of counter space, airy and well-lit, stocked with everything under the sun, from anchovies to zolfini beans. Valter was incredibly well organized and specific during class, delivering our instruction in a clear, flat voice, but he didn't do well, it seemed, with group chatter. When people got goofy, as vacationers always do, his back stiffened like a cat; he was unable to hide his irritation. A whisk accidentally dropped on the floor drew a sharp reproachful stare. Silly questions were curtly deflected or ignored. There was no room for horseplay, which erupted from the start.

The older couples were especially loose. They'd come to Italy to unwind, using the cooking school as a layover between sightseeing tours. There was a consensus among them that the experience should be fun. They were good-natured participants, all except for Wendy, a housewife from Detroit who would have preferred a public flogging to pasta-making.

"Oh, what have you gotten me into?" she moaned, blinking at her husband as if it might make him disappear. She held up her apron as if it were a burka. "Well, I'll wear it, but I'll never really use it."

Normally, I might have stepped forward to offer some friendly reassurance. I was, after all, something of a veteran of these situations. But I had my own demon to contend with. During a demonstration of *puttanesca* sauce, one of the single southerners, a meaty gal named Cheryl Lynn, tapped me on the shoulder. "You have to move so everyone can see," she said in a drawl as thick as polenta. Not: "Would you mind moving?" Or: "Sorry, honey, but I can't see around you." *You have to move so everyone can see.*

Strangely, no one, aside from Cheryl Lynn, was standing within five feet of me. I didn't even have time to react, when she tapped me again, this time digging in with a steely little finger. "You obviously didn't hear me."

Later, while I was taking a picture of the sauce, she stuck her paw in the frame, ruining the shot. "Oh, why 'scuse me," she said. Her smirk appeared pleased.

I made every effort to stay out of Cheryl Lynn's way. Nonetheless she managed to get under my skin. Often, during class, she refused to pass me a necessary ingredient I'd requested; she'd pretend not to hear me or look away with an annoying little gesture. A flicker of satisfaction played on her lips. Sometimes, when I was talking, I'd see her mimic me to a friend. I was determined to ignore it, but it made my blood boil.

The next day, on the way to a vineyard in Greve, we made a pit stop at a rest station and I somehow got locked in the bathroom. It took some doing to extricate myself, and once settled back on the bus, I related the story with plenty of comic touches. "Man," I said, "I was worried no one would find me."

"Or no one would care,"Cheryl Lynn said.

I don't know what I had done to offend this toad, but this was going to end badly.

Valter, who had watched this episode unfold, walked alongside me to a *trattoria* where we were having lunch. "It seems like you and Cheryl Lynn have gotten off on the wrong foot," he said.

"Which foot would that be, Valter?"

"Please don't make this any more difficult. She seems to have some kind of grudge against you." He looked around uncomfortably. "Did you, perhaps, come on to her?"

"You must be joking!"

"Then maybe you should."

"I'd sooner come on to a porcupine. Really, Valter, that woman is a menace. I'm usually a good sport when it comes to these group dynamics, but I'm warning you, if she keeps this up, you may find her floating in the *bollito misto*."

Cheryl Lynn's presence in the class formed the perfect opportunity to concentrate on the cooking. Social interaction seemed out of the question. It was a practical solution, but it annoyed me; the world's downward spiral seems to be perpetuated by such jerks.

Our late-afternoon class offered plenty to distract me. We made pasta the old-fashioned way, by dumping a mountain of semolina onto the counter, cracking eggs into a well in the center, and incorporating the flour from inside the well, slowly working outward until the eggs had been absorbed. I'd done this before, kneading the dough until it was smooth and then feeding it into a little hand-cranked pasta machine. But Valter had an attachment for the KitchenAid mixer that did all the hard work. You just pressed a button and—instant pasta! It was a huge shortcut, just about foolproof, and we made perfectly smooth ribbons that begged for a creative twist. But—what?

Bud and Sally, who were from Florida, suggested spaghetti and meatballs. Valter stared at them, blank-faced, as if they had said Twinkies. In the end, he didn't even respond, which was probably a good thing. Thankfully, Ed, who was from Boston, bailed him out by mentioning that he loved ravioli, which jarred Valter from his trance. He had just the recipe—a wild–asparagus–filled ravioli with truffle butter. Once we had the pasta, it seemed like a perfect match, and we set about the process with liveliness.

WILD-ASPARAGUS RAVIOLI WITH TRUFFLE BUTTER

1/2 red onion	salt and freshly ground
1 garlic clove	pepper
9 oz. very thin asparagus	1/2 cup grated Parmesan
extra-virgin olive oil	pasta for ravioli
1 chili pepper, minced	1 egg, beaten
7 oz. ricotta cheese	3/4 stick unsalted butter
	black truffle, shaved

Prepare the filling: Chop the onion, the garlic, and the asparagus and sauté in 2 tablespoons of olive oil, adding a little bit of water (or stock) after a minute of cooking. Cook until vegetables are soft. Add the chili pepper and combine. Transfer to a metal bowl, add the ricotta, and mix thoroughly with a wooden spoon. Season to taste with salt, pepper, and 1/4 cup Parmesan. Combine.

Prepare homemade pasta, rolling out the dough into thin sheets.

Take one sheet of pasta and lightly wash the surface with the beaten egg. Mark, but do not cut, the positions of the ravioli with a cutter or knife, and place a teaspoon of filling in the center of each one. Cover with another thin sheet of pasta. Using a cookie cutter or knife, cut and seal into the desired shape. Cook in salted boiling water until al dente, about 4 minutes.

Combine the butter with 1/4 cup Parmesan in a saucepan until just melted. Mix with the ravioli and serve immediately, with a few light shavings of truffle on top.

Serves 4

We also rolled out a few pasta sheets and cut them into fine ribbons of *tagliolini*, which we served with a simple cherry-tomato sauce that, according to Valter, "you cannot beat." There was nothing to it; everything came together in a little over five minutes.

CHERRY TOMATO AND BASIL SAUCE

extra-virgin olive oil
1 garlic clove, minced
1 3/4 lb. cherry tomatoes, quartered

salt and freshly ground pepper
handful of whole basil leaves
homemade pasta
grated Parmesan

Heat the oil in a frying pan and lightly fry the garlic. Add the cherry tomatoes, salt and pepper well, and top with basil. Cook 5 minutes. Mix with fresh homemade pasta and top with fresh basil leaves and grated Parmesan.

We'd been cooking for almost two hours without a break when Valter said, "Tonight, one more classic: risotto." He spoke in a respectful, rhapsodic voice when describing the legendary preparation, which I instantly related to, having spent countless nights doubled over a steaming pot, stirring like a maniac in an attempt to produce the creamiest possible consistency. It was a mainstay of my repertoire. Short of a great roasted chicken, there was nothing more comforting than well-made risotto. The sweet butter, perfumey wine, savory stock, nutty rice, and any number of assorted mix-ins—they were an aphrodisiac to those of us for whom eating was a sensual experience.

"I must tell you . . . ," Valter said, pausing to great effect and looking meaningfully into our eyes with something close to indecency, "I am a lover—a *lover* of risotto."

Amen, brother.

"And to capture my heart, to make my insides explode with pleasure . . ."

Uh-oh, this was getting weird.

". . . you need patience. Patience, and the right stuff."

"Exactly *what* right stuff?" a woman named Deanna asked on cue.

A flurry of titters leaked out when Valter said, "Rice, for one thing. You need a good starchy rice, like Carnaroli or Arborio, which adds the proper glue. Basmati, or any other type, doesn't have the right texture, and the essential ingredients don't blend with it. The same goes for stock. It has to be very good, no cutting corners, otherwise you sacrifice all flavor."

Earlier, he had started a vegetable stock for our benefit, infusing a huge pot of water with a sliced zucchini, three carrots, a stalk of celery with its leafy crown, an onion that had been cut in half and roasted in a dry pan, and a few denuded parsley stems that were otherwise headed for the bin. There were several other ingredients at our disposal as well, although it was not a foregone conclusion whether we would use any of them. Everything depended on the type of dish we desired. Risotto, in a funny way, was something of a kindred spirit to pizza; it tasted wonderful on its own, but there were times when that plain cheese pie begged for pepperoni, peppers, or mushrooms. Likewise, you could dress the risotto in almost any accessory, so long as you didn't go too wild, like the "special" at my local Rowayton Pizza, which was the works, just about everything in the shop. In the past, I had been partial to saffron and sea scallops. Valter suggested we start more simply, perhaps sticking to some sliced *porcini* mushrooms, which we had admired in the Pistoia market. They were flawless, the color of deerskin, with massive meaty stems and a good peaty scent.

The stock made from those few timid vegetables was a bit too pallid for my taste—perhaps they needed more time to release their flavor into the water, or maybe a chicken to punch up the character—but Valter blended it so skillfully with the other ingredients that it flattered the rice without compromising the overall brightness. What it lacked in tanginess, he made up for with panache and pleasure, managing to convey the romance he felt to all of us who were stirring away at our stations.

On paper, my risotto technique must have resembled a fancy football play, what with all the *x*'s and arrows scrawled over my recipe, the crossovers to and from the stove, furtive hand checks, and deep passes of the ladle, with the occasional fumble. I felt like a quarterback under siege, everything coming at me in a flash.

"You seem too high strung, too on edge," Valter said as he came up behind my *mise-en-place*. "Relax. You're not doing brain surgery here. Risotto is very forgiving, as long as you are well organized." He poured two generous glasses of nebbiolo and handed one to me. "Let's have a little drink, enjoy the evening. In the meantime, we can tend to things, keeping an eye on our risotto."

In what seemed like slow motion, we made another portion together: shallots sizzling in a pool of butter and oil; rice glistening in the fat; a glass of wine reduced to a faint, flowery whiff; six cups of stock trembling just below the boiling point; grated Parmesan as fine as talc; dull gray sea salt; more sweet butter, *more*; a generous sprinkling of chopped mint leaves; and, of course, the mushrooms, firm, smooth, beautifully shaved, and just wilted.

It was nothing more than an assembly-line operation, not at all worth the nervous breakdown I'd been cultivating, and a crowdpleaser that managed to boost our collective mood.

After dinner, everyone drifted off into separate areas of the villa, some to read, others to play backgammon. A few even elected to watch TV, which seemed almost disrespectful to the magnificent surroundings. There was no great urge to talk, no effort made to get to know one another. Even at Le Mas, where guests eventually squared off like Afghan tribal factions, there had been a tug of curiosity that drew us into each others' lives. That was the beauty, I realized, of these vacation-oriented cooking schools. The social aspect, the camaraderie, was an attraction all its own. The diversity here in Tuscany might provide a compelling little sideshow, but aside from the two older couples traveling together, no one wanted anything to do with anyone else.

Like anything else, I decided, it came down to the right mix of personalities and serendipity. Why couldn't the Yankees win with a lineup of Jeter, A-Rod, Giambi, and Mussina? My guess is that after the games, some went to read, others to play backgammon or to watch TV or . . . In any case, this group wasn't headed to the World Series.

This was not good news for me. The last thing I needed was solitude, to be alone with my thoughts. Instead I decided to take a walk through the village. The full moon was so bright it seemed to live on the rooftops, shifting through the line of the trees, revealing a cluster of narrow pathways on the other side of the road. Stefania, the local kitchen assistant, lived somewhere over there, and I volunteered to keep her company on her way home.

She was a pretty young thing, olive-skinned and so solemn, with wispy chin-length hair that fell over one eye. Her slight frame was boyishly bony; even in her twenties, more girl than woman. I had watched her grind along in the kitchen, where her presence seemed almost ghostlike, chastened. A guardedness had claimed her, and we walked in silence for much of the way. As we came to a juncture near a ruin, she stopped suddenly, as if deciding whether to go on.

"I wonder . . ." Stefania said, with studied seriousness, "would you like to have a drink at the bar in the village?"

It was a very sweet invitation. Lissa's *Caffè* was the only game in town, the place everyone eventually passed through at some point in the night. The phone booth in its courtyard served the entire scene. At a little after nine, Lissa's was already packed; Stefania knew all the kids who hung out there, probably from childhood, since they had all been schoolmates. Still, she had no compunction about walking in with me, a man more than twice her age, and talking earnestly at the bar over ice-cold *prosecco*, without any distraction.

Was this, I wanted to know, a place her friends always came back to when they were in town?

"You assume we move away," she said in careful, unaccented English.

"Well, yes. It's usually the natural life cycle in towns like these. The younger generation goes off to school and returns sporadically to visit."

"That would be the case in a perfect world. Maybe in America, where everything goes according to plan." She smiled wryly, and we both laughed. "But you are in Tuscany, which is small and mostly poor, and we don't have the wherewithal to move on like that."

"Perhaps when you are finished with your apprenticeship . . . ," I suggested.

A look of discontent tinged with irony crossed her face: "Is that what you think I am doing? An apprenticeship in the kitchen of Villa al Boschiglia?"

I let my silence pass as affirmation.

"You don't know how funny that sounds," Stefania said humorlessly. "It may seem that way, but it is nothing more than the most menial position. Something to keep me from going mad." She lit a cigarette and inhaled, wearied by any discussion of her situation. "An apprenticeship! I should have thought of that when I was a teenager, before . . ."

An acquaintance caught her attention in the mirror over the bar, and waves were automatically exchanged.

"Before what?" I said, prompting her.

She looked directly into my face and seemed to know that whatever was written there had already missed the point.

"Before I took my vows. It is an Italian girl's duty; we dedicate ourselves to service, solitude, and poverty. No matter what goal we reach for, it always comes to that." She took a sip of *prosecco,* looking over the top of the flute to see if I was following the spirit of her remarks. "Do you know, I speak five languages? And there were four years at university, where I trained to be an elementary-school teacher, for which there is no vacant job. The one school in Vorno is permanently closed. So I took the only position available: setting tables and washing up. That is the extent of my apprenticeship, as you call it. Otherwise, I live with my parents, which is like living in a box. It would be wonderful to—how did you put it?—to move on, but without any prospects, I cannot afford even to go to another town on my own. I am trapped here."

She talked to me, drinking and smoking, for at least another hour. At one point, there was a commotion in the bar as another young woman barged in, sobbing uncontrollably. A swirl of available bodies converged around her, clinging. Stefania went to see what was wrong, weaving her way inside the huddling crowd.

"She accidentally hit Bella, Villa Lucia's dog, with a car, and killed her," Stefania reported.

The hair on my arms touched all nerves. Two days earlier, I had rung the bell at Villa Lucia, hoping for an invitation to cook there, and a sweet, goofy-looking mutt bounded out, jumping playfully at me.

A few minutes later, the girl stumbled toward us and collapsed, weeping, in Stefania's arms. We folded her into a seat and got her a drink, something strong and homemade, as she buried her head and tried to smother cries in a tangle of shirtsleeves. She held a napkin to her face and moaned into it. Young couples followed the action from tables, uncertain whether to approach. Eventually, I enlisted one of the boys to take the girl back to the villa, where someone could keep an eye on her.

I returned to the bar. "She'll be okay; she just needs something to distract her," I said to Stefania, with too much apparent empathy. Her face responded, curious. *What? I obviously missed something.* To change the subject, I gave Stefania a thumbnail sketch of my ongoing cooking odyssey, then instantly regretted it. The words that tumbled out of my mouth sounded privileged and proud.

"You have a perfect life," she said, without a trace of irony.

"You must be kidding. Really, it's not at all what you think, and certainly it's anything but perfect." There was no point in dredging up the whole sad story, but I shared a bit of the kind of turmoil the last three years had wrought.

She listened, occasionally nodding, without revealing much of what she was thinking. When I had finished, she said, "You will get past it, and then you will resume your perfect life."

Stefania's words continued to resonate during the next few days in Vorno. Even though they were far from the mark, there was an element of truth in what she had said. However you gauged it, I was a survivor, ahead of the game, doing what I love, healthy, and free. There was no box out of which I couldn't crawl; I wasn't out of prospects—or trapped. Over time, I'd gotten some clarity on my messy life, there was some daylight. The divorce, as friends assured me, would turn out to be a blessing in disguise. I could rebuild my life, emerge from under the pile of debt. As far as my romantic portfolio went, more rebuilding was in order. The worst anyone could lay on me was a gift for chaos. Or my inability to perfect an Italian meringue.

My life was anything but perfect, but plenty of promise lay ahead. I decided to enjoy the rest of my travels. I owed myself that much.

The remaining cooking scheduled for our sessions was straightforward. We made steaks grilled with *porcini* mushrooms, arugula, and zolfini beans; eggplant Parmesan; chicken *cacciatore* (in place of rabbit, which the others flat-out refused) on cakes of polenta studded with green beans; more sea bass baked *en papillote*; a high-octane *limoncello*; pear-and-marzipan tart; Amaretto peaches with cinnamon ice cream; and chocolate biscotti. Valter conducted the classes with as much enthusiasm as possible, but I could tell from experience that he was going through the motions, like an accomplished jazz musician moonlighting in a wedding band.

"Should we make a chicken stock for an extra blast of flavor?" I asked, during the preparation for a wild mushroom soup that had the old-world elegance of *vichyssoise* about it.

"We could," he said, "but I don't think it will make much difference. We'll use water instead, to save everyone the extra work."

This seemed a bit perfunctory coming from Valter. Since we'd arrived at Villa al Boschiglia, he had stressed using only the best ingredients in our cooking, so cutting corners like this seemed out of character.

There were other signs that indicated his frustration. A few times, on the verge of introducing a new recipe, he'd look up from the page, scan the gallery of wide-eyed empty faces, and ultimately scrap a preparation in favor of something simpler, something I'd already learned elsewhere that required no practice. Usually the class would respond with enthusiasm. They would snap into action, completing each detail with mechanical precision, but it never inspired much enthusiasm in Valter. He was a dedicated teacher, but he drew his energy from the students and, in this case, there just wasn't enough intensity to wind him up.

Once, he brought out an orange-scented ricotta grain tart, tucked lavishly into a hand-painted tin that anyone could tell was a family heirloom. He was flushed and impish for a change, and it was clear that he felt like a character in a Hallmark special, sharing a treasure that had been given to him by some revered guru. Serving with exaggerated ceremony to the chatter of indiscreet mouths, he gave each triangle a sprinkling of confectioner's sugar like pixie dust from a sorcerer's magic wand. Everyone dug in with gusto, as Valter's eyes danced with anticipation, but it was impossible to disguise the letdown.

Deanna leaned into me and whispered, "What are we going to do? He'll be insulted, but I just can't eat this."

"I could pretend to pass out," I offered. "While everyone is reviving me, you can launch this stuff."

She turned colors, trying hard not to laugh. We were beginning to attract Valter's attention when Cheryl Lynn, to her credit, bailed us out. With a loud whoosh, she pushed her plate to the middle of the table and groaned.

"I can't put this stuff in my mouth! Y'know, Walter, Americans don't consider rice pudd'n any special kinda dessert."

He stared at her darkly, frowning, unable to speak.

"It's not rice, Cheryl Lynn," I said. "It's spelt, a kind of grain."

"Then why don't you just say *grain*? Talk plain English, instead of using all these highfalutin words. No one is impressed."

"Calling it *grain* would be like reducing this glass of wine to a color, red, instead of calling it *pinot noir*, which would be more than you could grasp."

"Am I going to have to separate you two?" Ed asked, only half-joking.

Deanna leaned toward me and whispered, "I think you're entitled to take a whack at her."

Cheryl Lynn stood there openmouthed, a hand to her chest, as though wounded. I had to admire her performance.

Before anyone knew it, the other couples inched closer, waiting to see which of us drew blood, and Valter, having recovered, was urging us diplomatically, but firmly, away from the counter and toward the upstairs drawing room, where there was some *prosecco* waiting to be served.

Later, Valter discussed the menu for our next class, and upon hearing it was gnocchi, I knew it was time for me to move on.

If I had any second thoughts, they were eliminated at breakfast the next morning. Cheryl Lynn smiled dismissively at me as I pulled up a chair, then launched into a monologue about the travel demands of her corporate job and how she softened the grind by staying at the same hotel chain in every city.

"Explain to me about these Courtyards," Valter suggested, triggering a treatise on the amenities and how one could "always get a big batch o' eggs in the mornin' with hash browns, grits, and lotsa buttered toast."

As she was explaining this, Tiberio, the kitchen assistant, brought me some strong Italian coffee in a thimble-size cup. As he put it down, Cheryl Lynn interrupted her piece, glowered, and wrinkled up her nose.

"I don't know how you can drink that stuff," she said, without looking at me. "It's awful."

"You ought to try it," I said. "It's the way Italians drink their coffee."

"I don't have to try it. I can *smell* it, and it stinks."

Valter gave me a pleading look, and I shrugged to let him know he had nothing to worry about. Instead, I thanked Tiberio for making the coffee especially for me.

I stood looking at Cheryl Lynn across the table, not saying anything, just wishing I had a whipped-cream pie in my hand. Finally I broke out laughing. I couldn't help myself. She was as unpleasant as anyone I'd met, but it had gone past that; it was so irrational I was becoming amused.

"Cheryl Lynn," I said, "you are just great! It's a shame we can't spend more time together. Something tells me I could grow to like you."

"You're nuts!" she said, and I laughed more heartily than before. Then she flapped both hands at me and turned back to the others, extolling the bounties of the Courtyards' mini-bars.

I set out after breakfast, leaving earlier than planned. Even so, I felt satisfied that I had scored some great recipes and, despite the odious Cheryl Lynn, an appreciation for the mellow approach of the others. In a way, I kind of envied the way they enjoyed themselves without taking the work too seriously or especially to heart. Unlike so much of French cooking, which demanded precision, many Italian recipes invited a more casual, improvisational touch, and my uptight approach was beginning to melt away. I had seen that the payoff for my classmates was, perhaps, the breezy spirit in the kitchen, the understanding that their cooking will never win Michelin stars or even forks, but that it will also never fail to please. For most people, that payoff is enough, it makes the entire experience worthwhile. There wouldn't be gnocchi and tiramisu if that weren't so.

I kept turning that over on the slow train to Naples. Surprising as it seems, I was questioning my mission to cook as the great French and Italian chefs cook. It was hard to imagine, considering the goals I'd set for myself: mastering technique, perfecting new recipes, staging a dining experience *extraordinaire*. All of those things still mattered, perhaps had even intensified over the long months on the road, but I had to admit that here in Italy my outlook had changed.

I was beginning to understand that there are two kinds of cooks. There are the perfectionists, who spend their entire lives chasing down the green flash, the moment when all the lessons they have learned, all the mysteries penetrated by trial and error, come together on the plate and send a jolt of rapture to the senses. And then there are the enthusiasts, those who cook for pure selfish pleasure, to make something delicious and satisfy whatever creative impulse drives them toward that end. For the longest time, the perfectionist in me had prevailed, but that strategy, as you've seen, didn't always bring me satisfaction.

Some of my old anxiety had resurfaced in Valter Roman's kitchen. I still felt compelled to learn as much as possible in the limited time allotted, and the energy I put out, my single-mindedness, obviously ruffled the Cheryl Lynns of the world. I had no interest in making vanilla ice cream (again), biscotti (again), *pesce al cartoccio* (sea bass in parcels– *papillote!*— again), or arugula-filled Parmesan baskets. (Hadn't everyone seen Martha Stewart's or Rachael Ray's version?) I had nothing to gain from a polenta demo. Did I say that—or was I merely thinking it? No doubt I was giving off some antsy vibes. In any case, the "farewell dinner," an event I missed by leaving Vorno a day early, would be rife with comments about my intensity and impatience.

Still, the enthusiast in me had emerged at Claudio's and in the last couple of days at Valter's. I found myself watching a few of his demos without taking notes, just leaning against the counter, appreciating the rhythm of the cooking process, the syncopation of steps, the music of pots hitting the stove, the movement of the class, like a repertory company, across the kitchen floor. Everything moved at a nice, easy pace. The scene, to me, was like good theater—or at least a rehearsal. The actors kind of knew their lines and had a general idea where to stand, how to move, when to take a bow. You could tell that everything was coming together. And me— I felt like an understudy in the wings, waiting to make my entrance.

Near the end of the week, Valter had taught us how to make a pear-and-marzipan tart slathered with a creamy dark-chocolate sauce that turned a group of innocent bystanders into full-fledged cooks. I had been lusting after just such a recipe. Kate Hill had a similar version, but we'd never gotten around to making it. But something about this one caught everyone's attention. My classmates pitched in with exuberance and delight, even Wendy, who volunteered to undertake the final assembly. We had a lot of fun putting that baby together: cooking the pears in a simple sugar syrup, rolling out a *pâte sucrée*, making the marzipan and the chocolate sauce. It was a group effort from top to bottom. We all worked together in a calm, relaxed manner, and when we clinked glasses in a post-show toast, everyone, even Cheryl Lynn and I, found an encouraging word to say.

Rain beat against the windows as the train rolled through Umbria toward the palatial contours of Rome. The hills were slick and stained with dampness, as if someone had just given them a second coat of paint. Somewhere after Assisi, my compartment emptied out and a new cast clambered aboard: a mother and her pregnant daughter, who began unwrapping sandwiches the moment they entered; a dashing older man with a persistent cough who helped me move my bags into the corridor every time someone needed to pass; and Aislinn, a very pretty Irish woman who was something of a mentor in her dissociated way. She had just been laid off from her job at a mortgage firm and was kicking off a yearlong odyssey through Europe and Africa, blowing her retirement account to keep from ever feeling indebted to that company, although when she talked about the place it reminded me of the way I talked about my failed marriage. Aislinn was tense and disoriented and bitter, but there was something courageous about her that I admired . . . another lesson in how to keep moving forward, looking for more.

She loved to cook, it ran in the family, of course, and she spent the next hour paging through the folio of recipes I'd collected. It felt reassuring, explaining them to her; each one had a story attached that was like a snapshot of my trip. I started with an impressionistic portrait of Bob Ash, whom she happened to know by reputation, and I had her laughing, even indignant for me, by the time we got to Cheryl Lynn, whose accent I'd perfected even if I laid it on a bit thick. Aislinn seemed charmed, even moved, by these odd, endearing sketches, and we opened a Super Tuscan I had picked up in Lucca that was intended as a gift.

"You must be quite a cook," Aislinn said, while perusing the list of ingredients that went into Claudio's gangrenous *francizina*.

The remark sounded ludicrous, and I swatted it away like a mosquito. But . . . I wondered. What was the upshot of all these exploits, this handiwork?

The variety of recipes, seeing them through Aislinn's eyes, had caught me off guard. I'd forgotten how much cooking had been done on my odyssey, and all of the ways it had been presented and explained to me. The concentration of work, the range of experiences was even richer than I'd realized. Meanwhile, I'd benefited from an extravagance of advice currently rumbling around my head. Baffling observations that had been neatly filed away—the proper trussing of a roast, the browning of meat, paring of citrus fruit (a technique Fred Rivière taught me called *pelé à vif*)—seemed profound, profoundly enlightening in this context. All that dabbling, the groping and fumbling, the embarrassment, coalesced into a foundation that seemed impressive, even if I knew it was as unstable as plutonium. Quite a cook? I wasn't at all sure, but somewhere along the way, I'd become a decent work in progress.

In any case, I needed to practice what I'd learned, to crank out a few dishes that were fresh in my mind. Where would I start? Kate Hill's rabbit stew? Yannick's omelet? Valter's eggplant Parmesan? Arpège's *tarte Tatin*? I fantasized a few fabulous menus that would tantalize my friends. Those Friday-night dinners, it occurred to me, would never be the same. Could I pull it off? Would my soufflé rise or tank? *You've got soup! You idiot!* It was anyone's guess.

I continued to shuffle the possibilities on the gorgeous but hair-raising drive from Naples, bypassing Sorrento, and up the slender switchbacks that lead to the mountaintop village of Sant'Agata. On either side lay a sheer drop with a corresponding drop-dead view worthy of being the last one I might see in this lifetime. We were *sui due Golfi*, the driver told me—between two gulfs: Salerno to the left and Naples on the right, with a commanding view to the south of sirenic Capri.

It was stunning, like a painted 1950s movie backdrop, a turquoise paradise, but difficult to absorb. The car took the turns like a juiced-up Wild Mouse. Before leaving Naples, I had wolfed down a prosciutto-and-cheese sandwich, and now I struggled to keep it down as we rocked and rolled our way upward. My stomach lifted as if in flight above the receding city of Sorrento, which twinkled in the late-afternoon light. "It is only seven kilometers," I mumbled through tightly clenched teeth. "How long will it take us to get there?"

Augusto, my driver, threw me a wicked little smile. "About half an hour. The roads are very narrow. It takes time. Enjoy the view."

The view. I couldn't focus on anything that might require motion. The slightest movement, this way or that, would lead to an embarrassing accident via the open car window. Instead, I folded my slack body into the crease of the seat and tried to hypnotize myself with a silent singsong mantra. *Sooey-dewy-golfi . . . sooey-dewy-golfi . . . above the coast of Amalfi . . . sooey-dewy-golfi.*

It worked for a while, until Augusto lurched into a lower gear. I needed another drastic tactic, aside from screaming, *Stop the fucking car!* I remembered a remedy my boating friends used to ward off seasickness, entailing a fixed point on the horizon. Frantically, my eyes sought out something rock solid that would buy a little time.

"I thought Mount Everest was in Tibet," I said, acknowledging a cloud-capped peak occupying the middle of our windshield.

"That is Vesuvio," said Augusto, with appropriate respect. "The black stretch underneath it is lava and rock."

Information was exchanged about its last recorded eruption, which, if I got it straight, amounted to a Richter-size hiccup. "It is supposed to have small discharges every eight years," Augusto said, "but the last one was in 1941. As you can expect, we are worried about the next one. Everyone thinks that when it comes it will be big."

I did the math—sixty-three years. Could I be *that* unlucky? I wondered.

Incredibly enough, my luck was already changing. The Relais Oasi Olimpia in Sant'Agata was a sight for sore eyes, a renovated mansion transformed by a pale-peach wash that glinted like a jewel in the setting sun. Right off the bat, I realized I had come to a magnificent place, a hidden gem. The hotel was perfectly sited at the top of a knobby rise, with views of Capri through a copse of trees. The grounds surrounding it were vast and lushly landscaped, with bougainvillea growing up the walls to sweeten the air and lavender lining each of the practical quarry-stone paths.

"The pool is beyond those trees," Augusto said, pointing to a thick oasis of palms, "and behind it, the heliport and tennis courts. If you feel like a swim, I will organize a lifeguard and a bartender, though not necessarily in that order."

A Campari would have done nicely to rinse the nausea from my mouth, but before I had time to answer, another voice rang out.

"*Ciao,* Bob—I am Carmen, and you . . . you are *late.*"

The woman, Carmen Mazzola, was surprisingly young to be the executive chef and manager of such a posh hotel. Just twenty-seven, dark and strong, with Valentine-shaped lips and a full figure that she used to good effect, she looked as though she had stepped out of an Italian family comedy. She was exotic and offbeat and warm and high-spirited, as if she were trying to supply enough enthusiasm for two. In every respect, she was a full-fledged character, a natural, who traded on her personality as a way of compensating for her age.

"Here is what you are going to do, Mr. Late Pants," she said, eyeing my luggage with pop-eyed astonishment. "Get settled in your room. There is a bathtub there as big as a pond. Take a little dip. I will send up a glass of wine, which you undoubtedly will pay for. And then come down to where the rest of us are waiting for a get-acquainted dinner."

The room was fantastic, a lovely honey-yellow mini-suite, with a bed that looked big enough to hold André the Giant, a tiled terrace the size of Hoboken, and the enormous tub with a Jacuzzi that I immediately swung into action. A moment later, a knock at the door brought the wine, an icy Livia Felluga pinot grigio no less, in a balloon-shaped snifter. Perfect: Screw the cooking school; I was never leaving my room.

Instead, I did a mental inventory of Neapolitan specialties. At their most basic, they are an American's idea of Italian food, like the dishes we encounter in those red-checkered tablecloth joints in the Little Italys of this world: spaghetti and meatballs smothered in red sauce, stuffed tomatoes and eggplants, deep-fried mozzarella (*in Carrozza*), Caprese salad, *braciola,* and, of course, pizza. As the Italians say: "Chow, baby!"

When I finally struggled into the dining room, it was alive with unusual spirit—a vibrant, sophisticated energy that I hadn't encountered on the circuit until now. There were six people seated at a table with Carmen: two couples from the West and a pair of women from Chicago, all of whom were around my age, attractive, well dressed, and already acquainted. They were engaged in a lively conversation and rolled me right into it, a debate about the vicissitudes of American pasta.

"The dried variety doesn't do it for me," a woman said gently. "It's not at all sensual."

"You find pasta sensual?" asked her seatmate, a man whose kind amused smile invited her to take the plunge without fear.

"Honey, you just haven't lived until *tortelli* turns you on."

Another man who sat next to Carmen said, "Now that you mention it, I always suspected Tortelli, a lawyer from the Heights. He and you must have gotten it on while I was away on business, that trip to Singapore."

"Relax, we just noodled around. Anyway, as we were saying, I prefer getting fresh."

Encouraged, everyone played along and exchanged barbs, political views, opinions on books and music and art and, of course, food. It was a welcome relief from the crew at Villa al Boschiglia. This was my kind of table talk, like good theater. By the end of the night, we were all fast friends.

Some time after dessert, as Carmen replenished the *limoncello* in our pencil-thin glasses, Giuseppe, the pale young desk clerk with almond-shaped Picasso eyes, drifted over to our table and stood at attention, with his hands clasped behind his back. He fixed his stare at a place on the wall behind us and without any fanfare broke into a gorgeous rendition of "O Sole Mio." In any other restaurant and with any other group, this might have devolved into a sidesplitter, but Giuseppe had a rich, beautiful tenor and he sang the familiar ballad so convincingly, and with such passion. The tender liquid lines of his delicate mouth formed each word as if it were poetry. It was a moving performance, and when he finished, we broke into spontaneous and sincere applause.

Giuseppe's face blazed with joy as he bowed slightly before heading back to his post at the reservation desk.

"Have you ever experienced anything like that?" asked Jeff, an IT manager with a secret artistic dash to him. He was a dedicated blues guitarist
with an encyclopedic knowledge of rock 'n roll.

All of us nodded in incredulous agreement. We decided not to belabor
it, so as not to talk away the magic. At any rate, for the next four nights
we never failed to summon Giuseppe to the table after dinner, to which
he eagerly responded. "I believe you like 'O Sole Mio,'" he'd say gallantly,
before reprising the song. One night, we begged for an encore, and he
delivered an equally lovely version of "Come Back to Sorrento."

The cooking classes benefited from the same kind of civility, with
everyone pulling for one another and lending sympathetic hands. It would
be safe to say that the facility contributed to the overall good mood, an
airy glass-enclosed conservatory attached to the kitchen that was the gold
standard as far as places like these went. There were clean, stainless-steel
work surfaces with acres of elbow room, good natural lighting, state-of-
the-art equipment, and unlimited varieties of food, all just steps from the
master kitchen, where we gravitated after prep. All of us enjoyed cooking
in that felicitous room. Through it all, Carmen Mazzola set the tone with
her brand of manic gregariousness. She kept up a hilarious running commentary that combined elements of teaching with social direction that
gave the enterprise a loose salon-type feel.

"I've been thinking that you and Carmen might get something going,"
suggested Debbie, a wiry, dark-haired woman from Chicago with a boyish
boniness who had taken me on as her personal reclamation project.

"I'm sure she'd be a terrific companion at any father-daughter function," I said. "Besides, if I am not mistaken, she's already involved."

There had been mounting speculation about Carmen's relationship
with the owner of the hotel, a lovely mutt of a guy named Salvatore, whom
she ordered around like the hired help.

"*What!*" Carmen, listening in, nearly lifted off her bar stool like an
Orion space capsule. "He's so . . . *old!*"

"Really?" I asked, dispirited by her explanation. If we had guessed correctly, Salvatore was somewhere in his mid to late fifties, possessed of

an eternally youthful spirit. "Exactly how old is old? Are there any great-grandchildren in the picture?"

"He's forty-six . . ." I knew I shouldn't have asked. ". . . and I am a mere child. What would I do with such a whiskery geezer?"

"Well, that leaves me out," I said, looking my most pitiful.

Carmen draped an arm playfully over my shoulder. "On the contrary," she said, displaying a brilliant grin. "Haven't you heard? Americans are my weakness. C'mon, baby, why do you think there is no lock on your bedroom door?"

As it was, I had nothing to worry about—or secretly wish for. I had it on good word that Carmen and Salvatore had been carrying on a longtime torrid romance. There was a wife stashed somewhere nearby, attached irrevocably by Church doctrine, but the marriage, from what I'd been told, had been finished for years. Salvatore had, in effect, bought the hotel for Carmen, sent her to Accademia della Cucina in Rome to cultivate her passion for cooking, and endured her constant needling, playing Desi to her Lucy.

"He adores her," said Lynn, another classmate. "Just look at the way he follows her around."

The night before, I noticed Salvatore sitting by himself at a table in the corner of the dining room, pretending not to keep an eye on us, and waved him over to join our group.

"Yes, yes, Salvatore," Carmen insisted, "be friendly to these lovely Americans."

He nodded in agreement, even though he didn't understand a word of English. And then I had seen the adoring look for myself and knew for sure they were in love.

"Today, we start by making tomatoes stuffed with risotto," Carmen said, as we filed behind our places in the test kitchen. Also on the agenda was a spicy *calamari* casserole, and roasted peppers stuffed with an olive, caper, and Parmesan paste, all of which were simple and delicious recipes, though fairly unchallenging. It didn't matter. The class was captivated and Carmen proved patient and capable, but I had done this kind of cooking before, and with more flair. One recipe, however, grabbed me by the short hairs. It was an attractive starter called *fagotino di zucchini*, which I have made consistently since returning from Italy and routinely share with friends who refuse to leave without the recipe.

FAGOTINO *di* ZUCCHINI

2 long zucchini, sliced lengthwise	1 Tbl. mozzarella, chopped
1/2 cup olive oil	1 Tbl. ham, chopped
	2 Tbl. butter, cut in pieces
	grated Parmesan

Preheat oven to 350 degrees.

Slice each zucchini lengthwise into four pieces and sauté in olive oil over high heat until golden brown but not crisp. Immediately drain the zucchini on plenty of paper towels.

On a flat surface, arrange the four pieces of each zucchini in an asterisk shape—two pieces crossed over each other, two on the diagonal so that a little mound forms in the center—overlapping each. In the middle of the asterisk, place a teaspoon of chopped mozzarella and an equal amount of ham. Press down slightly with the heel of your hand.

Fold over the flaps of zucchini and secure with a toothpick. Dot each package with a tablespoon of butter. Sprinkle with grated Parmesan, and bake 10 minutes.

Makes 3–4

I loved making these appetizers because they combined so many decadent flavors in one fell burst and because they drew a smile each time they were served. But, when it came to the nitty-gritty, they didn't deepen my understanding of Italian cooking.

The truth was, I was growing bored. It had set in while I was in Vorno, making more *salsa di pomodoro* and more tiramisu, and my prospects in Sant'Agata seemed no more promising than that. Carmen's classes were lively and well taught, but they were loaded with introductory technique—

browning onions slowly, so they wouldn't burn; making risotto with enough hot stock; peeling and seeding tomatoes; removing pinbones from fish. I knew all this, more or less, even if Carmen's methods improved slightly on those of others before her. In a quiet moment, while my class-mates were stuffing their tomatoes, I asked to see the syllabus for the rest of the week.

It was a good program, from what I could tell, with plenty of cooking mixed in among the excursions, but it was familiar terrain: more eggplant Parmesan, more fresh pasta-making, more *braciole*, more stuffed vege-tables, and, just in case I had doubts, more *gnocchi* and more tiramisu. Carmen must have read the disappointment on my face.

"You don't know everything, Mr. Kitchen Wizard," she said, after I had paged through the schedule and respectfully pronounced it excellent. "I've seen you in the *cucina*; you could use some good advice."

It was hard to argue that point. There was plenty I didn't know, plenty to learn about handling food and combining ingredients and the way things cook, even kitchen etiquette. But, not to take anything away from Carmen, I wouldn't add much more to my knowledge here. These classes were structured for the beginner; it was a wonderful introduction to Italian cooking, certainly a lot of fun for a week, but I needed to practice and apply what I'd learned. I realized that my most fulfilling experiences, if also the hardest, had been working in the restaurant kitchens, cooking food for other people to eat. I needed to cook—on my own, in my own kitchen, experimenting with the recipes that were already spewing out of my notebook like overdue homework.

In any case, I needed to get home, to put everything together. I wanted to cook for my daughter and my friends, to show off all the amazing things I'd learned. To bring some order to my kitchen, some calm to my life. I needed to sort things out—at least for myself.

That evening, before dinner, I wandered down to the hotel lounge and had a glass of wine with Debbie, who had just gotten married and posi-tively glowed with contentment. Needless to say, I envied how she felt, being so happy and in love. I was reluctant to throw any kind of cloud over that, to discuss the depth of my loneliness and how disoriented I was still. Besides, I felt a little ashamed of the enduring sadness and the shadow it cast.

"You know, a few of us have been talking and we think you're a great guy," she said, indifferent to my embarrassment. "We really enjoy your company, all of us. I really mean it. In fact, just an hour ago," and she named one of the wives, "was saying that if she wasn't already married, you would be a great catch, and we all, the four gals, pretty much agreed with her. It's really a shame that you are in such a terrible place. That woman who did a number on you . . . Any woman worth your heart doesn't treat a man that way, or send him a 'Dear John' letter by email. Especially after you planned to take her on a four-month vacation. That's too damned cruel, and besides, it's just not classy. In any case, you deserve better."

I let Debbie speak her piece without saying a word. I knew she was right. I'd probably known it all along. Here in the free-spirited kitchens of Italy, I was beginning to come to terms with my need to let go of the anger and frustrations of the last several years. In any case, I wanted some closure. I wanted to return to my real life, refreshed and ready to be on my own, or, if it wasn't too much to hope for, to find something crucial that was mine.

"It's time to put your life back together," Debbie continued. "It's time to be happy for a change. You've got so much going for you. It'd be horrible to waste a minute pining after someone who doesn't love you. Take it from me—I can't get enough of my husband, and I'm willing to bet he'd say the same about me. You know the feeling. My guess is it was all one-sided with you and that woman. . . ."

Debbie continued to talk, but I was no longer listening. Suddenly jumping up, I said, "Excuse me, Deb, but I have to go to my room." I darted off toward the staircase near where Giuseppe was tending the bar.

"Hey . . . *wait!* You're not going to do anything drastic, are you?" she called after me, worried she'd said too much, had pushed too hard.

I spun around and gave her a radiant smile. "You bet I am," I practically shouted. Then I took the stairs two at a time.

There wasn't much to work out. I had a handful of cooking schools left on my itinerary: two in Sicily—in Catania and Taormina—an *enoteca* in

Parma, followed by a one-day *stage* with Paola Budel in Milan before fly-ing back to the States at the end of next month. I managed to cancel them all without sparking a vendetta. Something told me there would be other gnocchis and tiramisus on a future plate.

I took care of all these things and many more, and when Carmen finally cornered me after dinner, I stood without speaking for a minute.

She wore a sympathetic look on her face, and said, "You need to do something fabulous tomorrow so that you remember this week at Oasi Olimpia."

I had opted out of the scheduled group excursion to Capri, a place more suited to lovers, wondering if, instead, Carmen and I might spend the day together, working on something special at the stove.

"I've done better than that," she said, with an enigmatic grin. "Meet me in the lobby after you've had your breakfast."

The next morning, after the others left for Capri, I reported to the front desk, where Carmen was already lingering by the door. "We're walking," she said, hooking her arm through mine and leading me off the prop-erty. We made our way with caution along the pavement, careful to side-step the Vespas buzzing like angry hornets as they took the sharp turn up the hill toward the Amalfi coastal roadway. A few blocks away, on Via Deserto, she detoured into Lo Stuzzichino, a modest *trattoria* right off the main drag. We pushed through strands of plastic beads that obscured the doorway into a little *caffè* with a small communal dining room located off to one side. The place was deserted, aside from a few saucepans simmer-ing noisily on the stove.

"Hello, everybody—I'm here!" Carmen sang out, as she cruised behind the counter and opened a few refrigerated display cabinets, poking through the dishes of cold *antipasti*. "Where are you all hiding?"

"Jesus, Carmen, you're going to get us shot," I said, pulling her by a sleeve toward the door.

"Look at all this pretty stuff," she said, wrinkling her nose comically. "Let's take a fork and help ourselves."

"You'd better not." A bear of a man loped around the corner from a room in the back.

"Mimmo!" Carmen cried, jumping into his arms. "I've brought you Bob from America, who knows absolutely nothing about Italian food."

He wrapped my hand in his huge paw and welcomed me to his family *cucina*. "My father will be here in a moment. This is my cousin," he said, acknowledging another man who paraded through the kitchen balancing a metal tray on each hand. Mimmo's wife, Dora, was preparing the front room for lunch. "You are going to cook with us?" Mimmo asked.

I glanced at Carmen, who nodded wilily.

"I would . . . *love* that," I said, accepting a folded apron.

The whole family converged on me like a sacrifice, and for two high-speed hours we cooked up a storm. Paolo De Gregorio, the *padrone,* was a small, wiry man with the energy of a teenager, ever more peculiar considering he'd cooked all day long for sixty years running. It left him no time for anything as frivolous as learning English, so we covered all bases in his mother tongue. Paolo spoke slowly, with comic emphasis, and pointed fitfully as he talked, enabling me to understand and follow directions—lucky for me, because we worked at a breakneck pace.

Paolo had a culture to uphold. It may have been lunch, but no one was going to leave his place with an inch of room remaining under his belt.

We made mouthwatering potato croquettes, oozing mozzarella and strong green olive oil, coated in a light batter of herbed bread crumbs; a typical well-salted *bruschetta,* that found the perfect balance of tomato, garlic, and olive oil; knuckle-size marbles of *bocconcini* wrapped in basil leaves and transparent pink curls of prosciutto, skewered and grilled until nicely browned, which Paolo called *spiedino*; big plates of sliced, spongy local mozzarella draped with roasted peppers and sun-dried tomatoes and gently bathed in oil; a thick hand-kneaded *tagliatelle*-like pasta called *scialatielli*—"shall-ya-tyel-li," Paolo enunciated, hitting each syllable like Mel Torme—that he sauced with *salsa di pomodoro* and slabs of sautéed eggplant; a powerful emulsion he called *zuppa di verdure del colle "Deserto"* that was so thick he served it, reheated, on slices of Parmesan-encrusted *crostini*; a couple of those sumptuous *tartino di melanzana,* filled with chopped ham, eggplant, mozzarella, tomato *bruschetta,* and Parmesan; and a local specialty of shrimp grilled on fragrant lemon leaves and crusted with a dense layer of chopped capers, peppers, and oil.

My favorite preparation was a Neapolitan variation of *arancini,* the traditional breaded risotto balls that were deep-fried until the molten mozzarella core erupted like Vesuvio. I'd made one in Vorno, with Valter Roman, that was less elaborate and not as jeweled with bits of ham and onion, or as creamy. This version was unforgettable and fairly easy to prepare.

ARANCINI

1/2 onion, chopped finely	1 lb. Arborio rice
1/2 cup plus 2 Tbl. olive oil	1/4 cup Parmesan, grated
2 oz. ham, chopped finely	4 oz. mozzarella, small dice
1/4 cup dry white wine	1 egg, beaten lightly with a
3 Tbl. fresh tomato sauce	little salt
2 1/2 cups beef stock	fine bread crumbs
salt and freshly ground black	
pepper	

In a medium saucepan, sauté the onion in 2 tablespoons olive oil. When softened, add the ham and cook a few minutes, then add the wine and the tomato sauce and reduce by half.

Add the stock and season to taste with salt and pepper. When it comes to a boil, add the rice all at once and boil vigorously until the water is absorbed, about 10 to 12 minutes. Stir in the Parmesan to taste. Transfer the rice to a metal bowl and cool thoroughly. Adjust seasoning if necessary.

Wet your hands with water and roll the rice into golf-ball shapes. Poke a hole in each with a finger, push in a few dice of mozzarella, then spackle over the hole with more rice. (These can be prepared to this point and kept refrigerated up to one day in advance.)

Wet your hands with water and wipe a little around each rice ball.

Dip each one into the beaten egg and then roll in the bread crumbs.
Deep-fry batches of arancini in olive oil heated to 330 degrees, until
the rice turns a rich golden brown (about 4 minutes). Serve piping hot.
Makes between 22 to 30, depending on size of *arancini*

Of course, someone should have warned me about the molten mozzarella, because I blistered the roof of my mouth with the first impetuous bite. The antic little dance I did between the stove and the watercooler struck everyone there as funny, an indication, I suppose, of Neapolitan humor. In any case, I left plenty of time before the next bite, which Paolo hastened by plying me with flutes of *prosecco*.

He spun me from recipe to recipe with hardly a breath in between, feeding me the luscious spoils of each until I thought I would burst. Cooks like Paolo can't help themselves, I concluded. They are compelled by the urge to feed people, and the generosity to share their kitchens with anyone who aspires to cook as their Italian ancestors did.

I realized I wasn't anxious. I was having fun. My broken hand didn't even hurt anymore.

"We did well for a morning," Mimmo said, as he walked me around the corner to a coffee bar run by yet another cousin. It was a hot October afternoon, and the combination of food, alcohol, and sunshine were working their languorous spell.

"For a morning!" I said, laughing at the absurdity of his reflection. "My friend, I've done well enough for a lifetime."

We hugged each other and said our good-byes. With considerable effort, I beached myself at a table on the terrace, a contented solid creature learning to thrive on his own. Then I put my head on my hands and fell into a deep, satisfied sleep.

EPILOGUE

Judy Garland has nothing on me. All she had to do was wake up on that little farmhouse featherbed and discover her Emerald City odyssey had been a dream. Symbolically, every oddball character wound up on the right side of the bubble. Even the Wicked Witch, for all the havoc she wreaked, came out smelling sweet. Of course, upon Dorothy's return from Oz she was still the same sweet girl, facing the same saccharine prospects.

For me, on the other hand, everything had changed.

You can be sure that Alain Llorca, Frédéric Rivière, and Claudio Piantini weren't camped out around my bed, grinning like Dorothy's Kansas pals. Their effect on me had been mighty—and mighty real. Nor had that wreck of a rental car been a figment of my imagination; a bill for outstanding damages lingered on my nightstand. In truth, no one was waiting for me when I staggered back from Europe. Call me pathetic, but I harbored a little hope that Carolyn would meet me at the airport. She didn't, nor did she call during my long drive back home. There were two cartons from the post office stuffed inside my front door. The papers finalizing my divorce sat atop the towering stack of mail.

Cold reality jolted me back to the here-and-now, but that wasn't to say that the outlook appeared bleak. The uncertain world I'd inhabited before I left hadn't vanished. The unreturned calls from concerned friends. The accordion shades always drawn to ward off drop-in visitors. The wide-screen TV tuned to the Yankees game so that the crowd sound filled empty rooms. The unopened boxes of vinyl records, once a source of instant pleasure, gathering dust along the baseboards. Sheaves of a coffee-stained manuscript, pages I'd pored over, anguished about, and shed blood upon, scattered on every available surface, and then some. The matching volumes of photo albums chronicling a courtship, a marriage, family vacations, another life. The secondhand furniture I'd borrowed from friends, a lover's nightgown hanging in the closet, those wire casings on the windowsill from Champagne bottles opened to celebrate even the most insignificant event: yet it all looked different to me now. I'd gone to Europe to reclaim something. Cooking—its endless combination of tastes and contrasts of flavors, its kitchens alive with the symphonic ruckus of pots—represented something fixed and durable that couldn't be pulled out from under me.

Somewhere along the way I had learned how to cook. Of course, I couldn't claim very much in the way of experience, certainly less when it came to creativity or accomplishment. But I had gotten great advice from wonderful teachers, studied every detail of their preparations, written down everything they said, learned to respect tradition, smelled and touched all the ingredients, and tasted, tasted every dish in every stage of preparation, until an awareness, a kind of intimacy, developed that I grew comfortable with.

I had learned how to cook. Different ways in France and Italy, but all good lessons for life, in general. In France, where I was ordered around by martinets, I'd learned the importance of discipline and technique. (I left France like a whipped dog—although, oddly, I kind of enjoyed the experience. As a result, I'd become a foot soldier for cuisine.) In Italy, I'd learned the importance of simplicity, authenticity, and, of course, *love*. And having mastered, or at least laid, these foundations, I had learned to settle into a kind of unforced ease—that calm quality I observed and envied in the best chefs.

I had learned how to cook. I learned how to *be* in the kitchen, to think and act like a cook, to anticipate and respond. I had learned how to trust my instincts—whatever my natural culinary ability. Somehow I had learned the secrets of the universe, and I was eager, I was burning, to put them to the test.

And I couldn't wait to play with my new toys. Within hours of landing in the States, I filled the car with the entire spectrum of chef's wares. It must have looked like I had knocked over a Williams-Sonoma store. The back seat and trunk overflowed with boxes: a new food processor, a food mill, a nonstick frying pan, a stick blender, a deadly mandoline, a *chinoise,* silicone baking mats, a net scoop for deep frying, a blender, a tart pan, a porcelain soufflé dish, a food scale, all sorts of molds, a pastry bag, an oyster knife—*an oyster knife!*—a vegetable shredder, metal mixing bowls, ramekins, an apple corer, a knife sharpener, spatulas, kitchen twine, cookie cutters, cutting boards, and enough plastic wrap to give Christo a hard-on. I was ready to roll.

A lavish dinner, *la grande bouffée,* would mark my homecoming with style. But . . . the menu had to be perfect, a kind of whistle-stop tour of all the places I'd been. I spent a week shaping it, shuffling and reshuffling dishes, putting them into as proper a regional context as possible. It would be a feast of gastronomic proportions. After great deliberation, the stage was finally set: a selection of irresistible appetizers (Paolo De Gregorio's *tartino di melanzana,* Samira Hradsky's lemon-lime marinated salmon, and Fred Rivière's scampi *mille-feuilles*), followed by Bruno Söhn's silky zucchini soup. For the main courses: Kate Hill's duck *confit* and Claudio Piantini's pork fillet stuffed with sage and Tuscan ham in a fennel cream sauce, accompanied by Robert Ash's leek-and-potato *dauphinoise* and Valter Roman's *verdura alla griglia.* Dessert was tougher to narrow down, but there were three dishes that were not to be denied: Arpège's exotic tarragon *tarte Tatin,* which I dared to attempt without a net, Jean-Michel Llorca's peach melba, and, of course, Madame's strawberry soufflé (in Doug's honor, I wouldn't drink wine beforehand). I thought through who among my friends would most appreciate this bounty and planned accordingly.

For three long days I relocated to my tiny, steam-filled kitchen, turning out stocks and sauces like a madman. Still . . . there was a rhythm to it that I settled into, a frame of mind that allowed me to keep the wolves at bay. In any other time, I would have smashed two or three plates in an effort to appease the tension gods. But I whistled while I worked, answering the phone and playing air guitar along with the radio, as if nothing could shake my inner *wa.*

Lily wondered if I was having a breakdown. "You seem weird, Dad," she said.

"Weird . . . how?" I wondered, too gaily, hoping to allay any doubts.

"Weird scary, like Hannibal Lecter weird. Like the front page of the *Post.*"

The absence of hysteria punctuated by profanity had thrown her a curve. Meanwhile, the workplace was orderly and neat, no bandages had been pressed into service, no cold packs or aloe extract to counteract scarring.

"Who helped you do all this work?" Lily asked.

My spirits lifted further as I dispatched half a dozen gnarly potatoes, establishing an even, steady motion with the mandoline: all in the wrist. Behind me, four burners sizzled and chuffed, though nary a complaint. Nothing to worry about, liquid bubbling, nice even browning, let's hear it for patience. Order reigned.

With plenty of time on my hands, a late addition to the menu took shape. I sent Lily out to cut what was left of the mesclun growing in pots on the patio and searched through the cupboard for a tin of Mediterranean anchovies. Luckily, I remembered to buy fresh eggs. In a large metal bowl, I pounded a pinch of salt and some pepper into two cloves of garlic, added a few anchovies, and worked it into a grainy paste. After I'd whisked in enough Provençal olive oil and some lemon juice, I fried thick slabs of bacon until nicely crisp and set them aside to drain, while I arranged the salad loosely on plates. Later, when we sat down, I would fry the eggs and deglaze the pan with sherry vinegar before adding it to the dressing. Lily's favorite—just in case there wasn't enough to eat.

Lily set the table around six o'clock. It was a chore she particularly loathed and avoided like math homework, although this time she exercised great care in the details, an effort, I suspected, that was meant to keep an eye on me.

"You don't seem too concerned," she said, looking up from the work, "I mean, considering this is kind of like a reunion."

She knew the whole woeful state of my rocky personal life and no doubt shouldered her share of its tremors. There was no escaping it, no matter how I'd tried to shield her.

"I'm cool." The big toothy smile couldn't have been all that convincing. "You know how I am under pressure: serene, rock- solid, master of Zen."

"Puh-*lease!*"

We fenced and parried like that for most of an hour, our dependable version of stand-up to dodge the tougher issues. There was a lot of catching-up for us. I had been away from Lily for almost a third of a year, an eternity, especially in light of the divorce. She had grown up in that time, grown ever more beautiful, branching into abstract realms of young womanhood. She needed extra attention from me now, which is why I'd included her in the festivities. Neither of us intended to let the other out of their sight.

By seven, the preparations had reached a harmonious crescendo. I opened Champagne and a bottle of Monthélie that would stand up to the duck and pork. Candles were lit, roses rearranged. The kitchen felt dream-like, always a refuge in its familiarity. On the counter, in the enveloping shadows, I laid out on four rectangular trivets serving platters heaped with food. Everything, including the soufflé, had turned out exactly as planned. How was that possible? I stepped back against the wall and admired the spectacular scene. The success of my pursuit was everywhere in evidence.

It was sublime. The combination of colors, textures, and smells was so intense that even in a restaurant it would dazzle. There wasn't a doubt in my mind that it would taste as good as it looked.

Lily poked her head in the room and let out a gasp. The variety of food on display was shocking.

"What do you say we get started?"

"What about the gang?" Lily wondered. "Shouldn't we wait until everybody gets here?"

I straightened the silverware on the other place settings. "I don't think so, Sweet Thing," I said. "This is all for you and me."

A BRIEF AFTERWORD

"To everything, turn, turn, turn . . ."

I had been listening to that old Byrds single to excess after I got home, as the tides of my life shifted this way and that. Something about its groove lifted my spirits beyond the exuberant beat, and the lyric—well, that lyric morphed conveniently to signify any message or deed.

There was plenty of time to kill, as I put the trip behind me and sifted through its bulky residue. The volume of recipes I'd amassed was daunting, and for a while, I have to admit, it was relegated to a shelf in the kitchen, strategically out of eyesight. I didn't go anywhere near the stove, fearing that a misfire might render the entire experience a megaflop.

Instead, I reverted to old standbys, ordered in pizza, Chinese, anything that could be reconstituted in a microwavable bag.

Gradually, however, it was a time to build up, and, tentatively, uneasily, I began to cook again. Gnocchi to warm up, then a few pasta dishes, those pesky *tartes Tatins,* eventually duck. Carolyn came back into my life for a short time. I suppose she was curious about the journey's effect on me, whether I found what I was looking for. Like everyone else, she was eager to know what I'd learned. A sampling of my culinary showpieces drew little in the way of response, aside from her observation that I'd become slave to the demon butter. Nothing I did measured up to that chunk of cheese. In any event, Debbie had been right: I deserved better, and after a while I put that entire episode behind me.

It was a time to cry, and a time to heal. Lily tended to me throughout two years of recovery, while I picked up and mended the pieces of my life. I tried dating a few women I met here and there, but no one seemed right and I let it drop. By now I'd learned enough to know that some combinations just don't work. It's no use trying to force them. Patience—I thought of Claudio and his long-simmering sauces. I decided to be content with what I had in life—my daughter, my writing, my cooking. My biography of the Beatles finally came out. Still, something was missing. I couldn't put my finger on it.

In the midst of this flux, I got a call from Fred Plotkin, the gifted writer and a friend, who checked in from time to time. It had been two years since we'd last spoken, the usual chitchat about our work, new places we'd eaten. He'd served as my Italian food guru, so it was natural that he'd expect a recap of my trip. We met for dinner at one of those joints in Manhattan that everyone was talking about. But, hard as it is to believe, Fred wasn't interested in food. There was someone he wanted me to meet. A woman.

I've sworn off, I should have replied. Matter of fact, I'm in a twelve-step program.

"She's one of my closest friends," he said. "Besides, I've been thinking about this for a long time. Several years, in fact."

How odd. This was a man with whom I had but a passing professional relationship. He knew nothing about what I'd gone through, where I was in my life. It took incredibly large stones to think I'd welcome an unsolicited fix-up.

"I don't introduce people often," he went on, "but when I do, rest assured, it always works. Always."

The man was a crackpot. I should have walked out or at least informed him of my new address: a leper colony off the coast of Honduras. Instead, I said okay. As in: "Okay, here's my heart, just stomp on it now."

Her name was Becky, and, as it turned out, it was a time to laugh, a time to sigh. She was a writer, of all things, talented and kind. She was also gorgeous, delightfully slender, and made it clear, right off the bat, that her figure demanded she eat three good meals a day. Oh, and in case Fred hadn't already mentioned it, she loved food, loved the idea that a man would cook for her.

This was a trap.

Well, you know how it goes: One meal led to another. I cooked my ass off for that woman, whipped up everything I'd learned. Even my disasters had a satisfying, comic appeal. Becky was besotted, so she said; everything in my repertoire pleased her no end. Everything just worked. The kitchen at Arpège had nothing on us. From the beginning, our relationship had all the giddy fun of a peach *blanc-manger* at Moulin de Mougins, all the unforced compatibility of a simple Italian sauce. Magically, my life started to turn around. My entire outlook took on a sanguine glow. I was calm in the kitchen, handled the chores with confidence and poise. It helped to know that she appreciated everything I made. Alas, she lived an hour away, but, like Claudio, nothing interfered with my making that trip.

Which brings me to this point: Relationships this late in life are like soufflés. They need the right ingredients to start with, lots of loving care, and the wisdom to realize that if you have to work too hard at it, the air goes out. Otherwise, as every idiot knows, you just have soup.

ACKNOWLEDGMENTS

I wish to express my thanks and indebtedness to the many individuals whose kind assistance and encouragement were invaluable to the success of this project.

I am deeply grateful to Karen Herbst of The International Kitchen, in Chicago, who arranged many of the cooking *stages* and who helped shape the itinerary, coordinate the arrangements, and made excuses for my behavior on the road. For anyone interested in a cooking-school vacation, her website (theinternationalkitchen.com) is indispensable, the gateway to culinary paradise. My thanks to Julie Mautner, Alice Marshall (Alice Marshall Public Relations), Nina Lora and Kristen Vigras (the Brandman Agency), Clay Chapman (Mason Rose USA), and Cullen International PR, all of whom arranged for me to cook with some of the best chefs in Europe. I wish also to thank Brenda Homick and her assistant Sarah Lechvalier at Relais et Châteaux for setting up apprenticeships at several of their fabulous properties (Pierre Orsi in Lyon; Moulin de Mougins in Mougins; and Arpège in Paris).

For a wealth of favors, I am indebted to Maria Woodley at the Italian Trade Commission and Louise O'Brien, formerly of the French Government Tourist Office; also to Mike and Terri Rhode; Delphine Boutier of Kobrand; Jacques Lardiere at the Jadot winery in Beaune; Claudia Schall at Le Meurice; Sabrina Piantini in Figline Valdarno; Pierre Orsi, one of Lyon's most inventive chefs and luminous personalities; Jean-Luc Rabanel; Adriano Cavignini, head chef at the Hotel Eden in Rome; Attilio Fabrizio and Luca Drini at the Villa San Michele; and to the splendid chefs, teachers, their assistants, and fellow students whose appearances and contributions throughout the book enriched the story.

Lanie Goodman, my onetime neighbor and longtime friend, provided shelter and, as always, thoughtful guidance to steer me through very tough times. Kathy Kukkula and Rosa Lowinger read early drafts of chapters when I needed keen insight and encouragement. Sandy D'Amato, the best friend anyone could ask for, once again provided valuable advice, to say nothing of his boundless expertise, and showed faith in me throughout the long haul. I owe a great debt to Sandy for proofreading and correcting the recipes that appear in the text. Jim Falsey lived through it all—many times over! I am especially grateful to Mary Finnegan, who stood by me through the writing of the book, invested it with her enthusiasm, and gave me the courage to see it through. I wish also to thank my agent, Sloan Harris of ICM, who supported me throughout the project and repeatedly reminded me: "We're a team here." Don't I know it! He read and critiqued, he pushed me to sharpen my pencil, to dig in and go to places I'd been scrupulously avoiding. Above all, he devoted himself to the quality of the book and its fate.

At W. W. Norton, my publishing house, Star Lawrence, who has been an advocate of my writing for what seems like half a lifetime, provided expert editorial guidance and the kind of barbed marginalia that forces the Supreme Court to revisit the obscenity laws every few years. My gratitude (and condolences) to his assistant, Molly May, for performing so many thankless tasks, to Maria Guarnaschelli for scrutinizing the recipes and bringing clarity to the directions, and to the entire creative team at Norton whose tireless group endeavor streamlined every phase of the process.

Lily, my daughter, is the shining star, my beacon. Her love of food and exquisite palate were the inspiration for this book. I would never have gotten through it—the adventure or the writing—without knowing she was rooting me on, waiting for me on the other side. A few nights ago, Lily and I were watching a video of Paul Simon singing "Father and Daughter." When he hit that gem of a line—"There could never be a father/ Who loved his daughter as much as I love you"—Lily turned to me and said, "Except for you, Dad." So, she knows—she knows. I feel the same from my parents, who have shared many fabulous meals over the years, urged me to follow my dreams, and supported all of my efforts.

Thanks is nowhere near enough gratitude to lavish on Becky Aikman, to whom this book is gratefully dedicated. She was instrumental in its outcome, reading every word twice, three times—okay, four!—making important cuts and suggestions with her sensible judgment and critical eye. The cover concept was all hers. In her spare time, she rescued me from the brink, restored my faith in romance, and somehow put a permanent smile on my face. *What took her so damned long?* In any case, I knew she always had my back. And my heart.

Lastly, to all the lovely folks I met along the way, even those who considered me a royal pain in the ass, my apologies and thanks.

Bob Spitz
July 2007
Darien, Connecticut, and Joucas, France